THE NATURE OF PERSONALITY:

SELECTED PAPERS

by

GORDON W. ALLPORT

Professor of Psychology
Harvard University

GREENWOOD PRESS, PUBLISHERS
WESTPORT, CONNECTICUT

Library of Congress Cataloging in Publication Data

Allport, Gordon Willard, 1897-1967.
    The nature of personality.

    Reprint of the 1950 ed. published by Addison-Weseley
Press, Cambridge, Mass.
    Bibliography of the author's works, 1921-1950: p.
    Includes bibliographies.
    1. Personality--Addresses, essays, lectures.
I. Title.
BF698.A38 1974 155.2   74-2795
ISBN 0-8371-7432-5

Originally published in 1950 by Addison-Wesley Press, Inc.,
Cambridge, Mass.

Reprinted with the permission of Mrs. Ada R. Allport.

Reprinted in 1975 by Greenwood Press,
A division of Congressional Information Service, Inc.
88 Post Road West, Westport, Connecticut 06881

Library of Congress catalog card number 74-2795
ISBN 0-8371-7432-5

Printed in the United States of America

10 9 8 7 6 5 4 3

CONTENTS

PREFACE v

ATTITUDES 1
   Chapter 17 in *A Handbook of Social Psychology* (edited by
   C. C. Murchison). Worcester: Clark University Press, 1935.

THE PSYCHOLOGIST'S FRAME OF REFERENCE 48
   Psychological Bulletin, 1940, 37, 1-28.

THE FUNCTIONAL AUTONOMY OF MOTIVES 76
   American Journal of Psychology, 1937, 50, 141-156.

MOTIVATION IN PERSONALITY: REPLY TO MR. BERTOCCI . . . 92
   Psychological Review, 1940, 47, 533-554.

THE EGO IN CONTEMPORARY PSYCHOLOGY 114
   Psychological Review, 1943, 50, 451-478.

THE PSYCHOLOGY OF PARTICIPATION 142
   Psychological Review, 1945, 53, 117-132.

GENETICISM *versus* EGO-STRUCTURE IN THEORIES OF PERSONALITY . 158
   British Journal of Educational Psychology, 1946, 16, 57-68.

EFFECT: A SECONDARY PRINCIPLE OF LEARNING 170
   Psychological Review, 1946, 53, 335-347.

PERSONALISTIC PSYCHOLOGY AS SCIENCE: A REPLY . . . 183
   Psychological Review, 1946, 53, 132-135.

SCIENTIFIC MODELS AND HUMAN MORALS 187
   Psychological Review, 1947, 54, 182-192.

PERSONALITY: A PROBLEM FOR SCIENCE OR A PROBLEM FOR ART? . 198
   Revista de Psihologie (Cluj, Rumania), 1938, vol. 1, No. 4,
   1-15.

BIBLIOGRAPHY 211

PREFACE

For some years I have been unable to supply reprints of most of the papers that are here republished. People who request copies often do not have access to the original sources where the articles were first printed. Furthermore, there is a certain logical coherence among these eleven studies that seems to justify bringing them together in an orderly and convenient series. Except for the final paper in the series, the articles have been photographed exactly as they first appeared in print.

With few exceptions, these papers have been printed since 1937, the year that marked the publication of my book *Personality: a psychological interpretation*. All of them represent in one way or another clarifications or amplifications of the theory of personality presented in that volume. Some of the articles were written explicitly in answer to critics who expressed their disagreements and misgivings in print. Others represent expansions in theory or application provoked by my own dissatisfaction with my previously stated position.

———————

Since the papers were written over a period of years and for various occasions there is no strict continuity among them. Yet a common orientation to the science of psychology in general, and to the theory of personality in particular, marks them all. The present arrangement places those papers that are most closely related in theme adjacent to one another. The fact that the order is at the same time roughly chronological is perhaps a sign that the logical development of an author's thought is of necessity temporally conditioned.

The opening article on *Attitudes* gives a standard account of the status of this concept up to the year 1935. Instructors sometimes refer students who are preparing themselves on the backgrounds of social psychology to this paper. Attitudes are here viewed as important (often the most important) determiners of the social behavior of the individual. Although there have been various attempts since 1935 to dislodge the concept, one wonders whether its critics (learning theorists, phenomenologists, field theorists) have done more than help refine it. For example, one may agree wholeheartedly that attitudes are learned, that they operate at any given time through a convergent perception, thus reflecting the impact of the situation upon the individual, and that they always serve a functional role in the economy of a person's life as a whole — without surrendering the concept. Insofar as social behavior of the individual reflects organization, recurrence, and similarity, the doctrine of attitude (or some close equivalent) seems indispensable. Since 1935 a whole new realm of attitude research has opened up in social psychology, namely, public opinion polling. While this research is generally regarded as having a practical and applied bent, the logic of its procedures and its underlying theory raise many old and many new problems of attitude psychology. All things considered, the concept of *attitude* remains central to the field of social psychology.

The second paper is an address delivered before the American Psychological Association at Berkeley in 1939. It reports historical research on changing trends in American psychology over a period of fifty years. It likewise argues, as do other articles in the series, for a clearer recognition of the patterned personality of the single individual as a basic datum for the science of psychology. It insists that if *understanding, prediction,* and *control* are the criteria of science, then the sustained study of the single case may advance the science of psychology.

The remaining papers are closely knit in subject matter and in theory. *The functional autonomy of motives* (essentially the same as Chapter VII of *Personality: a psychological interpretation*) sets forth the argument that contemporary motives in an individual's life may be quite independent, dynamically speaking, of earlier (e.g., childhood) motives. This unassuming proposition has aroused considerable controversy. It is uncongenial to strict Freudians, to instinctivists, to some learning theorists, and to other psychologists whose thinking runs more readily toward "reduction" than toward "emergence." A. H. Maslow has drawn a helpful distinction between "deficiency-motivation" and "growth-motivation." Reductionist doctrines of drive and deprivation, now so prevalent, allow only the former; functional autonomy allows also the latter. Some of the remaining papers· of the series defend functional autonomy, but primarily are concerned with its implications for various central issues in personality theory.

Motivation in personality: reply to Mr. Bertocci faces the question whether functionally autonomous adult motives are at bottom sustained by instincts, or whether they themselves may be the ultimate forms of motivation in a mature life. This same issue underlies the later paper, *Geneticism and ego-structure in theories of personality.* Both Mr. Bertocci and certain British writers (to whom the latter article replies) prefer a McDougallian foundation of personality in terms of hypothesized instincts. These replies argue that such an assumption of underlying propensities is both unnecessary and insufficient in accounting for the structure and functioning of developed personalities.

Critics have complained with good reason that a certain atomism, or extreme particularism, flavors the theory of functional autonomy as originally presented. Motives seemed autonomous not only of their origins but of each other. Later papers in the series, especially *The ego in contemporary psychology, The psychology of participation,* and *Geneticism versus ego-structure,* try to remedy the blunder. The concept.of ego-involvement is advanced to handle both the unification and the forward thrust that characterize mature motivation. The concept of ego-involvement likewise seems unavoidable in order to account for the experimental findings summarized in *The ego in contemporary psychology.*

Effect: a secondary principle of learning attempts to escape from the excessive geneticism of modern theories of learning, especially those that pretend to account for all present behavior in terms of previous rewards and punishments. Fashionable as this formula is at the present time, one may question whether it applies to more than primitive forms of learning as encountered most clearly in animals and in children. Ego-involved interest is the key required to an improved learning theory.

In the brief paper, *Personalistic psychology as science: a reply,* I have taken pains to clarify the meaning of the term "personalistic." It is easily misunderstood. Within the broader sense of the term the approach of the present series of papers is certainly "personalistic." Yet there are distinct differences between their line of thought and other doctrines marked by this label. It would, no doubt, assist the reader and lighten the task of the student if a conspicuous tag — an "ism" of some sort — could be attached to the present series of papers. But it would be misleading to do so. The tag "personalistic" — if broadly appropriate — yet fails to convey the eclectic and empirical character of the approach that characterizes the articles in this volume.

Scientific models and human morals raises a basic issue. It inquires whether certain currently popular models, such as the child, the animal, the machine, are suitable prototypes for the functioning of the developed personality. These root-metaphors, so well established in psychological thinking today, may be seriously misleading. To enhance our understanding and our powers of prediction and control we seem now to require a model of personality that stresses active intention rather than passive expectation, contemporaneous rather than past motivation, interest rather than reward, and cognitive as well as reactive dynamisms.

The final article, *Personality: a problem for science or a problem for art?* is the most popularly written in the series. It treats the contrasting methods of literature and of psychology — the two ultimate avenues to the study of human personality. It forms a bridge between the papers in the present series and a separate monograph that explores the problem of the idiographic method in psychology in detail (*The Use of Personal Documents in Psychological Science,* 1942).

A bibliography, compiled with the kind assistance of Mrs. Eleanor D. Sprague, has been added in the hope that it will assist readers who may wish to locate a reference to some publication not reprinted in this volume.

GORDON W. ALLPORT

Cambridge, Massachusetts
September 1950

ATTITUDES

Reprinted from *A Handbook of Social Psychology*, Clark University Press, 1935, pp. 798-844.

The concept of attitude is probably the most distinctive and indispensable concept in contemporary American social psychology. No other term appears more frequently in experimental and theoretical literature. Its popularity is not difficult to explain. It has come into favor, first of all, because it is not the property of any one psychological school of thought, and therefore serves admirably the purposes of eclectic writers. Furthermore, it is a concept which escapes the ancient controversy concerning the relative influence of heredity and environment. Since an attitude may combine both instinct and habit in any proportion, it avoids the extreme commitments of both the instinct-theory and environmentalism. The term likewise is elastic enough to apply either to the dispositions of single, isolated individuals or to broad patterns of culture. Psychologists and sociologists therefore find in it a meeting point for discussion and research. This useful, one might almost say peaceful, concept has been so widely adopted that it has virtually established itself as the keystone in the edifice of American social psychology. In fact several writers (cf. Bogardus, 1931; Thomas and Znaniecki, 1918; Folsom, 1931) *define* social psychology as the scientific study of attitudes.

As might be expected of so abstract and serviceable a term, it has come to signify many things to many writers, with the inevitable result that its meaning is somewhat indefinite and its scientific status called into question. Among the critics (e.g., Bain, 1927-28; McDougall, 1933; Symonds, 1927), McDougall has been the most severe:

> American social psychologists and sociologists have recently produced a voluminous literature concerning what they call "social attitudes"; the term is used to cover a multitude of facts of many kinds including almost every variety of opinion and belief and all the abstract qualities of personality, such as courage, obstinacy, generosity and humility, as well as the units of affective organization which are here called "sentiments." I cannot see how progress in social psychology can be made without a more discriminating terminology. (1933, p. 219)

It is undeniable that the concept of 'attitude' has become something of a factotum for both psychologists and sociologists. But, in spite of all the animadversions of critics, the term is now in nearly universal use and plays a central rôle in most of the recent systematic studies in social psychology. It is therefore a concept which students must examine with unusual care.

History of the Concept of Attitude

Like most abstract terms in the English language, *attitude* has more than one meaning. Derived from the Latin *aptus*, it has on the one hand the significance of "fitness" or "adaptedness," and like its byeform *aptitude* connotes a subjective or mental state of preparation for action. Through its use in the field of art, however, the term came to have a quite independent meaning; it referred to the outward or visible posture (the bodily position) of a figure in statuary or painting. The first meaning is clearly preserved in modern psychology in what are often referred to as "mental attitudes"; and the second meaning in "motor attitudes." Since mentalistic psychology historically precedes response psychology, it is only natural to find that mental attitudes are given recognition earlier than motor attitudes. One of the earliest psychologists to employ the term was Herbert Spencer. In his *First Principles* (1862) he wrote,

> Arriving at correct judgments on disputed questions, much depends on the attitude of mind we preserve while listening to, or taking part, in the controversy: and for the preservation of a right attitude it is needful that we should learn how true, and yet how untrue, are average human beliefs. (vol. I, 1, i)

Similarly in 1868 Alexander Bain wrote:

> The forces of the mind may have got into a set track of attitude, opposing a certain resistance as when some one subject engrosses our attention, so that even during a break in the actual current of the thoughts, other subjects are not entertained. (p. 158)

Somewhat later, when psychologists were forsaking their exclusively mentalistic point of view, the concept of *motor attitudes* became popular. In 1888, for example, N. Lange developed a motor theory wherein the process of a perception was considered to be in large part a consequence of muscular preparation or "set." At about the same time Münsterberg (1889) developed his action theory of attention, and Féré (1890) maintained that a balanced condition of tension in the muscles was a determining condition of selective consciousness. In 1895 Baldwin proposed motor attitudes as the basis for an understanding of emotional expression, and later writers such as Giddings (1896) and Mead (1924-25) expanded still further the rôle of motor attitudes in social understanding.

In recent years it is uncommon to find explicit labeling of an attitude as either "mental" or "motor." Such a practice smacks of body-mind dualism, and is therefore distasteful to contemporary psychologists. In nearly all cases today the term appears without a qualifying adjective, and implicitly retains both its original meanings: a mental aptness and a motor set. Attitude connotes *a neuropsychic state of readiness for mental and physical activity.*

Attitudes in Experimental Psychology. Perhaps the first explicit recognition of attitudes within the domain of laboratory psychology was in connection with a study of reaction-time. In 1888 L. Lange discovered that a subject who was consciously prepared to press a telegraph key immediately upon receiving a signal reacted more quickly than did one whose attention was directed mainly to the incoming stimulus, and whose consciousness was not therefore directed primarily upon the expected reaction. After Lange's work, the task-attitude, or *Aufgabe,* as it came to be called, was discovered to play a decisive part in nearly all psychological experiments. Not only in the reaction experiment, but in investigations of perception, recall, judgment, thought, and volition, the central importance of the subjects' *preparedness* became universally recognized. In Germany, where most of the experimental work was done, there arose a swarm of technical expressions to designate the varieties of mental and motor "sets" which influence the subjects' trains of thought or behavior during the experiment. In addition to the *Aufgabe,* there was the *Absicht* (conscious purpose), the *Zielvorstellung* (or idea of the goal), the *Bezugsvorstellung* (idea of the relation between the self and the object to which the self is responding), the *Richtungsvorstellung* (or idea of direction), the *determindierende Tendenz* (any disposition which brings in its train the spontaneous appearance of a determined idea), the *Einstellung,* a more general term (roughly equivalent to "set"), the *Haltung* (with a more behavioral connotation), and the *Bewusstseinslage* (the "posture or lay of consciousness"). It was perhaps the lack of a general term equivalent to "attitude" that led the German experimentalists to discover so many types and forms.

Then came the lively controversy over the place of attitudes in consciousness. The *Würzburg* school was agreed that attitudes were neither sensation, nor imagery, nor affection, nor any combination of these states. Time and again they were studied by the method of introspection, always with meager results. Often an attitude seemed to have no representation in consciousness other than a vague sense of need, or some indefinite and unanalyzable feeling of doubt, assent, conviction, effort, or familiarity. (Cf. Fearing, 1931; Titchener, 1909.)

As a result of the *Würzburg* work all psychologists came to accept attitudes, but not all believed them to be impalpable and irreducible mental elements. Marbe's conception of the *Bewusstseinslage* as an "obvious fact of consciousness, whose contents, nevertheless, either do not permit at all of a detailed characterization, or are at any rate difficult to characterize" became a particular bone of contention. In general, the followers of Wundt believed that attitudes could be accounted for adequately as *feelings,* particularly as some blend of striving and excitement. Clarke (1911), a pupil of Titchener, found that attitudes in large part *are* represented in consciousness through imagery, sensation, and affection, and that where no such states are reported there is presumably merely a decay or abbreviation of these same constituents.

However they might disagree upon the nature of attitudes in so far as they appear in consciousness, all investigators, even the most orthodox, came to admit attitudes as an indispensable part of their psychological armamentarium. Titchener is a case in point. His *Outline of Psychology* in 1899 contained no reference to attitude; ten years later, in his *Textbook of Psychology,* several pages are given to the subject, and its systematic importance is fully recognized:

> Behind everything lies a cortical set, a nervous bias, perhaps inherited and permanent, perhaps acquired and temporary. This background

may not appear in consciousness at all; or it may appear as a vague, conscious attitude (passive imagination), or again as a more or less definite plan, aim, ambition, intention (active imagination). Whether conscious or not, the nervous disposition determines the course of consciousness. (1916, Sect. 119)

The meagerness with which attitudes are represented in consciousness resulted in a tendency to regard them as manifestations of brain activity or of the unconscious mind. The persistence of attitudes which are totally unconscious was demonstrated by Müller and Pilzecker (1900), who called the phenomenon "perseveration." The tendency of the subject to slip into some frame of mind peculiar to himself led Koffka (1912) to postulate "latent attitudes." Washburn (1916) characterized attitudes as "static movement systems" within the organs of the body and the brain. Other writers, still more physiologically inclined, subsumed attitudes under neurological rubrics: traces, neurograms, incitograms, brain-patterns, and the like.

Psychoanalytic Influence. The contribution of the Würzburger and of all other experimental psychologists was in effect the demonstration that the concept of attitude is indispensable. The discovery that attitudes are to a large degree unconscious, however, tended to discourage them from a further study of the problem. Once a phenomenon has been driven, as it were, to take refuge in nervous tissue, and identified with cortical sets and brain fields, the psychologist, at least the introspectionist, is disinclined to pursue it further. The tendency of experimental orthodoxy is to admit the crucial part played by attitudes in all mental operations, but to consign them to the mysterious limbo of "motivation" and there to leave them.

It was the influence of Freud, of course, that resurrected attitudes from this obscurity and endowed them with vitality, identifying them with longing, hatred and love, with passion and prejudice, in short, with the onrushing stream of unconscious life. Without the painstaking labors of the experimentalists attitudes would not today be an established concept in the field of psychology, but also without the influence of psychoanalytic theory they would certainly have remained relatively lifeless, and would not have been of much assistance to social psychology which deals above all else with full-blooded phenomena. For the explanation of prejudice, loyalty, credulity, patriotism, and the passions of the mob, no anemic conception of attitudes will suffice.

Attitudes in Sociology. For a number of years sociologists have sought to supplement their cultural concepts with a psychology which might express in *concrete* terms the mechanisms through which culture is carried. At first, under the influence of Bagehot, Tarde, and Baldwin, a somewhat vaguely postulated instinct of imitation (or suggestion) was thought adequate. Somewhat later the basis was sought in a more varied native equipment of men. It is interesting to note that of the first two textbooks in social psychology, both published in the year 1908, the one, by Ross, marks the demise of the "simple and sovereign" psychology of imitation-suggestion, and the other, by McDougall, marks the commencement of the still more vigorous social psychology of instincts.

The instinct-hypothesis did not satisfy social scientists for long, for the very nature of their work forced them to recognize the importance of custom and environment in shaping social behavior. The instinct-hypothesis has precisely the contrary emphasis. What they required was a new psychological concept which would escape on the one hand from the hollow impersonality of "custom" and "social force," and on the other from nativism. Being committed to *some* psychological doctrine and dissatisfied with instincts they gradually adopted the concept of *attitude*.

The case of Dewey may be taken as fairly typical. In 1917 he professed to see in the doctrine of instincts an adequate basis for a social psychology. Five years later (1922) he no longer found instincts suitable and sought to replace them with a concept that would

> express that kind of human activity which is influenced by prior activity and in that sense acquired; which contains within itself a certain ordering or systematization of minor elements of action; which is projective, dynamic in quality, ready for overt manifestation; and which is operative in some subdued subordinate form even when not obviously dominating activity. (p. 41)

To express this complex type of mental organization he chose "habit," but admitted as its equivalent either "disposition" or "attitude."

The credit for instituting the concept of attitude as a permanent and central feature in sociological writing must be assigned to Thomas and Znaniecki (1918), who gave it systematic priority in their monumental study of Polish peasants. Before this time the term had made only sporadic appearances in sociological literature, but immediately afterward it was adopted with enthusiasm by scores of writers.

According to Thomas and Znaniecki the study of attitudes is *par excellence* the field of social psychology. Attitudes are individual mental processes which determine both the actual and potential responses of each person in the social world. Since an attitude is always directed toward some object it may be defined as a "state of mind of the individual toward a value." Values are usually social in nature, that is to say they are objects of common regard on the part of socialized men. Love of money, desire for fame, hatred of foreigners, respect for a scientific doctrine, are typical attitudes. It follows that money, fame, foreigners, and a scientific theory are values. A social value is defined as "any datum having an empirical content accessible to the members of some social group and a meaning with regard to which it is or may be an object of activity" (p. 21). There are, to be sure, numerous attitudes corresponding to every social value; there are, for example, many views or attitudes regarding the church or the state. There are also numerous possible values for any single attitude. The iconoclast may direct his attacks quite at random upon all the established social values, or the Philistine may accept them all uncritically. To a large extent, of course, new social values are created by the attitudes which are common to many men, but these attitudes themselves depend upon pre-existing social values. Hence in the social world, as studied by the sociologist, both values and attitudes must have a place. Primarily it falls to the ethnologist and philosopher to examine values; but it is social psychology which is "precisely the science of attitudes."

The authors draw a distinction between attitudes of temperament and of character; the former include what psychologists have been accustomed to speak of as instincts and innate aptitudes; the latter are the acquired operations of the socialized mind—the plans, interests, and sympathies which characterize the average citizen. The authors admit likewise a distinction between natural attitudes (toward the physical environment), which are of slight interest to social psychology, and the social attitudes proper which are far more numerous and which constitute the distinctive subject-matter of the new science.

Following closely in the same vein of thought, Faris (1925) proposed additional refinements. He would distinguish between conscious and unconscious attitudes, between mental and motor attitudes, between individual and group attitudes, and between latent and kinetic attitudes. Park (see Young, 1931), who is likewise in essential agreement with this school of thought, suggests four criteria for an attitude: (1) it must have definite orientation in the world of objects (or values), and in this respect differ from simple and conditioned reflexes; (2) it must not be an altogether automatic and routine type of conduct, but must display some tension even when latent; (3) it varies in intensity, sometimes being predominant, sometimes relatively ineffective; (4) it is rooted in experience, and therefore is not simply a social instinct. Bernard (1930) has recently prepared a synthesis of the conceptions found in current sociological writing:

> Social attitudes are individual attitudes directed toward social objects. Collective attitudes are individual attitudes so strongly inter-conditioned by collective contact that they become highly standardized and uniform within the group. . . The attitude is originally a trial response, i.e., interrupted, preparatory or substitute behavior arising within an incompleted adjustment response, but it may become the permanent set of the organism. It ranges from concrete muscular response to that which is abstract, inner or neural. . . . Attitudes form the basis of all language and communication. In them is implicit all finished social behavior and through them practically all social adjustment is consummated. . . Public opinion is the highest form of collective attitudes.

Conclusion. This brief review of the history of the concept of attitude has established three important facts. (1) After the breakdown of intellectualistic psychology the phenomena of "determination" came slowly but certainly to be admitted to unquestioned standing in experimental psychology. *Attitudes* came into fashion. (2) Under the influence of psychoanalytic theory the dynamic and unconscious character of attitudes became more fully recognized. (3) In sociological writing there was a gradual turning of interest to attitudes considered as the concrete representations of culture. The effect of these three convergent trends within the past fifteen years has been the creation of a vigorous doctrine of attitudes, which today is bearing most of the descriptive and explanatory burdens of social psychology. Whether the concept is being overworked to such an extent that it will be discarded along with the past shibboleths of social science remains to be seen. It seems more probable that the ever increasing number of critical and analytical studies will somehow succeed in refining and preserving it.

ATTITUDES AS A FORM OF READINESS

Let us now consider a representative selection of definitions and characterizations of attitude.

[An attitude is] readiness for attention or action of a definite sort. (Baldwin, 1901-05)

Attitudes are literally mental postures, guides for conduct to which each new experience is referred before a response is made. (Morgan, 1934, p. 47)

Attitude=the specific mental disposition toward an incoming (or arising) experience, whereby that experience is modified, or, a condition of readiness for a certain type of activity. (*Dictionary of Psychology*, Warren, 1934)

An attitude is a complex of feelings, desires, fears, convictions, prejudices or other tendencies that have given *a set or readiness to act* to a person because of varied experiences. (Chave, 1928)

. . . a more or less permanently enduring state of readiness of mental organization which predisposes an individual to react in a characteristic way to any object or situation with which it is related. (Cantril, 1934a)

From the point of view of Gestalt psychology a change of attitude involves a definite physiological stress exerted upon a sensory field by processes originating in other parts of the nervous system. (Köhler, 1929, p. 184)

An attitude is a tendency to act toward or against something in the environment which becomes thereby a positive or negative value. (Bogardus, 1931, p. 62)

By attitude we understand a process of individual consciousness which determines real or possible activity of the individual counterpart of the social value; activity, in whatever form, is the bond between them. (Thomas and Znaniecki, 1918, p. 27)

The attitude, or preparation in advance of the actual response, constitutes an important determinant of the ensuing social behavior. Such neural settings, with their accompanying consciousness, are numerous and significant in social life. (F. H. Allport, 1924, p. 320)

An attitude is a mental disposition of the human individual to act for or against a definite object. (Droba, 1933)

[An attitude] denotes the general set of the organism as a whole toward an object or situation which calls for adjustment. (Lundberg, 1929)

[Attitudes] are modes of emotional regard for objects, and motor "sets" or slight, tentative reactions toward them. (Ewer, 1929, p. 136)

An attitude, roughly, is a residuum of experience, by which further activity is conditioned and controlled. . . . We may think of attitudes as acquired tendencies to act in specific ways toward objects. (Krueger and Reckless, 1931, p. 238)

When a certain type of experience is constantly repeated, a change of set is brought about which affects many central neurons and tends to spread over other parts of the central nervous system. These changes in the general set of the central nervous system temper the process of reception. . . . In terms of the subjective mental life these general sets are called attitudes. (Warren, 1922, pp. 360 f.)

An attitude is a disposition to act which is built up by the integration of numerous specific responses of a similar type, but which exists as a general neural "set," and when activated by a specific stimulus results in behavior that is more obviously a function of the disposition than of the activating stimulus. The important thing to note about this definition is that it considers attitudes as broad, generic (not simple and specific) determinants of behavior. (G. W. Allport, 1929)

We shall regard attitudes here as verbalized or verbalizable tendencies, dispositions, adjustments toward certain acts. They relate not to the past nor even primarily to the present, but as a rule, to the future. Sometimes, of course, it is a hypothetical future. . . The "attitude" is primarily a way of being "set" toward or against things. (Murphy and Murphy, 1931, p. 615)

It is not difficult to trace the common thread running through these diverse definitions In one way or another each regards the essential feature of attitude as a *preparation or readiness for response*. The attitude is incipient and preparatory rather than overt and consummatory. It is not behavior, but the precondition of behavior. It may exist in all degrees of readiness from the most latent, dormant traces of forgotten habits to the tension or motion which is actively determining a course of conduct that is under way.

Some writers prefer to characterize attitudes in neurological and physiological terms. They regard attitudes as neural sets which in some cases may be as definite as a physical posture or muscular contraction, and in some cases diffuse and non-identifiable. Bernard (see Young, 1931, pp. 48 ff.) calls the identifiable bodily sets "neuromuscular attitudes" and the more diffuse mental sets, "neuropsychic attitudes." The former are fully prepared to issue into action, their final common path is determined. The neuropsychic attitudes on the other hand involve primarily the complex mechanisms of the cortex, which make delay and substitute forms of action possible. In principle, both mental and motor attitudes are alike. Both are expressions of a preparedness for adjustive behavior, and both ultimately are related to the neural substrata. What these neural substrata are, however, is a problem which remains almost wholly in the sphere of speculation. Only in the simplest instances can the direct involvement of definable regions of the body be determined. For the most part attitudes are diffuse and pervasive. That they involve skeletal, visceral, cortical, and subcortical activity probably no psychologist would deny, but what these correlates are none can tell.

Time and again the phenomena of perception, judgment, memory, learning, and thought have been reduced largely to the operation of attitudes (cf. e.g., Ach, 1905; Bartlett, 1932; Chapman, 1932; Pyle, 1928). Without guiding attitudes the individual is confused and baffled. Some kind of preparation is essential before he can make a satisfactory observation, pass suitable judgment, or make any but the most primitive reflex type of response. Attitudes determine for each individual what he will see and hear, what he will think and what he will do. To borrow a phrase from William James, they "engender meaning upon the world"; they draw lines about and segregate an otherwise chaotic environment; they are our methods for finding our way about in an ambiguous universe. It is especially when the stimulus is not of great intensity nor closely bound with some reflex or automatic response that attitudes play a decisive rôle in the determination of meaning and of behavior.

Since reflex and automatic response have little place in social psychology, it is with attitudes that social psychology must be concerned. The whims of fashion, the success and the failure of propaganda, the swing of public opinion, the depredations of a mob, and a change in moral standards, are all alike unintelligible excepting in terms of the attitudes of individual men and women. It is knowledge of our associates' attitudes which enables each of us innumerable times every day to anticipate their behavior, and to insult, console, persuade, flatter, or amuse them, as we choose.

DIFFERENTIATION FROM OTHER TYPES OF READINESS

In contemporary literature *attitude* has a wide range of application, from the momentary mental set, or *Aufgabe,* to the most inclusive and permanent dispositions, such as a philosophy of life. This broad usage can neither be denied nor remedied. The psychologist must accept the fact that the concept is very general, but he should not for that reason be content to use it loosely. Some writers seem to prefer to attach to *attitude* a vague and omnibus significance that will "involve instincts, appetites, habits, emotions, sentiments, opinions, and wishes" (Park and Burgess, 1924); but such a generous connotation surrenders a valuable term to the ravages of mere verbalism, and is not to be recommended. Fortunately the majority of social psychologists do not employ the term as an omnibus. They have many other words at their disposal to connote other forms of readiness, and wisely prefer to restrict the use of "attitude." Readiness-for-response is the *genus proximum* to which "attitude" belongs. What are the *differentia* by which "attitude" may be distinguished from the numerous other forms of readiness?

Attitudes and Reflexes. Although the latent reflex tendency, like the attitude, is a potential determinant of behavior, it is much more invariable in its operation and much more limited by the conditions of the stimulus..

Its neural "trace" is presumably more specific and less diffuse. Furthermore, the reflex unlike the attitude is entirely innate or congenital.

Attitudes and Conditioned Reflexes. Both of these determinants of behavior are acquired in the course of experience, but the distinction as in the preceding case is one of scope, diffuseness, and variability.

Attitudes and Habits. Although Dewey equates these two concepts (cf. p. 802), it is ordinarily supposed that habits are more specific in their dependence upon the stimulus and are more invariable in their expression. Habits, furthermore, lack the *directedness* which is characteristic of attitudes, that is to say, they are not accompanied by a customary feeling of favor or disfavor; they are more automatic and less partisan.

Attitudes and Instincts or Propensities. The differences here are striking. Unlike the innate tendency the attitude is (1) always, at least in part, acquired, (2) highly individual, varying from person to person, and not universal, (3) as a rule considered to be more "directive" than "driving," and (4) has more cognitive content.

Attitudes and Needs, Wishes, or Desires. Like attitudes, needs, wishes, and desires are ordinarily supposed to reflect considerable organization under the influence of environmental forces, but, unlike attitudes, they are generally offered in neat classified lists and regarded as universal motives of men. Attitudes are more numerous, more personal, and more variable, and are commonly regarded as *modi operandi* in conduct rather than as original sources of motivation.

Attitudes, Vectors, and Quasi-Needs. In the theory of Lewin (1931) a vector, like an attitude, becomes an expression of attraction and repulsion, in other words, an expression of the directed relationship of the organism to some environmental object which has for him value or 'valence.' The vector, however, seems in part to be extra-organic, whereas the attitude is always considered to be an internal condition of the organism. The internal conditions, Lewin refers to as either *genuine* needs or as *quasi*-needs. The latter are tensions engendered by the situation or undertaking in hand. They are indeed attitudes, but attitudes of a somewhat specific order, limited by the *Vornahme,* and regarded as relatively transient. Quasi-needs, therefore, are essentially temporary attitudes.

Attitudes and Sentiments. According to McDougall:

> The theory of sentiments is the theory of the progressive organization of the propensities (instincts) in systems which become the main sources of all our activities; systems which give consistency, continuity and order to our life of striving and emotion; systems which in turn become organized in larger systems, and which, when harmoniously organized in one comprehensive system, constitute what we properly call *character.* (1933, p. 211)

McDougall contends "that an adequate theory of the sentiments must be the main foundation of all social psychology." The present chapter, on the contrary, is engaged in proving that an adequate theory of *attitudes* must be the main foundation of all social psychology.

The objections which McDougall raises against attitude are two in number. He finds (1) that "the term is used to cover a multitude of facts of many kinds," and (2) that it "literally means some particular expressive position of body and limbs, and when used metaphorically of the mind, it can only mean some particular actual, incipient, or potential reaction." Sentiment on the other hand, he believes, is a less ambiguous term and designates a more varied and purposive behavior. For the majority of psychologists "attitude" has long since lost its specific postural connotation. It serves exactly the purpose which McDougall reserves to "sentiment," viz., the designation of breadth of receptivity and versatility of response.

Specifically, the differences between attitude and sentiment, which are at the same time grounds for preferring the former as "the main foundation of all social psychology," are the following: (1) A sentiment, in Mc-Dougall's sense, presupposes definite underlying propensities; whereas an attitude is an *actual* disposition within the organism considered without regard to its origins. (2) An attitude may be specific or general, that is to say, it may be directed toward a very special object or value, or may be highly diffuse in its reference; whereas the sentiment is considered as a system of emotional tendencies centered about some *definite* object. The object of an attitude is usually less definite and more abstract. It may be proper to speak of either an attitude or a sentiment toward John, but it is clearly an attitude and *not* a sentiment which one possesses towards John's untidiness, his laziness, his nonchalance, or his affected speech. It is an attitude and not a sentiment which makes us despise affected speech in general. It is an attitude and not a sentiment which leads us to a gentle tolerance or a profound cynicism. It is an attitude and not a sentiment which makes us prey to the ravages of advertisers and propagandists. (3) Sentiments are conceived as more lasting and more hierarchical than attitudes need be. Some attitudes indeed may be lasting and architectonic, but they may be, and frequently are, transient and dissociated from the main emotional centers of personality. (4) Finally, McDougall considers the sentiment on the whole to be both conscious and benign in its operations. In these respects it differs from the *complex* which is a morbid and repressed sentiment (1926, pp. 227 f.). The term "attitude" refers indistinguishably to both the conscious and unconscious aspects of a disposition, and likewise has the added advantage of presuming no normative distinction between what is healthful and what is unhealthful.

Attitudes and Motor Set. Psychologists long ago recognized the functional importance of muscular tonicity in determining both the content of consciousness and the response. The term "attitude," of course, is still used to refer to this obvious condition of motor preparedness. Response-psychologists prefer on theoretical grounds to identify attitudes with motor set (Washburn, 1916), but other psychologists who are unwilling to reduce all phenomena to the motor levels prefer to regard motor sets as only one type of attitude.

Attitudes, Interests, and Subjective Values. Interests are a special type of enduring attitudes which refer, as a rule, to a *class* of objects rather than to a single object. They are dynamic attitudes, rich in ideational content, and involve a recognition and understanding of the objects which have satisfying properties. Subjective values are essentially the same as interests, except that they are more properly spoken of when the individual is mature and has reflected upon and organized his interests within a comprehensive and consistent system of thought and feeling.

Attitudes and Prejudices or Stereotypes. Attitudes which result in gross oversimplifications of experience and in prejudgments are of great importance in social psychology (cf. pp. 814-816). They are commonly called biases, prejudices, or stereotypes. The latter term is less normative, and therefore on the whole to be preferred.

Attitudes and Concepts. The concept, like the attitude, betokens a preparation to receive and to interpret the data of the external world. It is, however, clearly a more intellectualistic term. It suggests preparation only for thought and never directly for action.

Attitudes and Opinions. Psychologists conceive the relation of opinion to attitude in two ways. (1) Thurstone (1927-28) considers an opinion to be the accessible portion, or external expression, of the attitude. (2) Others believe that the opinion is at best a distortion of the true attitude. Park writes;

> An individual's own account of his attitude is his opinion; but opinions are after all largely what the psychoanalysts call a "rationalization." They are his explanations and justification of his attitudes, rather than his actual tendencies to act. (1924)

Similarly Bogardus writes:

> An opinion may be merely a defense reaction which through over-emphasis usually falsifies consciously or unconsciously a man's real attitude. (1931, p. 54)

Attitudes and Traits. As ordinarily used the term "trait" does not imply as definite a relation between the self and the external or conceptualized object or value as does "attitude" (cf. pp. 836-838). A trait is a form or manner of behaving; an attitude is a directed tendency. One may have an attitude of fear *toward* objects, persons, qualities, or classes of ideas, but one *is* in one's very nature yielding, shy, submissive, retiring, or bashful.

A Definition of Attitudes. It is not easy to construct a definition sufficiently broad to cover the many kinds of attitudinal determination which psychologists today recognize, and at the same time narrow enough to exclude those types of determination which are not ordinarily referred to as attitudes. The definitions considered above (pp. 804-805) contain helpful suggestions, and yet none alone is entirely satisfactory. The chief weakness of most of them seems to be their failure to distinguish between attitudes, which are often very general, and habits, which are always limited in their scope.

Any attempt at a definition exaggerates the degree of agreement which psychologists have reached, but is justified if it contributes toward securing greater agreement in the future. The following definition has the merit of including recognized types of attitudes: the *Aufgabe,* the quasi-need, the *Bewusstseinslage,* interest and subjective value, prejudice, stereotype, and even the broadest conception of all, the philosophy of life. It excludes those types of readiness which are expressly innate, which are bound rigidly and invariably to the stimulus, which lack flexibility, and which lack directionality and reference to some external or conceptual object. *An attitude is a mental and neural state of readiness, organized through experience, exerting a directive or dynamic influence upon the individual's response to all objects and situations with which it is related.*

Genesis of Attitudes

Four Common Conditions for the Formation of Attitudes. One of the chief ways in which attitudes are built up is through the accretion of experience, that is to say, through the *integration* of numerous specific responses of a similar type. It is not, as a rule, the discrete and isolated experience which engenders an attitude; for in itself the single experience lacks organization in memory, meaning, and emotion. An attitude is characteristically a fusion, or, in Burnham's terms (1924, p. 285), a "residuum of many repeated processes of sensation, perception, and feeling."

It is a favorite doctrine of mental hygiene that *wholesome* attitudes are those which are the product of *all* experience that is relevant to a certain issue, without repressions or dissociations to mar their inclusiveness. Thus Morgan writes:

> A hasty generalization based on a very few incidents should be viewed with suspicion, [whereas if the attitude] grew from actual experiences, and is a correct abstract formulation of the lessons learned from a large number of these experiences, it should be rated high. (1934, p. 49)

Important as the mechanism of integration unquestionably is in the formation of attitudes, it has in recent years been criticized for its one-sided emphasis. The motto of integration is *e pluribus unum.* It inevitably implies that the infant is totally specific and fragmentary in his responses, and that in childhood his attitudes become gradually "pieced together," and that in adulthood he becomes still more thoroughly unified.

Certain recent developments in psychology have brought a quite contrary emphasis in their train. Integration, it is said, is not the only mechanism of development. It is supplemented by an equally important mechanism which has been variously called *individuation, differentiation,* or *segregation* (Holt, 1931; Lewin, 1935; Ogden, 1926; Pratt, Nelson, and Sun, 1930). According to this doctrine the original matrix of all attitudes is coarse, diffuse, and non-specific; it is the mass-action found in infancy, which tends only to have a general positive (adient) or negative (abient) orientation. From this point of view it might be said that in the beginning the infant has two primordial, non-specific attitudes, namely, approaching and avoiding. From this matrix, he must segregate action-patterns and conceptual systems which will supply him with adequate attitudes for the direction of his adaptive conduct.

A third important source of attitudes is the dramatic experience, or *trauma.* It is well known that a permanent attitude may be formed as the result of a compulsive organization in the mental field following a single intense emotional experience. Probably everyone can trace certain of his fears, dislikes, prejudices, and predilections to dramatic incidents of childhood. Sometimes, as Freudians have shown, the source of these early fixations are suppressed and forgotten, and the resulting attitude, though strong, seems to be of mysterious origin. But sometimes the whole process of traumatic fixation is accessible to memory. The recovery of the traumatic origins to consciousness does not necessarily weaken the attitude. The autobiography of W. E. Leonard (1927) illustrates the tenacity of early attitudes of fear in spite of the insight acquired into their origin. Although the traumatic experiences of childhood seem to be especially important, there is all through life a susceptibility to the influence of emotional shock. In *Days without End* Eugene O'Neill traces the genesis of a young man's atheistic attitude to the death of his parents, and the restoration of his religious attitude to the critical illness of his wife many years later. Even in old age radical changes of attitude through circumstances of dramatic moment are not unknown.

There is a fourth common condition under which attitudes are formed. Through the imitation of parents, teachers, or playmates, they are sometimes adopted *ready-made.* Even before he has an adequate background of appropriate experience a child may form many intense and lasting attitudes toward races and professions, toward religion and marriage, toward foreigners and servants, and toward morality and sin. A parent's tone of voice in disapproving of the ragamuffins who live along the railroad track is enough to produce an uncritical attitude in the child who has no basis in his experience for the rational adoption of the parent's point of view. It frequently happens that *subsequent* experience is fitted into the attitude thus uncritically adopted, not—as the mental hygienist advocates—made the basis for the attitude. In such cases every contact is prejudged, contradictory evidence is not admitted, and the attitude which was borrowed second-hand is triumphant. Few men have actually encountered "tricky Japanese" or "cruel Turks," few have known tragedy to follow a dinner party of thirteen, or the lighting of three cigarettes from the same match. And yet thousands of such attitudes and beliefs are adopted ready-made and tenaciously held against all evidence to the contrary.

Genetic Studies of the Formation of Attitudes. Illustrations of the four conditions just described can be found in several recent investigations. Vetter and Green (1932) studied the genesis of anti-religious attitudes of 350 members of the American Association for the Advancement of Atheism. Many of these cases reported that the accumulation (integration) of influences derived from the reading of history and science resulted in the gradual formation of their attitudes. Others spoke of their atheism as a by-product (differentiation) of a more general, preceding point of view, e.g., a philosophy of materialism. Still others traced their convictions to sharp (traumatic) experiences of disgust or grief. Occasionally they reported the influence of a friend whose atheistic views they adopted (ready-made).

In a study of children's attitudes toward race, Lasker (1929) found that cumulative experience (integration) is a relatively minor factor. The dramatic (traumatic) experience likewise occurs but is not usually the principal cause. More often the ostracism or segregation of a given race is observed by a child before he has any clear prejudice of his own. In these cases it may be said that the specific prejudice develops from the preceding attitude toward exclusion or toward the separation of what is "desirable" from what is "undesirable" (through differentiation). But the outstanding source of racial prejudice is the assumption of the attitudes of others (ready-made). The white child who has as yet no convictions of superiority is not slow in interpreting his parents' amusement at Mandy's gay new Easter hat or her use of a blond face-powder. Through derogatory and derisive names, through humorous stories, through persecution, and through legend, "the social order itself conveys lessons that are absorbed without conscious learning" (Lasker, 1929, p. 102).

In his study of the genesis of revolutionary attitudes among 163 outstanding communist leaders in Russia, Davis (1930) listed twenty-five formative influences. Of these the most important were teachers, fellow-students, fellow-workers, books, periodicals, and the family. Three-quarters of the leaders began radical activity by the time they were twenty-one years of age, and virtually all of them by the age of twenty-six. This fact is an illustration of the decisive effects of the attitudes formed in youth. Most of the incomparably important attitudes not only toward politics, but toward the home, toward religion, sex, social welfare, vocation, marriage, and personal duty, are formed in adolescence, and for the most part endure throughout life. Barring unusual experiences of conversion or crisis, attitudes are likely to be confirmed and enriched rather than altered or replaced.

Davis found that the cumulative experiences of persecution had an *integrative* effect upon the attitudes of the revolutionists. *Traumatic* in-incidents are also frequently listed. (The hatred of the father sometimes led a man into radical activity, a fact which lends some support to the Freudian theory that revolutionary attitudes are provoked by repressed aggression.) The turning of vague discontent into revolutionary channels is an instance of *differentiation;* and the influence of associates undoubtedly signifies in some cases the adoption of attitudes *ready-made*.

Fixity and Change in Attitudes. It has been said that "it is characteristic of attitudes to be modified by every experience which relates to them" (Morgan, 1934). This is a statement of the condition which *would* prevail if integration were the only mechanism concerned in the formation of attitudes. Day by day our varied encounters would be absorbed into our pre-existing store of knowledge, and would modify in direct proportion to their number and relevancy our "pictures" of the world we live in. This orderly procedure, so desirable from the point of view of mental hygiene, is a flattering overstatement of the rationality of mental operation. An attitude seldom contains all of the experience which is relevant to it, and seldom changes as rapidly as a faithful following of experience would require.

Attitudes are often as rigid as habits. They are, to paraphrase William James, a fly-wheel and a conservative agent in society; they save the privileged classes from the envious uprisings of the poor; and cause the poor in spite of their bitter experience to think and to vote in ways that are inimical to their own interests. The attitude, like the habit, "keeps the fisherman and the deck-hand at sea through the winter; it holds the miner in his darkness, and nails the country man to his log-cabin and his lonely farm through all the months of snow." Professional attitudes, like professional mannerisms, are set early in life.

> You see the little lines of cleavage running through the character, the tricks of thought, the prejudices, the ways of the "shop," in a word, from which the man can by-and-by no more escape than his coat-sleeve can suddenly fall into a new set of folds. On the whole it is best he should not escape. It is well for the world that in most of us, by the age of thirty, the character has set like plaster, and will never soften again. (James, 1890, vol. 1, p. 121)

The inflexibility of attitudes has formed the basis of Lippmann's theory of public opinion (1922). It is not possible, as he points out, for human beings to respond to every stimulus-event with complete and intelligent discrimination. People have neither the time, the knowledge, the inclination, nor the requisite intelligence for meeting adequately the subtle and varied demands of their intricate environments. The best they can do is to classify the events of life and to respond to them, not on their own individual merit, but according to their assumed membership. *Clichés* are made to cover the facts of life. In place of rational adaptation, there is called into play merely an approximate, rough-and-ready attitude. The newspaper reader who is bewildered by the challenge to his feeble powers contained in the day's news conveniently protects himself with stereotyped attitude and says, "I never believe what I read in the papers." The conservative man who is aware of, but confused by, the injustices of society rationalizes his inability to think things through and protects himself from personal discomfort by the reflection that "you cannot change human nature." A few amiable souls are able to dispose of the totality of life's puzzles with one simple and salutary attitude: "It's a great life if you don't weaken." Such attitudes serve as a safety-valve when pressure upon human reason becomes excessive.

Because they save both time and effort, stereotyped attitudes offer great resistance to change. They resist the inroads of new contradictory experience and are retained as long as they satisfy and protect the individual. But sometimes an attitude proves to be so distressingly inadequate that it can no longer be retained. Likewise, there are men who are plastic and open-minded and who seriously try to keep their attitudes abreast of their experience.

If the experience contradicts the stereotype, one of two things happens. If the man is no longer plastic, or if some powerful interest makes it highly inconvenient to rearrange his stereotypes, he pooh-poohs the contradiction as an exception that proves the rule, discredits the witness, finds a flaw somewhere, and manages to forget it. But if he is still curious and open-minded, the novelty is taken into the picture, and allowed to modify it. Sometimes, if the incident is striking enough, and if he has felt a general discomfort with his established scheme, he may be shaken to such an extent as to distrust all accepted ways of looking at life, and to expect that normally a thing will not be what it is generally supposed to be. (Lippmann, 1922, p. 100)

Undoubtedly the occasion most favorable to an alteration of attitudes is a period of emotional disorganization. At such times pre-existing attitudes are found to be unsuitable. New attitudes emerge which, according to Faris, represent "a resolution of a crisis, the solution of a difficulty, the end of a period of chaos, the termination of a moment of disorganization" (see Young, 1931, p. 11). When in a crisis old attitudes are found to be worthless they no longer offer effective resistance to the new. Conversion, the shock of grief, economic disaster, and falling in love are typical occasions during which old attitudes are abandoned and new attitudes come into being.

By way of summary it may be said that attitudes do not, as the simple principle of integration would imply, grow only through the orderly accretion and arrangement of experience. They are often merely rough-and-ready mental sets through which diverse experiences are channelized. They are so saving of time and mental effort that they often persist throughout life in the way in which they were fixed in childhood or in youth. An attitude is retained so long as it satisfies the individual, but is likely to be modified under the provocation of serious affective disorganization.

PREJUDGMENT AND PREJUDICE

Whenever a pre-existing attitude is so strong and inflexible that it seriously distorts perception and judgment, rendering them inappropriate to the demands of the objective situation, the social psychologist usually designates this tenacious attitude as a *stereotype,* a *prejudice,* or sometimes, more loosely, as a *logic-tight compartment.* These three concepts, which are more or less interchangeable, are of great value in the explanation of social phenomena. They explain why the skilful propagandist chooses solidified emotional attitudes to play upon. They tell why human beings persevere in ancient ruts of thought and action, and why "facts" are of relatively little importance in shaping public opinion, and why the dead hand of the past is permitted to fashion the social policies of the present day. They explain why the banal remarks of a famous man or woman are widely circulated and reverently quoted, and why the cleverer epigrams and shrewder pronouncements of an unknown sage are ignored or discounted. They help one to understand the characteristic conservatism and the "cultural lag" of society.

Experimental Studies of Prejudgment. In a simple way, Zillig (1928) demonstrated the effect of personal likes and dislikes upon observation and report. She had secretly instructed some children who were very popular with their schoolmates to make a certain error during a classroom demonstration of physical drill (for example, to raise their left arms instead of their right). Unpopular children in the same demonstration performed the exercise correctly. When the class was asked to report the names of the children who made mistakes during the exercise, the faultless but unpopular pupils received the blame! Working with the older students, Lund (1925) discovered an agreement between *desire* and *belief*. It is not knowledge, he found, which determines the strength of a conviction but rather the desirability of this conviction from the point of view of the individual holding it. Sargent (cited in Murphy and Murphy, 1931, pp. 681-683) discovered that the more intensely emotional an attitude the less flexible is the meaning or definition of the object of that attitude. For example, if one has a marked attitude toward socialism, the meaning of the concept is more stereotyped and less susceptible of change than if one possesses no strong feelings concerning the matter. Probably the best-known work in this field is that of Rice (1926-27). He demonstrated by the use of photographs the existence of visual stereotypes concerning vocational and racial types (e.g., the senator, the bootlegger, and the Bolshevik), as well as the effect of these stereotypes upon judgments concerning the intelligence and craftiness of the men whose pictures were employed.

A demonstration of aesthetic stereotypes has been made by Sherif (1935). This investigator secured, as a first step in his study, the rank-order preferences of his subjects for sixteen English and American authors (such as Barrie, Conrad, Cooper, Dickens, Poe, Scott, Stevenson, and Wilder). After an interval of several weeks he submitted sixteen literary passages, all from Stevenson, but each passage ascribed to one of the authors included in the first list. The subjects were then required to rank these passages in order of their literary merit. In no case did any subject suspect the deception.

A few judges reported that in ranking the passages they ignored altogether the names of the "authors" which appeared underneath each passage. In these cases, as might be expected, the correlation between the original preference for the authors and the rating for the merit of the passage was zero. But for the remaining subjects, nearly two hundred in number, the average correlation was +.46. Work attributed to a favorite author is considered good, and work attributed to an uncongenial author is considered bad. Since the passages are in fact from a single author, and since the same results are secured whatever author's name is appended to a passage, it is clear that the correlations obtained can only be a measure of prejudice.

Racial Attitudes. By asking "which of these two nationalities would you prefer to associate with?" Thurstone (1928) determined by the method of comparative judgment the relative popularity of twenty-one national groups for a population of university students. Establishing for the preferred group, the American, a scale value of zero, and for the least preferred a sigma value of 5.86, the relative standing of each of these racial groups was determined:

American	0.00	Russian	4.10
English	1.34	Pole	4.41
Scotch	2.09	Greek	4.62
Irish	2.18	Armenian	4.68
French	2.46	Japanese	4.93
German	2.56	Mexican	5.10
Swede	2.90	Chinese	5.30
South American	3.64	Hindu	5.35
Italian	3.66	Turk	5.82
Spanish	3.79	Negro	5.86
Jew	3.92		

Although Thurstone's results were obtained for a limited population of subjects, they are strikingly similar to results obtained in various parts of the United States. With but few local variations the "social distance" with which different racial groups are regarded is the same from coast to coast. Katz and Braly (1933) attribute this uniformity of racial attitudes largely to the acceptance of ready-made attitudes, and they studied the stereotyped associations which accompany each of the racial labels. Using a check-list of adjectives they determined the percentage of their subjects who thought of certain qualities as attributes of each race. The Germans, for example, were regarded as predominantly scientific, industrious, and stolid; the Negroes as superstitious, lazy, happy-go-lucky; the Irish as pugnacious, quick-tempered, and witty; the English as sportsmanlike, intelligent, and conventional; the Italians as artistic, impulsive, and passionate; the Jews as shrewd, mercenary, and industrious; Americans as industrious, intelligent, and materialistic; Chinese as superstitious, sly, and conservative; Japanese as intelligent, industrious, progressive; Turks as cruel and very religious. One noteworthy feature of this study was the finding that degree of acquaintance with a racial group did not enchance the degree of agreement concerning its outstanding characteristics. The qualities of the Americans, who surely were the best known, were less agreed upon than the qualities of the Jews, Germans, or Italians.

Another study of the uniformity of prejudice is that of Katz and Allport (1931). In a large population of students it was found that certain antipathies were almost universal. Less than 10 per cent of the students signified their willingness to admit to their fraternities or rooming-houses such groups as the Negroes, Turks, Hindus, Chinese, Japanese, Bolsheviks, anarchists, students of unconventional morals or of low intelligence; Greeks, Armenians, Poles, Jews, agnostics, socialists, and lazy or unattractive students fared little better. A number of these groups have no racial implications, but the force of the symbol in all cases evokes avertive attitudes. The prejudice toward unpopular group labels seems to be practically universal.

Have Attitudes Motive Power?

As a rule in psychological literature attitudes have been regarded as determining tendencies and not as the main-springs of conduct. They are generally considered to be channels through which a motive is expressed but not in themselves to be true motives. Thus Droba (1933) writes, "Attitudes point out the direction an activity will take; motives are the starters of the activity." McDougall likewise regards attitudes as mere motor sets or postures which are provoked and sustained by the action of sentiments which in turn derive their energy from the instincts, "the main-springs of all human and animal activity" (1933, p. 225). All psychologists who postulate an underlying scheme of instincts, needs, desires, or drives are inclined to regard attitudes as formal and determinative rather than as motivational. Even Thomas, who was so instrumental in securing the adoption of the concept of attitude, seems to consider it necessary to postulate an underlying stratum of "wishes" which will instigate and sustain the activity of the attitudes (1923).

On the other hand it is not difficult to find opinions on the other side. Dewey (1922), for example, regards habits (attitudes) as self-active; they are "positive forms of action which are released merely through the removal of some counteracting 'inhibitory' tendency, and then become overt." According to Köhler (1929, p. 323) "the most compulsory organization which can occur in experience is a dynamical event or attitude." Warren and Carmichael (1930, p. 326) have an equally dynamic emphasis: "The idealistic man, the practical man, the scientist, and other types are distinguished on the basis of certain underlying attitudes which govern their behavior and conduct." North (1932) defines attitude to include motive: it is "the totality of those states that lead to or point toward some particular activity of the organism. The attitude is, therefore, the dynamic element in human behavior, the motive for activity."

This second group of writers have the support of common sense. One says, "I voted for him because I am a Republican," "I will not do business with him because I distrust his race," "I have a strong prejudice against commercial advertising and so I try never to buy an advertised product," or "I am an admirer of such-and-such an author, and read everything he writes." In these instances and in numberless others it seems to be the attitude which itself is the efficient cause of the activity.

On page 802 attention was called to the tendency in contemporary social psychology for the concept of attitude to displace the concepts of need, instinct, and drive. Many writers prefer to emphasize the concrete, personalized motives, such as attitudes represent, rather than abstract uniformities of motives, such as need or instinct. John's personal beliefs and attitudes respecting some national policy are surely a more tangible "cause" of his behavior than is his "instinct of gregariousness," and Mary's mature affection for her father is a more proximate and intelligible cause of her devoted behavior than is "infantile sexuality," "a filial instinct," or a "wish for security."

Psychoanalysts, instinctivists, and geneticists in general, of course, protest that it is superficial to consider an attitude as a motive. They say that it is only in the deeper energic streams of life, or in the unconscious, that motive power is to be sought. Here, it must be admitted frankly, is a controversy. Dynamic psychology, which is interested above all else in motivation, divides on this issue into two camps. The following paragraphs outline and defend the position of those who, contrary to the views of psychoanalysts and instinctivists, believe that acquired attitudes may serve as fundamental and irreducible motives.

The original drives, instincts, or libidinal strivings of early childhood, whatever they may be, are quickly overlaid by experience and are organized into a personal system of attitudes. Their roots are absorbed into the new individualized motives. One recalls in this connection how James declared all instincts to be transitory and overlaid in childhood with habits which in turn became the primary factors in the motivation. It is impossible in adult life to designate the basal instincts or universal needs, for each person is driven by his own beliefs and ambitions, by his own prejudices and desires. So great is the diversity of motives that in no concrete or intelligible sense can they all be referred to "sex energy," or to "instincts." In order to account for the infinite variety of human motives it becomes necessary to admit that the very process of learning is a process of forming new motives, which in time lose their functional dependence upon the antecedent motives from which they were derived.

The question now arises whether these new motives are properly to be called "attitudes." Can one speak, for example, of "being driven by an attitude?" The answer is that *sometimes* one can do so. A strong anti-Fascist attitude, for example, may involve a tension which *provokes* the individual to some aggressive behavior in order to express or to satisfy it. Ever so many similar attitudes could be enumerated. The bridge-enthusiast, the loyal lodge member, the inveterate fisherman, the philanthropist, the esthete, the church-goer, the red-baiter, the muck-raker, the cynic—all behave as they do because they have developed dynamic attitudes. In these cases it becomes impossible to distinguish between motive power and direction, between the drive and the form of expression which the drive takes, or between the energy itself and the way in which the energy is guided. These attitudes both motivate and guide; they supply both drive and direction.

On the other hand, it must be admitted that *some* attitudes seem to be merely directive and not motivational. For example, when a subject comes into a psychological laboratory he is motivated by curiosity, emulation, or obedience (themselves deep-lying attitudes), but he may assume additional attitudes which are incidental to the occasion. The *Aufgabe* which he adopts, for instance, is not itself the motive in the situation. To press a key when a red light appears is an attitude but not a motive. This attitude merely directs or guides a course of conduct which has been otherwise motivated.

It seems necessary, therefore, to distinguish two types of attitudes: one which is so organized and energized that it actually *drives*, and the other which merely *directs*. Both of these types are conditions of readiness-for-response, both are in a sense dynamic, for both enter into the determination of conduct. The first, however, is specifically *motivational*, the second (which includes besides the *Aufgabe* such "postures of consciousness" as are involved in skills and in the manner and modes of response) are merely *instrumental*. The true motive underlying an instrumental or directive attitude is often some other driving attitude, or sometimes it is of so primitive and unorganized a nature that it may be called instinctive.

The distinction between a driving and a directive attitude is not always clear-cut. What is a directive attitude today may become a driving attitude in the future, and what is today a true motive may in time degenerate into a mere habitual directive attitude. The first of these mutations is described by Woodworth (1918) as the transformation of "mechanisms" into "drives," and the second by Voelker in his theory of the degeneration of ideals to the status of mere habit (1921, p. 56).

POSITIVE AND NEGATIVE ATTITUDES

An attitude characteristically provokes behavior that is acquisitive or avertive, favorable or unfavorable, affirmative or negative toward the object or class of objects with which it is related. This double polarity in the *direction* of attitudes is often regarded as their most distinctive feature. It has a central place in Bogardus' definition (1931, p. 52): "An attitude is a tendency to act toward or against some environmental factor which becomes thereby a positive or negative value." Likewise, Thurstone defines an attitude as "the affect for or against a psychological object" (1932).

This point of view is a modern version of an ancient dialectic. For centuries the opposed categories of "attraction" and "repulsion" have in one form or another played a decisive part in psychological theory. Empedocles assumed as the explanation of all activity the two contrasting immaterial principles of Love and Hate. The same opposed forces are prominent in the psychological theories of Mantegazza, Brentano, and Lindworsky. On a physiological plane one again encounters the dialectic of attraction and repulsion in the opposition of the flexors and extensors (Sherrington), in facilitation and inhibition (Münsterberg), in resistance and conductance (Troland), in outreaching and withdrawing behavior (Watson), in alliance and combat (Tarde), in acquisitive and avertive tendencies (Kempf), in adient and abient responses (Holt), and in pleasure and pain. One recent textbook of social psychology bears the subtitle, *The Psychology of Attraction and Repulsion* (Smith, 1930), and the same pair of concepts underlie the sociological system of Roguin (1931 and 1932). It is no wonder that many writers find it possible to classify all attitudes as either *positive* or *negative*. It is undoubtedly true that the majority fit easily into these categories.

And yet some attitudes are not readily classified. What shall one do, for example, with a detached, impersonal, or judicial attitude, or with an attitude of neutrality? Complacency, amusement, tolerance, and open-mindedness are not easily reduced to "affect for or against" an object. Two bridge-players may have the same "degree of affect" toward the game, and yet differ qualitatively in their attitudes toward it. Two radicals may be equally in favor of change, but disagree in the *modus operandi* of reform. Two people equally well disposed toward the church may differ in their sacramental, liturgical, esthetic, social, Protestant, or Catholic interpretation of the church. Is the degree of positive or negative affect aroused by the concept of "God" as significant as the *qualitative* distinctions involved in theistic, deistic, pantheistic, agnostic, intellectualistic, or emotional attitudes? When one speaks of attitudes toward sex, it is obviously only the qualitative distinctions that have any intelligible meaning. What is a "serene and benevolent mind"? Certainly not one devoid of attitudes, nor yet one that is a battle-ground of tendencies "for" and tendencies "against." All of these objections to the unidimensional view argue strongly for the recognition of the *qualitative* nature of attitudes.

There is, however, one way of meeting these objections, namely, by reducing attitudes to small enough components. If they are divided up into artificialized units, the unidimensional conception is saved. The two radicals, for example, who are equally "against" the present social system, but who differ in their policies, may conceivably be compared in respect to the attraction or repulsion they show for each of the disputed policies. The bridge-enthusiasts who differ in their attitudes toward the game *can* be compared quantitatively in their attitudes for or against conversation during the play. Church-goers may be found to vary quantitatively in the degree to which they favor every specific practice: baptism by immersion, intincture, genuflection, or the use of vestments. And even the man who has a neutral attitude may be found to have a positive and measurable attachment to the *ideal* of neutrality. If such rigid analyses are pursued, all of the complex, qualitative attitudes can be broken down and measured in *fragments*. The price one must pay for bi-polarity and quantification in such cases is, of course, extreme, and often absurd, *elementarism*.

SPECIFIC AND GENERAL ATTITUDES

There are two quite clearly opposed points of view regarding the breadth or range of attitudes. Some writers maintain that attitudes are specific, that they represent tendencies to make particular responses in particular situations. From this point of view "attitudes are as numerous as the objects to which a person responds" (Bogardus, 1931, p. 54). Other writers, however, consider attitudes as capable of "spreading" until they represent extensified and broadly generalized dispositions. The issue which is involved in this lively controversy is of the greatest practical and theoretical importance, for upon its solution depends not only the proper choice of methods for investigating attitudes, but likewise the theory of mental organization and of the structure of personality itself.

The Case for Specificity. In the older experimental psychology it was customary to regard attitudes as temporary mental or motor sets, prepared at one time and applied to one and only one act of adjustment. There is therefore a certain tradition in favor of the view that attitudes are specific, momentary integrations. The modern argument rests, however, more directly upon impressive recent experiments—those, for example, carried out by the Character Education Inquiry (Hartshorne and May, 1928; Hartshorne, May, and Maller, 1929; Hartshorne, May, and Shuttleworth, 1930).

The results of this extensive investigation have entrenched the specificistic point of view. Among the problems studied was the tendency of children to cheat. It was found, for example, that school children who overcome the greatest resistance in order to cheat while correcting their own arithmetic papers will overcome also weaker resistances, and that those who overcome only the least resistance will not cheat when cheating is more difficult. This clear quantitative expression of the readiness to cheat holds, however, only for a specific type of cheating (in this case, grading school papers). Those who will go to great limits here for the sake of illicit gain do not necessarily go to the same limits for the sake of dishonest advantage in other tests. Since children have such different scores in different tempting situations, the authors are led to conclude that their moral attitudes must be limited by the particular situation in which they are called forth.

> Honesty or dishonesty is not a unified character trait in children of the ages studied, but a series of specific responses to specific situations. (Hartshorne, May, and Maller, 1929, p. 243)

Essentially the same type of finding and interpretation characterize the other "areas" of conduct studied, such as helpfulness, persistence, and inhibition. As a consequence of this monumental study, a didactic literature has arisen which advises that children be trained in specific moral habits rather than by precept or general principle (e.g., Hartshorne, 1932; Symonds, 1928).

Various criticisms have been advanced against the conclusions and applications of this investigation. It has been objected, for example, that a high degree of generality must not be expected in young children, and that in the older children the Inquiry did indeed find greater evidence of consistency. It has been objected that the moral habits studied are too few and too distantly related to give a reasonable opportunity for generality to emerge in the results. It has been objected that ethical rather than psychological conceptions were used, and that, although children may not be consistent in character, *socially defined,* they may be quite consistent in their own way in their own *personal* attitudes and traits. It has been pointed out that, although general moral attitudes have not been developed under our piece-meal method of education, there is no proof that such general attitudes cannot under proper conditions of instruction be produced. It has been objected, furthermore, that the theory of specificity rests ultimately upon an arbitrary interpretation of equivocal results. Treating the same data with different statistical tools, one may find evidence for a genuine consistency of moral attitudes.

Quite apart from the merits of this single study, which will long remain a classic of social research, a serious theoretical objection must be made to the doctrine of specificity. If an attitude be defined only as a tendency to make a particular response in a particular situation, it is clear that the number of attitudes will be as numerous as the totality of stimuli to which the individual has responded in his lifetime. Each separate connection would be a separate attitude, and there would be no consecutiveness in conduct or organization in personality. It must be that those who define attitudes so specifically cannot mean what they say, for without a certain *inner* organization of tendencies there would be neither consecutiveness nor intelligibility in behavior. The issues involved here are somewhat complex and have been treated elsewhere (G. W. Allport, 1932; Allport and Vernon, 1930).

The Case for Generality. The doctrine of generality maintains that attitudes are not merely constant dispositions to repeat precisely the same act in the same way when the same stimulus recurs in an old or new context. They are variable in the behavior they produce, and stable only in their significance. Faris writes:

> If they were predispositions to specific and definite acts the difficulty would be less, but attitudes are *tendencies toward modes of action and do not have any one-to-one correspondence to specific response to stimulations.* (see Young, 1931, p. 12)

Similarly, Dewey:

> Repetition is in no sense the essence of habit [attitude]. The essence of habit is an acquired predisposition to ways or modes of response, not to particular acts, except as, under special conditions, these express a way of behaving. Habit means special sensitiveness or accessibility to certain classes of stimuli, standing predilections or aversions, rather than the bare recurrence of specific acts. (1922, p. 42)

Some readers may find it difficult to conceive of attitudes as generalized tendencies having no specific relation either to the stimulus or to the nervous system. But in modern psychology it has become equally difficult to picture an attitude as residing in specified neural grooves, capable of activation only in an invariable way through stimuli that are always the same. It is now recognized that stimuli are never twice the same, and that the neural process is one of dynamic interplay rather than of mechanical rigidity.

The case for generality does not rest merely upon speculation. In an experimental study of the attitudes of white people toward the Negro, Likert (1932-33) found that whatever questions were asked these subjects tended to display a constant amount of favor or disfavor toward the rights of the Negro.

> Why the attitude toward the Jim Crow car and the attitudes toward a Negro's buying a home or farm should be closely linked is not apparent if one considers merely the *direct* social implications of the two. It is only when one realizes that both propositions touch off a general attitude toward the Negro that one sees the reason for the link-

age. Quite in contrast with our expectations, we are obliged to report that there exists a clear-cut pro- or anti-Negro sentiment, an emotional and conative disposition which runs through the entire fifteen items used to study white attitudes toward the Negro. (p. 38)

Likert's method and conclusions are typical of many recent studies. Every attempt to measure an attitude with a many-itemed scale implies, of course, that the investigator believes that the attitude in question is general. And whenever high internal consistency is obtained for such a scale the inescapable conclusion is that the separate items of which the questionnaire is composed represent merely so many aspects of a single coherent attitude (cf. Cantril and Allport, 1933). Still more striking evidence comes from the intercorrelation of *independent* scales. As an example, Likert (1932-33) demonstrated that his own test for internationalism and the Thurstone-Droba anti-war scale correlate +.67; and Pintner (1933) has found that measures of attitudes favorable to the church by the Thurstone-Chave scale correlate +.79 with the religious interest as measured by the *Study of Values*. Such facts do not fit the doctrine of specificity.

The direct experimental study of general and specific attitudes made by Cantril (1932) is most pertinent of all. Two of his conclusions follow: "General determining tendencies are more constant and enduring than specific content." A subject, for example, might display on various occasions, with quite different specific associations, the self-same attitude; or he might recall a previous attitude but be unable to report upon its earlier content. "A general attitude seems to serve as a dynamic or directive influence upon more specific attitudes and reactions." In support of this conclusion, he cites, for example, the fact that reaction times to stimulus-words are in direct proportion to the magnitude of the subject's interest in the value to which the word refers. A man with strong esthetic values responds more swiftly to such stimulus-words as "poem," "drama," "concert" than to words with a religious, political, or economic connotation. Similarly a man with strong religious interests responds more quickly to such words as "church," "prayer," "Christian."

Conclusion. There can be no doubt that *general attitudes* exist. They are discovered by tests, by experiment, and in everyday life. On the other hand, it is undeniable that attitudes of quite a specific order also exist. The task-attitude, or *Aufgabe,* and the underdeveloped moral dispositions of children are examples. Generality seems to be a matter of degree. Krueger and Reckless propose to distinguish

> two sorts of fixed or permanent attitudes: concrete attitudes which are directed toward specific objects, and *generalized* attitudes which are directed toward a class of objects. (1931, p. 270)

Similarly, Folsom, who however probably underestimates the frequency of general attitudes, writes:

> There seem to be certain attitudes, quite independent of temperament, which hold good throughout large classes of situations: *general attitudes.* These are fewer, more limited, less general, than most people suppose, but they exist. (1931, pp. 240 f.)

Likert (1932-33) presents the hypothesis that strong and well-integrated attitudes of ʽhe generalized type will dominate the mental field and take precedence over all specific determining tendencies. If no such strong general attitudes are available, the individual will be more influenced by the stimulus-situation and by such segmental habits as he may have at his disposal.

> The stronger the generic set toward one extreme or the other extreme of an attitude continuum, the more it influences the specific reactions. When the generic set is not strong then the specific items themselves largely determine the reactions.

This hypothesis, to which Cantril's work gives considerable support, has far reaching implications. To take but one example, if a criminal possesses a *generalized* anti-social attitude it may be safely predicted that under *any* circumstances he will be a menace if at large. On the other hand, a criminal without a generalized anti-social attitude is a creature of circumstance and is potentially a less dangerous character. But in either case the re-education of these delinquents in terms of specific habits is not enough, and this is especially true if they are of the anti-social type. Contrary to the opinion of specificists, what is essential is the building of dependable social attitudes of the *general* order which will dominate behavior in the face of varied temptations. Precisely this policy has been advocated by the German criminologist, Steckelings (1929).

Public and Private Attitudes

Most people reserve for themselves the right to say one thing and to think another. Caught off his guard, an individual may disclose his innermost attitude, but the direct frontal attack which many psychological inquiries make provokes him to give a merely conventional answer. For this reason the task of investigating attitudes is difficult and hazardous.

Not only is the individual inclined to give a safe and conventional answer, but, strange to say, he is often sincere in his answer, for he possesses two distinct sets of contradictory attitudes, one reserved for his personal and private life, and the other socially determined and quite honestly maintained in public. It is by no means certain that the inner private attitude is any more fundamental or significant than the outer, or public, attitude. Both may be sincerely held. William James tells of this conflict in the case of the magistrate who, in sentencing a prisoner, said, "As a man, I pity you, but as an official I must show you no mercy" (1890, vol. 1, pp. 294 f.). Everyone recognizes in himself precisely the same type of conflict between his public and his private attitudes. Ordinarily it is the public attitudes which are most readily and willingly disclosed. Any itinerant psychologist can elicit these by ringing doorbells and asking questions. Usually the private attitudes are discovered only through indirection, after a long period of acquaintanceship, or when the subject wholeheartedly and candidly cooperates.

Having made himself thoroughly acquainted in a rural community,

Schanck (1932) succeeded in studying *both* the public and private attitudes in the population. The results of his study are striking. To take a single example, he obtained from both Baptists and Methodists a statement of their attitude as *church members* toward the proper form of baptism, and likewise their *private feelings* about the matter. The following table shows in percentage the distribution of preferences for the forms of baptism among 51 Methodists and 46 Baptists:

| | As church member | | Private feelings | |
	Methodist	Baptist	Methodist	Baptist
Sprinkling only	90	0	16	0
Either	8	22	71	59
Immersion only	0	67	6	17
No attitude	1	11	7	24

In a similar way, he studied the public and private attitudes of the population toward a variety of institutional practices and policies. As a result of these investigations certain conclusions seem to stand out sharply: (1) As members of a group, people frequently hold attitudes that are quite opposed to their private feelings. (2) The institutional attitudes tend to be more uniform for all members of a given group than do their private attitudes. A skewed, or J-shaped, distribution results when the institutional attitudes are plotted, for members (as members) take the same distinctive and extreme view. But, left to themselves, their own experiences and preferences are diversified, and the resulting distribution of attitudes is on the whole less uniform. Members as members are homogeneous in their attitudes toward the objects with which their institution is concerned; but as private individuals they are more diversified, more liberal, and more tolerant. (3) The private attitudes of the members of these groups quite often resemble in moderateness and variability the attitudes of outsiders who are not members. It is only the individuals of the "in-group" who are self-conscious of their membership at the moment of responding who disclose the uniform "common segment" attitudes which are the psychological basis of institutional behavior. Schanck states the theory as follows:

> Institutional attitudes have been found to have a characteristic form. A distribution of institutional attitudes is found to be highly asymmetrical, usually J-shaped with the mode on the terminal step. Personality attitudes, on the other hand, tend to be normally or symmetrically distributed. The question arises as to the nature of the situations where we get a J-shaped distribution on a variable. It must be remembered that a bell-shaped distribution represents an instance of compound probability and suggests the presence of many unweighted items or at least items not weighted in the same direction. These many factors have a cancelling effect upon one another, throwing the distribution towards a central tendency. It must be evident that the institutional or J-shaped distribution does not represent an unloaded situation, but a situation where certain factors become dominant and tend to cause a uniformity of behavior. (See Black, 1933, pp. 20 f.)

The same point of view is developed at greater length by F. H. Allport (1932, 1934). This author points out that the institutional attitudes are usually controlled externally; they can often be elicited by machines (e.g., traffic lights) or by social and political symbols. They are likely to represent superficial and inharmonious segments of personality and are seldom well integrated with the individual's private philosophy of life.

> This collection of segmental habits, which we call the institution, is something we envisage as belonging more properly to Society than to particular individuals. But Society, if conceived as a being like a human organism, is a fiction. We, as individuals, are the organisms; institutional habits are really a part of *us*. And like all our other habits and dispositions, they must be made to harmonize not merely with the pattern of society, but with *our own characters as individuals*. If such a personal integration is not accomplished, no matter how expertly the "societal" pattern is conceived, our institutional habits (that is, our "institutions") will lead eventually to our ruin. (1933, pp. 471 f.)

The issue here is obviously one concerning the degree to which a man's public and private attitudes can be reconciled. As the author points out, they are frequently in conflict, and in extreme cases the institutional attitudes are so segmental that they prevent the wholesome integration of personality. In other cases, however, it seems that the institutionalized attitudes may become focal points in the integration. Through his loyalties and memberships the individual may find authentic means of self-expression.

COMMON AND INDIVIDUAL ATTITUDES

> Social psychology can study attitudes which it assumes are common to all conscious beings, and on the other hand, such as may be peculiar to only one individual member of the group. (Thomas and Znaniecki, 1918, p. 28)

In this statement Thomas and Znaniecki point out one of the most significant distinctions that can be made in the entire province of attitudes. Some attitudes are, roughly speaking, common to all conscious beings because they are based upon similar underlying conditions of inheritance, natural environment, and social influence. These common attitudes are so fundamental that they are sometimes confused with instincts. Bernard writes:

> The old classification of abstract or general so-called instincts were in reality classifications of acquired attitudes which undertook to name and evaluate classes or general types of behavior. Thus the so-called instincts of pugnacity, maternal care, self-assertion, self-abasement and scores of others, are but general classes of concrete forms of behavior which we have learned to think of together conceptually. (1926, p. 250)

Common attitudes may be defined as those attitudes which are essentially uniform owing to the operation of similar environmental and cultural conditions upon similarly constituted human beings. Physical environ-

ment, culture, and instinct cooperate in the production of common attitudes. For an example of such attitudes one may turn to Bernard's study
of the differences between farmers and city-dwellers (1916-17). The
attitudes of farmers, he finds, show certain common characteristics, namely,

> Individualism
> Religious and political orthodoxy
> Obtuseness to finer distinctions in humor
> More or less disregard for the scientific method
> Frugality and thrift which sometimes border on parsimony
> Emotional intensity with consequent high suggestibility along lines
>   of conventional interest

Many theories of the "social mind" are reducible essentially to the fact
that men have similar attitudes. These "common segments" of mental
life, when regarded apart from the personalities which contain them,
and when viewed in relation to the corresponding segments of the mental
life of others, give rise to an impression that the group itself has a mental
life of its own. But, psychologically considered, the "group mind" can
mean nothing more than the possession by a group of people of common
attitudes.

If all attitudes were common attitudes, it would be possible to construct
acceptable social laws, for in such a case all attitudes would be the same
for all people, and human nature would thus become a "constant." Since,
however, common attitudes are not the only type, social laws are merely
the statement of tendencies based upon the resemblance between *some* of
the attitudes of *some* of the individuals within any group. Prediction is
virtually impossible in social psychology largely because common attitudes
are not sufficiently universal to be depended upon. Social psychology
cannot afford to overlook the "individual perturbations" in social life. The
differences between human beings, in spite of all standardizing influences,
are more noteworthy than their resemblances. Personality everywhere
intrudes itself.

Although the attitudes which men share are fewer than their individual
attitudes, and are less universal than they are supposed to be, they retain
none the less a peculiar importance for social psychology. Whatever
stability society may have is clearly due to the similarity of men's attitudes.
A period of social disintegration such as we are at present living through
represents an ascendancy of individual over common attitudes. Since social
psychology is interested in both closely knit and in disintegrating societies,
it must, as Thomas and Znaniecki point out, take into account both common and individual attitudes.

The problem of the measurement of attitudes, which is the next topic
to be considered, clearly depends upon the distinction which has just been
drawn. It is only the common attitudes that can be measured, for
measurement requires a scale, and there is no scale which does not depend
upon the central tendencies and dispersions of opinions expressed by *many*
people. To measure an attitude requires the assumption that a large population of men shares the attitudes in question. Only if this assumpti n is
granted is it possible to study *quantitative* differences.

THE MEASUREMENT OF ATTITUDES

The interest of American social psychologists in fact-collecting and statistical methods has resulted in a rapid advance in the empirical study of attitudes, with the result that attitudes today are measured more successfully than they are defined. As has often been pointed out, the situation is not unlike that in the field of intelligence testing where practicable tests are an established fact, although the nature of intelligence is still in dispute. In recent years there has been a decline of interest in the measurement of intelligence (Goodenough, 1934) and an increase of interest in the measurement of attitudes. It seems as though militant testing, having won victories on one field of battle, has sought a new world to conquer. The numerous methods available for measuring attitudes have been often reviewed and do not require restatement here. The present abbreviated account, which confines itself to three methods, may be supplemented by the more complete summaries of Bain (1930), Droba (1932, 1934a), Katz and Allport (1931), Fryer (1931), Murphy and Murphy (1931), Stagner (see Black, 1933, pp. 115-127), Sherman (1932), and Symonds (1931).

The Census of Opinions. The simplest method for determining how common an attitude (really an *opinion*) may be in a certain population is by counting ballots or by tabulating answers to a questionnaire. Roughly, this method may be said to "measure" the range and distribution of public opinion, although it does not, of course, determine the intensity of the opinion of any given individual upon the issue in question. The application of this method may be illustrated by reference to a recent poll, widely reported in the newspapers, concerning pacifistic and militaristic attitudes among 22,627 students in seventy colleges. Thirty-nine per cent of these students declared that they would participate in no war whatsoever, 33 per cent would take part only if the United States were invaded, and 28 per cent were ready to fight for any cause that might lead the nation to declare war. A critic might remark that such a result expresses only "verbal" opinion, or at the most merely temporary attitudes, which would change under the pressure of propaganda. Whatever may be the force of this objection, it applies equally to *all* of the methods now existing for determining the strength and nature of personal attitudes.

A far more elaborate census of students' attitudes was made by Katz and Allport (1931). In this study 4248 students in Syracuse University responded to a questionnaire containing many hundreds of items. The students did not write their opinions, but under each topic checked one of several alternative opinions with which they felt themselves to be most closely in agreement. Obviously this method does not provide a true scale of measurement, since the alternative items are not scaled in respect to their intensity. The results obtained, however, can be turned readily into a study of the *percentages* of students who favor each of the opinions contained in the questionnaire. Two illustrations will be given.

In one place in the study, students who reported that loss of religious faith had taken away something essential to their peace of mind were contrasted with those who reported that in college they had found a new and more satisfying philosophy of life. Of the first group 41 per cent expressed a need for advice concerning personal problems (not of the religious order). Of the second group only 23 per cent expressed this need. In this case the difference between these percentages is 18 per cent and the P.E., 4.67; the critical ratio therefore is approximately 4 (1931, p. 98). The conclusion seems inescapable: students who feel maladjusted in respect to religious faith are worried and unsettled concerning their own personalities. In other words, disorganization in one set of attitudes is likely to be accompanied by disorganization in another.

In another portion of the study, the attitudes of fraternity members were investigated. Two-thirds of the students turned out to be "institutionalists" who believed that their fraternities were of the order of super-individual Beings; the remaining third were "individualists" who believed that their fraternities were mere collections of individuals. This latter group, as contrasted to the fraternity institutionalists, believed that varsity teams should not jeopardize individualized athletics, that athletic losses to outstanding rivals are not a serious detriment to the university, that professors should have considerable freedom of expression in the classroom, that some restrictions should be placed upon the privileges of fraternities, and that eccentric and unpopular student types should be admissible to fraternities. It is difficult to imagine a more convincing demonstration of the generality of attitudes. Individualists in one situation are individualists in others; and institutionalists in one are institutionalists in others. It will be noted that all of these students are members of fraternities, and yet not all are equally affected by such membership. One-third of them refuse to accept the cultural pattern at its face value. Their attitudes, therefore, are not determined, as some sociologists would argue, exclusively by the social influence to which they are exposed.

The a priori Scale. The so-called *a priori* scale is essentially a test devised on the basis of logical rather than empirical considerations. It is an economical method, widely used, and easy to apply, but in recent years it has been severely criticized. There are various forms of the *a priori* scale, but they are all alike in that their scoring is arbitrary. Sometimes the author presents a series of questions, each of which may have, say, five alternative answers from which the subject must select one. These alternative answers are conceived by the author to lie on a single continuum and to be equally spaced from the most favorable to the least favorable. To each item the author arbitrarily assigns a value of 1, 2, 3, 4, or 5, according to his opinion of its significance. Another variation allows the subject to place in rank order all of the alternatives according to his preference; these rank orders are then treated as though they were *equal* intervals in the scale. The statistical pitfalls of *a priori* scales have been pointed out by Thurstone (1927-28).

As an example of a widely used scale of this type may be mentioned the test for "social distance" devised by Bogardus (1925*a*, 1925*b*, 1927). In this test the subject is asked the degree of intimacy he would willingly sanction between himself and members of various races. The degrees of intimacy listed in one form of the test together with their "scale values" are as follows:

1—to close kinship by marriage
2—to my club as personal chums
3—to my street as neighbors
4—to employment in my occupation in my country
5—to citizenship in my country
6—as visitors only to my country
7—would exclude from my country

The weakness of the scale becomes at once apparent when it is realized that the distance between each of these degrees of intimacy is not necessarily comparable. The psychological difference between relationship in marriage and in a club is likely to be far greater than that existing between club relations and neighborly relations. It becomes therefore misleading to assign equally progressing arithmetical units to unequal attitudinal differences. Another difficulty arises in the assumption that each higher degree of intimacy necessarily implies all those that are lower; but there are cases where admission to neighborly relations, for example, is less distasteful than admission to one's occupation.

In spite of these handicaps, the scale has yielded interesting results. It shows, for example, that attitudes of Americans are most favorable toward the Canadians, the English, and the Scotch, less favorable to the Chinese, and least favorable to the Turks. This last antipathy is of special interest since few of the subjects studied with the scale had ever known or even seen a Turk. As the Murphys point out (1931, p. 632), it is unnecessary to go farther than history textbooks and war-time atrocity stories to explain this ready-made attitude. The lack of experiential basis for racial antipathies has been demonstrated also by Zeligs and Hendrickson (1933). Among sixth-grade children they found that, with the exception of the Negro, tolerance and favor were in direct proportion to familiarity, and that prejudice varied with unfamiliarity.

The Psychophysical (Rational) Scale. The most significant event in the history of the measurement of attitudes was the application of psychophysical methods by Thurstone. To apply psychophysical methods it is necessary first to conceive of an attitude as a "degree of affect" for or against an object or a value with which the scale is concerned. If this assumption is granted (cf. pp. 819 f.), it becomes possible to study the degree of favor or disfavor which each subject in a population has toward certain objects or values, such as the church, war, moving pictures, or government ownership. Within the past few years a large number of such scales have been devised and made available for general use (Thurstone and associates).

The scoring values for all of these scales are determined by combining the efforts of many judges who have arranged all the statements included in each scale according to their *discriminable* differences. If judges, by and large, agree that two statements express about the same degree of favor or disfavor it is obviously unnecessary to keep both statements in the scale; if the statements are widely different it is possible by comparing the judges' sorting of each statement in relation to all other statements to determine its position. The final, rational scale results when forty or fifty statements are secured whose distance from one another on a single continuum are known. This distance is essentially the discriminable difference between the statements as they appear to the standardizing group of judges. There are various methods by which the discriminable differences may be determined. The commonest is the "method of equal-appearing intervals." The directions for its use involve the following steps:

1. Specify the attitude variable to be measured.
2. Collect a wide variety of opinions relating to it, from newspapers, books, or from individuals.
3. Assemble on cards approximately one hundred such typical opinions.
4. Require at least 200-300 judges to sort these cards into piles (eleven being a convenient and commonly employed number), each pile representing equidistant degrees of the attitude according to each judge's estimation.
5. Calculate the scale value for each of the items by computing the median of the scale values assigned to it by the judges, and the dispersion of the judgments around the median.
6. Retain such statements as have small dispersions, and are on the whole equally spaced. Give approximately equal representation to each of the intervals secured. Clarity and brevity of wording may furnish additional bases for selection.
7. In applying the scale, the subject checks every statement with which he agrees, and his score is the mean scale-value for all the statements he has endorsed.

The most useful procedure in constructing such scales is to follow the models offered in the Thurstone-Chave (1929) or Peterson-Thurstone (1933) scale. Directions for uniform wording have been suggested by Droba (1932), Wang (1932), Kulp (1933), and Stagner (see Black, 1933, pp. 115-127). Further details concerning the construction and use of psychophysical scales may easily be traced through the literature (Black, 1933; Dockeray, 1932; Thurstone, 1927-28, 1929, 1932; Remmers, 1934).

As revolutionary as the rational scale undoubtedly is, certain criticisms must be made against the method as it is at present employed. (1) As has already been indicated on pages 819 f., attitudes are not necessarily arranged naturally upon a single continuum; they are often discrete and highly individual (cf. Katz and Allport, 1931). (2) There is also the question whether scale values for statements derived from one population of judges is applicable to other populations of subjects (Rice, 1930). For example, can the judgments of adults concerning the significance of a statement dealing with moving pictures be incorporated in a test that is to be administered to children? (3) Likert (1932-33) has shown that the simple *a priori* method of scoring in arbitrary units (1 to 5) when applied to these rational scales may yield results as reliable as do the psychophysical scores themselves. The agreement between the two methods is approximately .90. This fact may give comfort to investigators who wish to avoid the more complex procedures. Thurstone's strictures upon the logic of *a priori* scales are undoubtedly sound, but they do not necessarily invalidate these scales when only practical results are desired. Suppose, for instance, that a psychologically minded chairman wishes to determine at a certain meeting the temper of his audience in reference to some issue under discussion. He can quickly prepare and quickly (if roughly) score an *a priori* scale; whereas the preparation of a more carefully standardized test would be impracticable and unnecessarily fine-grained for his purposes.

Conclusions. The success achieved in the past ten years in the field of the measurement of attitudes may be regarded as one of the major accomplishments of social psychology in America. The rate of progress is so great that further achievements in the near future are inevitable. But there are inherent limitations in all methods of testing. Unless these are kept in mind the zeal for measurement may overstep reasonable bounds.

1. Measurement can deal only with attitudes that are *common,* and there are relatively few attitudes that are common enough to be profitably scaled. In forcing attitudes into a scale form violence is necessarily done to the unique structure of man's mind. Attitude scales should be regarded only as the roughest approximations of the way in which attitudes actually exist in the mental life of individuals.

2. Each person possesses many contradictory attitudes, and for this reason his mental set at the moment of submitting to a scale may tell only a part of the story. Furthermore, attitudes often change, and an investigation made under one set of conditions may not for long present a true picture of the attitudes of any given group. Stagner (see Black, 1933) reports a meeting of farmers in a village in northern Wisconsin who, under the influence of a persuasive speaker, voted unanimously one afternoon to call a milk strike. The same group met in the evening to hear a speaker with opposed views. They then voted unanimously not to strike.

3. Rationalization and deception inevitably occur, especially when the attitudes studied pertain to the moral life or social status of the subject. The difficulty of obtaining reliable information concerning attitudes toward sex is a case in point. So great is the tendency to protect oneself that even anonymity is not a guarantee. Lack of insight, ignorance, suspicion, fear, a neurotic sense of guilt, undue enthusiasm, or even a knowledge of the investigator's purpose may invalidate an inquiry.

ATTITUDES AND EVERYDAY LIFE

Social psychology, by its very nature, must be concerned with the problems of everyday life (cf. Cantril, 1934b). This chapter has already indicated the importance of attitudes in the study of racial relations, esthetic and moral prejudice, public opinion, the psychology of rural and student populations, and in other practical fields. One could extend very greatly this list of problems.

Changing Social Attitudes. Hart (1933) has surveyed in broad perspective the decline of public interest in religion and the growth of interest in science; he has studied also the growth and decline of sentiment favorable to prohibition, the increasing opposition in America to the interests of big business, and the increasing sentiment for disarmament. His method was indirect and consisted in the study of the circulation and contents of widely read magazines where one finds "precipitated layers of evidence about the intellectual and emotional life of past years."

It should be noted that in proportion as *common* attitudes are changed in the same direction social stability is essentially preserved, for all individuals alter their opinions together. The phenomenon in this case would be one merely of "social change." But in proportion as the common attitudes are disrupted and replaced by all manner of diverse and discordant *individual* attitudes there results inevitably a "social disintegration." The present century has witnessed the breaking-down of many common social attitudes, and the growth of very few new common attitudes to take their place. It must, therefore, be regarded as a period of social disintegration.

Criminality. The almost complete failure of both traditional and "enlightened" penology has intensified interest in the case-histories of individual delinquents (Glueck and Glueck, 1930, 1934). These histories reveal first and foremost the importance of attitudes. As a group, prisoners have intense attitudes of self-justification, loyalty, and belief in luck, as well as a tendency to exaggerate the defects of society and of their enemies (Field, 1931). Some reformers rest their efforts upon a policy of habit-training, assuming that re-education and rehabilitation are to be achieved only through a slow process of reconditioning each separate habit. Contrary to this policy, others insist that the best way to reform is to change an individual's point of view as a whole. If a new orientation can be acquired, the old and socially unsatisfactory habits will be dropped out and new ones will be automatically acquired. This point of view assumes that general attitudes exert a control over specific and subordinate attitudes (cf. pp. 820-824), an assumption which derives much support from Dunlap's discovery (1932) that the breaking of habits does not depend on the slow and painful process of reconditioning so much as upon the formation of a new controlling attitude.

The Influence of Moving Pictures upon Children. Using "rational scales" of the type described in the preceding section, Peterson and Thurstone (1933) studied the effect of films that treat controversial subjects in a partisan way. After seeing *The Birth of a Nation* a group of over four hundred children who had previously had little or no acquaintance with Negroes showed a pronounced shift of attitude in a direction unfavorable to the Negro, and after an interval of five months a large part of the prejudice remained. *The Son of the Gods* caused a shift of attitude in a direction definitely favorable to the Chinese; *Four Sons* made children more friendly toward the Germans; *The Criminal Code* caused a greater leniency toward criminals; *All Quiet on the Western Front* increased pacifism: *The Street of Chance* made children more severe in their judgment of gambling. Only one or two films failed to show some significant influence upon children's attitudes. It was clearly shown that the effects lasted over an interval of many months. In many cases they were undoubtedly permanent.

Vocational Psychology. Tests for attitudes seem destined to become an established supplement to tests for intelligence and skill. In the vocational field, interests (Fryer, 1931; Stone, 1933; Strong, 1927) are of great importance, likewise attitudes toward the occupation, the employer (Bogardus, 1927; Uhrbrock, 1933), and fellow workers. Although this type of study is still to a large extent experimental, it is supported by urgent demands from vocational counselors and from those engaged in personnel work.

Radicalism and Conservatism. One of the problems which has aroused considerable interest is the nature of radical and conservative attitudes. The varieties of human activity to which the designations of "conservative" and "radical" may be applied are so numerous that attitudes wholly and consistently generalized will be rarely, if ever, encountered. Not every act of a radical is uniformly rebellious, and no conservative is steadfast in his loyalties to every established custom and code. Several investigators (G. W. Allport, 1929; Droba, 1934b; Likert, 1932-33; Vetter, 1930a, 1930b), however, find so many instances where radical (or conservative) opinion pertaining to diverse issues are consistently combined in the same individuals that they favor the view that to a considerable extent these attitudes may be generalized. The fact, for example, that certain justices of the United States Supreme Court can be relied upon to give "dissenting" liberal opinions and that the others are safely on the side of tradition is proof of the point at issue. Kolstad (1933) found that members of conservative religious bodies were more nationalistic in their sentiments than members of the free and non-conformist sects; also students attending private, non-sectarian colleges were more radical in their outlook than students attending public or sectarian colleges. Finally, many investigators agree that the more radical students on the whole have higher intelligence than the conservative students (G. W. Allport, 1929; Kolstad, 1933; Moore, 1925; Vetter, 1930b).

Influencing Attitudes. Are attitudes influenced to a greater extent by the prestige of experts or by the prestige of the majority? This question has considerable practical significance. Moore (1921) found that in matters pertaining to speech and to morality college students more frequently change their own opinions to conform to those of the majority, but that in matters of esthetic judgment the expert is more influential. Boldyreff and Sorokin (1932) likewise found marked suggestibility to the esthetic opinions of experts. Following the false suggestion that musical critics preferred one of two *identical* Victrola records, the great majority of students actually "heard" these records as different and agreed that the one designated was preferable. Marple (1933) found that people are influenced greatly by both majority and expert opinion on social and political issues, and that the influence of the majority seems to be more marked than that of the expert. Considered psychologically, *propaganda* is altogether a matter of influencing attitudes. Among the writers who have treated propaganda from this point of view are Doob (1934), Biddle (1931, 1932), Dodge (1920), and Chen (1933).

Mental Hygiene. Elsewhere in this volume Dr. F. L. Wells considers the place of attitudes in the study of mental maladjustments. It is therefore unnecessary here to do more than call attention to this rich field for the application of the psychology of attitudes. Morgan's recent text in mental hygiene (1934) gives attitudes a place of central importance.

Classification-of Attitudes

In his textbook Titchener considered the possibility of classifying human attitudes, but he swiftly despaired of the task.

> There seems literally to be no end till we have exhausted the resources of the language, to the catalogue of possible attitudes. (1916, p. 506)

Recent writers, nevertheless, have attempted to establish at least a basis for such a classification. Droba (1933) groups attitudes according to their objects of reference, according to their individual or social significance, and according to their positive or negative direction. House (1929, p. 194) distinguishes four types of attitudes: the personal, the natural, the cultural, and the temporary social attitudes. Park and Burgess (1924) also have four fundamental classes: tendencies to withdraw, to approach, to dominate, and to yield. Bernard (1930) offers a five-fold basis: (*a*) the collective relationships which standardize conduct (resulting, for example, in nationalistic, racial, and occupational attitudes), (*b*) the aim or objective (as illustrated by humanitarian, protective, or exploiting attitudes), (*c*) the valuational significance (for example, attitudes of approving or discouraging), (*d*) objects of reference (attitudes toward money or toward sex), and (*e*) temporal reference (permanent, progressive, or temporary attitudes). Each of these proposals offers a framework for classification; none attempts to be complete.

Why is it that attitudes cannot be satisfactorily classified? The answer is simply that human personality, in which attitudes are imbedded, is an infinitely variable and constantly changing structure. In reality there are no absolute barriers between one attitude and others. For the sake of clarity in discourse, it is convenient to speak of attitudes (as of instincts, needs, desires, and traits) as well-segregated determinants of conduct, which, when appropriately stimulated, function independently, perhaps one at a time, much as the faculties of old were supposed to function.

The truth of the matter is that a man's conduct at any given moment is produced by an unanalyzable convergence of many determining tendencies. The final common path which results in overt behavior must be regarded as the product of the total "regnant" system of the mind, that is to say, of the complex pattern of all conscious and unconscious functions that are active at the time.   This total regnant system, which comprises innumerable forms of "readiness," issues always into *specific* activity, for only one act can be produced at a time.   Hence it is that probably no attitude is ever aroused singly, and that no attitude bears an invariable point for point relationship with any single motor act.

If attitudes never issue singly into action, if they are always interfused when they are active, if they cannot be considered to be well segregated even when they are latent, and cannot be counted, how does one know that they exist at all?   Only by necessary inference.   There *must* be something to account for the consistency of conduct.   It is the meaningful resemblances between activities and their congruence with one another that leads the psychologist inescapably to postulate some such generalized forms of readiness as the term "attitude" denotes.   These forms of readiness must not be thought of in absolutistic, singular terms.   One cannot say that a man has ten, a thousand, or a million independent attitudes which lie dormant waiting only to be activated by appropriate stimuli, for attitudes are not faculties.   They are dispositions whose boundaries are indefinite, and whose independence from one another is only relative.

Attitudes are not faculties, but neither are they fictions.   Without assuming them as actual neuropsychic facts no psychologist can give an intelligible account of human behavior.   Nor are attitudes a mere name for incoherent fragments of "specific stimulus-response tendencies."   If they did not exist as fairly *organized* and *coherent* dispositions in the mental life of each individual it would be impossible to account for the patent stability and consistency in human conduct.

The classification of attitudes is an impossible task: first, because it assumes a complete independence of attitudes, and, secondly, because it assumes that human beings are directly comparable with one another respecting the formal arrangement and content of their attitudes.   The utmost that can be done by way of classification is to select certain *common attitudes* which, in a highly approximate sense, most people may be said to share.   All objective studies of attitudes make just such a selection, and when one considers the fruitful consequences of this procedure the practice seems to be justified.   But behind the common attitudes, which comprise a major portion of research in social psychology (but a minor portion of human nature) there lies the immense margin of unique individual attitudes and traits.   These constitute the peculiarities of personality, and defy comparison, classification, and measurement.

THE PERSON AND THE SOCIUS

One final problem remains to be considered, namely, the relation between *attitudes* and *personality*.   There are two common but erroneous conceptions of this relation.   The first maintains that attitudes are the basic elements of personality:

> The integrated total of a human being's attitudes constitutes his personality.   (Bogardus, 1931, p. 52)
> Social attitudes are the elements of personality.   (Faris, 1925)

The second conception accepts the first and proceeds to declare that since attitudes are the basic elements of personality, and since they are determined largely by culture, then personality itself must be a cultural phenomenon.

A man's personality is the subjective aspect of the culture of the group. (Faris, 1925)

Both of these contentions represent an oversimplification of the nature of personality and must be examined critically.

Are Attitudes the Essential Elements of Personality? An attitude ordinarily has a well-defined object of reference (cf. pp. 806-810). The object may be material or it may be conceptual, but in any case it can usually be designated with considerable assurance. One may have attitudes toward modern art, the N.R.A., nudism, suicide, or parsnips. Besides having a definite object of reference, an attitude usually has a clear "direction" (cf. pp. 819 f.). It represents a tendency to act in favor of, opposed to, in behalf of, or in contradiction to, the object with which it is related.

There are qualities of personality, however, which have neither definite objects of reference nor clearly defined direction. They are dispositions which refer not to objects but to the *person;* their significance is not prepositional (directional), but adverbial. They are not attitudes, but rather *traits*.

The distinction between an attitude and a trait has been well drawn by Droba (1933):

An attitude has a definite object of reference, while a trait has a very vague object of reference or it has none at all. Honesty, aggressiveness, and trustworthiness are traits because the object to which they refer has a very wide range and hence is very vague. Racialism, militarism, and liberalism, are attitudes because they refer to definite objects, races, war, and social change, respectively.

Another definition of trait which likewise distinguishes it from attitude is that of F. H. Allport:

By a trait I mean a unique and important habit which an individual has acquired as a constant manner of adjusting himself to numerous situations differing widely in character. (1933, p. 324)

A trait, in short, is a man's personal and unique manner of responding to the myriad circumstances of life; it has very little reference to objects, for innumerable objects will arouse it. An individual's point of view toward war, liquor, the church, or capital punishment are clearly attitudes and not traits; but his talkative, shy, or emphatic *manner* of behaving are traits. The former are clearly less intimate and less personal than the latter.

Although this distinction between attitudes and traits is, by and large, both valid and useful, it cannot always be rigidly maintained. Psychological usage sanctions either "attitude" or "trait" for certain dispositions which seem to have a somewhat generalized object of reference and a vague directionality. Introversion and extroversion have been called both attitudes toward reality and traits of personality. Is radicalism an attitude or a trait? Probably it is the former if the object of rebellion can be clearly specified, but the latter if the radicalism is "temperamental." Is sociability, fair-mindedness, or esthetic interests, an attitude or a trait? The decision in these cases is difficult, perhaps impossible. The only helpful principle seems to be that *the more generalized the attitude becomes the more it resembles a trait.*

Is Personality the Subjective Side of Culture? Those who are impressed by the frequency with which attitudes refer to *social* values are inclined to answer this question affirmatively. But they forget two things: first, that traits and not attitudes are the primary qualities in personality; secondly, that by no means do all attitudes have social reference. Personality cannot then be regarded as dependent completely upon culture. Personality is conditioned not only by cultural surroundings, but by climate, heredity, disease, diet, glands, the natural beauty or austerity of the place of habitation, and the severity of the struggle for mere physical existence. Robinson Crusoe, Casper Hauser, the "wolf children," Itard's idiot, any hermit or solitary explorer, are deficient or else completely lacking in cultural contacts, and yet one and all they have personalities which are as interesting as they are intricate. Personality is not merely the subjective side of culture, and it is therefore not primarily a sociological problem. To be sure it is influenced by the cultural environment, but that fact does not assign it to the field of sociology, any more than its influence by climatic conditions assigns it to the science of meteorology.

The Socius. The personality of each man is a unique integration, and as such is a datum for psychology, and for psychology only. It is possible, however, to abstract from the unique personalities of any selected population those *common attitudes* which make men similar in their cultural behavior. It then becomes possible to study regional differences, the strength of tradition, and numerous problems related to the psychological aspects of institutions and the "social mind." To take a single illustration, Likert (1932-33) found that between 65 per cent and 75 per cent of the students in northern colleges believed that the lynching of a Negro was never under any circumstances justifiable; in an institution in Virginia only 31 per cent of the students held this view. Here is clear evidence for the determination of attitudes by membership in a regional and cultural group. In making this study, Likert was not dealing with personalities but with *socii,* that is to say, with men who have been "simplified" until they fit into a common mould for the purpose of some arbitrary comparison.

The *socius* might be defined as that part of personality which comprises common social attitudes, and which may for certain purposes be viewed independently. It is a useful abstraction, for it provides a large part of the subject-matter for all the social sciences. The *person,* on the other hand, is too involved and too unique a problem for any social science to treat. It is the subject-matter of a special branch of psychology. It should never be subsumed as a mere incident in the study of attitudes.

RÉSUMÉ

Within the past fifteen years the doctrine of attitudes has almost completely captured and re-fashioned the science of social psychology. The nature of attitudes, however, is still in dispute, and it may correctly be questioned whether a science reared upon so amorphous a foundation can be strong. What is most urgently needed is a clarification of the doctrine of attitudes, and to this task the present chapter has been addressed.

Because of historical considerations it is necessary to include a wide range of subjective determining tendencies under the general rubric of Attitude. Yet it is both possible and desirable to distinguish between attitudes and many correlative forms of readiness-for-response. Attitudes proper may be *driving* or *directive, specific* or *general, common* or *individual.* They characteristically have a material or conceptual object of reference, and are "pointed" in some direction with respect to this object. If they are so generalized that the object and the direction are not identifiable, they then merge into what may be called the "traits" of personality. Common attitudes can be roughly classified and measured, and when abstracted from the personalities which contain them they constitute the "socius" which is that portion of the unique personality of special interest to social science.

Attitudes are never directly observed, but, unless they are admitted, through inference, as real and substantial ingredients in human nature, it becomes impossible to account satisfactorily either for the consistency of any individual's behavior, or for the stability of any society.

BIBLIOGRAPHY

ACH, N. 1905. Ueber die Willenstätigkeit und das Denken. Göttingen: Vander-hoeck & Ruprecht. Pp. 294.

ALLPORT, F. H. 1924. Social psychology. Boston: Houghton Mifflin. Pp. xiv+453.

————. 1932. Psychology in relation to social and political problems. In *Psychology at work*, ed. by P. S. Achilles. New York: Whittlesey House. Pp. xiii+260.

————. 1933. Institutional behavior. Chapel Hill: Univ. N. Car. Press. Pp. xiii+526.

————. 1934. The J-curve hypothesis of conforming behavior. *J. Soc. Psychol.*, **5**, 141-183.

ALLPORT, G. W. 1929. The composition of political attitudes. *Amer. J. Sociol.*, **35**, 220-238.

————. 1932. Review of P. M. Symonds' *Diagnosing personality and conduct*. *J. Soc. Psychol.*, **3**, 391-398.

ALLPORT, G. W., & VERNON, P. E. 1931. The field of personality. *Psychol. Bull.*, **27**, 677-730.

————. 1933. Studies in expressive movement. New York: Macmillan. Pp. xiii+269.

BAIN, A. 1868. Mental science. New York: Appleton. Pp. 428.

BAIN, R. 1927-28. An attitude on attitude research. *Amer. J. Sociol.*, **33**, 940-957.

————. 1930. Theory and measurement of attitudes and opinions. *Psychol. Bull.*, **27**, 357-379.

BALDWIN, J. M. 1901-05. Dictionary of philosophy and psychology. (3 vols.) New York: Macmillan. Pp. xxiv+644; xvi+892; xxvi+542; viii+543-1192.

————. 1906. Mental development in the child and race. (3rd ed.) New York: Macmillan. Pp. xviii+475.

BARTLETT, F. C. 1932. Remembering. Cambridge, England: Univ. Press. Pp. x+314.

BERNARD, L. L. 1916-17. Theory of rural attitudes. *Amer. J. Sociol.*, **22**, 630-649.

————. 1926. Introduction to social psychology. New York: Holt. Pp. 651.

————. 1930. Attitudes, social. In Vol. 2 of *Encyclopedia of the social sciences*, ed. by E. R. A. Seligman and A. Johnson. New York: Macmillan. Pp. 305-309.

BIDDLE, W. W. 1931. A psychological definition of propaganda. *J. Abn. & Soc. Psychol.*, **26**, 283-295.

————. 1932. Propaganda and education. *Teach. Coll. Contrib. Educ.*, No. 521. Pp. 84.

BLACK, J. D. [Ed.] 1933. Research in social psychology of rural life. (Bull. 17.) New York: Soc. Sci. Res. Coun. Pp. 130.

BOGARDUS, E. S. 1925a. Social distance and its origins. *J. Appl. Sociol.*, **9**, 216-226.

————. 1925b. Measuring social distances. *J. Appl. Sociol.*, **9**, 299-308.

————. 1927. Race friendliness and social distances. *J. Appl. Sociol.*, **11**, 272-287.

————. 1928. Occupational distance. *Sociol. & Soc. Res.*, **13**, 33-81.

————. 1931. Fundamentals of social psychology. (2nd ed.) New York: Century. Pp. 444.

BOLDYREFF, J. W., & SOROKIN, P. A. 1932. An experimental study of the influence of suggestion on the discrimination and the valuation of people. *Amer. J. Sociol.*, **37**, 720-737.

BURNHAM, W. H. 1924. The normal mind. New York: Appleton. Pp. xx+702.

CANTRIL, H. 1932. General and specific attitudes. *Psychol. Monog.*, **42**, No. 192. Pp. 109.

————. 1934a. Attitudes in the making. *Understanding the Child*, **4**, 13-15.

————. 1934b. The social psychology of everyday life. *Psychol. Bull.*, **31**, 297-330.

CANTRIL, H., & ALLPORT, G. W. 1933. Recent applications of the study of values. *J. Abn. & Soc. Psychol.*, **28**, 259-273.

CHAPMAN, D. W. 1932. Relative effects of determinate and indeterminate *Aufgaben*. *Amer. J. Psychol.*, **44**, 163-174.

CHAVE, E. J. 1928. A new type scale for measuring attitudes. *Rel. Educ.*, **23**, 364-369.

CHEN, W. K. C. 1933. The influence of oral propaganda material upon students' attitudes. *Arch. Psychol.*, **23**, No. 150. Pp. 43.

CLARKE, H. M. 1911. Conscious attitudes. *Amer. J. Psychol.*, **32**, 214-249.

DAVIS, J. 1930. A study of one hundred and sixty-three outstanding communist leaders. Studies in quantitative and cultural sociology. *Proc. Amer. Sociol. Soc.*, **24**, 42-55.

DEWEY, J. 1917. The need for social psychology. *Psychol. Rev.*, **24**, 266-277.

————. 1922. Human nature and conduct. New York: Holt. Pp. vii+336.

DOCKERAY, D. C. 1932. General psychology. New York: Prentice-Hall. Pp. xxi+581.

Dodge, R. 1920. The psychology of propaganda. *Rel. Educ.*, 15, 241-252.

Doob, L. W. 1934. Psychological factors in propaganda. (Unpublished.) Cambridge: Harvard Univ. Library.

Droba, D. D. 1932. Methods for measuring attitudes. *Psychol. Bull.*, 29, 309-323.

————. 1933. The nature of attitude. *J. Soc. Psychol.*, 4, 444-463.

————. 1934a. Social attitudes. *Amer. J. Sociol.*, 39, 513-524.

————. 1934b. Political parties and war attitudes. *J. Abn. & Soc. Psychol.*, 28, 468-472.

Dunlap, K. 1932. Habits: their making and unmaking. New York: Liveright. Pp. x+326.

Ewer, B. C. 1929. Social psychology. New York: Macmillan. Pp. ix+435.

Faris, E. 1925. The concept of social attitudes. *J. Appl. Sociol.*, 9, 404-409.

Fearing, F. 1931. The experimental study of attitude, meaning, and the process antecedent to action by N. Ach and others in the Würzburg laboratory. In *Methods in social science*, ed. by S. Rice. Chicago: Univ. Chicago Press. Pp. 715-728.

Féré, C. 1890. Note sur la physiologie de l'attention. *Rev. phil.*, 30, 393-405.

Field, H. E. 1931. The attitudes of prisoners as a factor in rehabilitation. *Ann. Amer. Acad. Pol. Sci.*, 157, No. 2484.

Folsom, J. K. 1931. Social psychology. New York: Harper. Pp. xviii+701.

Fryer, D. 1931. The measurement of interests. New York: Holt. Pp. xxxvi+488.

Giddings, F. H. 1896. The principles of sociology. New York: Macmillan. Pp. xxvi+476.

Glueck, S., & Glueck, E. T. 1930. Five hundred criminal careers. New York: Knopf. Pp. xxvii+364.

————. 1934. One thousand juvenile delinquents. Cambridge, Mass.: Harvard Univ. Press. Pp. xxix+341.

Goodenough, F. 1934. Trends in modern psychology. *Psychol. Bull.*, 31, 81-97.

Hart, H. 1933. Changing social attitudes. In Vol. 1 of *Recent social trends*. New York: McGraw, Hill. Pp. 382-444.

Hartshorne, H. 1932. Character in human relations. New York: Scribner's. Pp. xiv+367.

Hartshorne, H., & May, M., *et al.* 1928-30. Studies in the nature of character: Vol. I. Studies in deceit. Vol. II. Studies in service and self-control. Vol. III. Studies in the organization of character. New York: Macmillan. Pp. xxi+306; xxiii+559; xvi+503.

Holt, E. B. 1931. Animal drive and the learning process. New York: Holt. Pp. vii+307.

House, F. N. 1929. The range of social theory. New York: Holt. Pp. 587.

James, W. 1890. The principles of psychology. (2 vols.) New York: Holt. Pp. xii+689; vi+704.

Katz, D., & Allport, F. H. 1931. Students' attitudes. Syracuse, N. Y.: Craftsman Press. Pp. xxviii+408.

Katz, D., & Braly, K. 1933. Racial stereotypes of one hundred college students. *J. Abn. & Soc. Psychol.*, 28, 280-290.

Koffka, K. 1912. Zur Analyse der Vorstellungen und ihren Gesetze. Leipzig: Quelle & Meyer. Pp. x+392.

Köhler, W. 1929. Gestalt psychology. New York: Liveright. Pp. xi+403.

Kolstad, A. 1933. A study of opinions on some international problems. *Teach. Coll. Contrib. Educ.*, No. 555. Pp. 95.

Krueger, E. T., & Reckless, W. C. 1931. Social psychology. New York: Longmans, Green. Pp. vii+578.

Kulp, D. H., Jr. 1933. The form of statements in attitude tests. *J. Sociol. & Soc. Res.*, 18, 18-25.

Lange, L. 1888. Neue Experimente über den Vorgang der einfachen Reaction auf Sinneseindrücke. *Phil. Stud.*, 4, 479-510.

Lange, N. 1888. Beiträge zur Theorie der sinnlichen Aufmerksamkeit und der activen Apperception. *Phil. Stud.*, 4, 390-422.

Lasker, B. 1929. Race attitudes in children. New York: Holt. Pp. xvi+294.

Leonard, W. E. 1927. The locomotive-god. New York: Century. Pp. 434.

Lewin, K. 1931. Environmental forces in child behavior and development. In *A handbook of child psychology*, ed. by C. Murchison. Worcester, Mass.: Clark Univ. Press; London: Oxford Univ. Press. Pp. 94-127.

————. 1935. Dynamic theory of personality. New York: McGraw-Hill.

Likert, R. 1932-33. Technique for the measurement of attitudes. *Arch. Psychol.*, 22, No. 140. Pp. 55.

Lippmann, W. 1922. Public opinion. New York: Harcourt, Brace. Pp. x+427.

Lund, F. H. 1925. The psychology of belief. *J. Abn. & Soc. Psychol.*, 20, 23-81, 174-196.

Lundberg, G. A. 1929. Social research. New York: Longmans, Green. Pp. x+379.

Marple, C. H. 1933. The comparative susceptibility of three age levels to the suggestion of group versus expert opinion. *J. Soc. Psychol.*, 4, 176-184.

McDougall, W. 1921. An introduction to social psychology. (14th ed.) Boston: Luce. Pp. 418.

————. 1926. Outline of abnormal psychology. New York: Scribner's. Pp. xvi+572.

————. 1933. The energies of men. New York: Scribner's. Pp. ix+395.

Mead, G. H. 1924-25. Genesis of self and social control. *Int. J. Ethics*, 251-277.

Moore, H. T. 1921. The comparative influence of majority and expert opinion. *Amer. J. Psychol.*, 32, 16-20.

————. 1925. Innate factors in radicalism and conservatism. *J. Abn. & Soc. Psychol.*, 20, 234-244.

Morgan, J. J. B. 1934. Keeping a sound mind. New York: Macmillan. Pp. ix+440.

Müller, G. E., & Pilzecker, A. 1900. Experimentelle Beiträge zur Lehre vom Gedächtniss. *Zsch. f. Psychol.*, Ergbd. 1. Pp. xiv+300.

Münsterberg, H. 1889. Beiträge zur experimentellen Psychologie. Vol. I. Freiburg: Mohr. Pp. 188.

Murphy, G., & Murphy, L. B. 1931. Experimental social psychology. New York: Harper. Pp. 709.

North, C. C. 1932. Social problems and social planning. New York: McGraw-Hill. Pp. x+409.

Ogden, R. M. 1926. Psychology and education. New York: Harcourt, Brace. Pp. xiii+364.

Park, R. E. 1924. Experience and race relations. *J. Appl. Sociol.*, 9, 18-24.

Park, R. E., & Burgess, E. W. 1924. Introduction to the science of sociology. Chicago: Univ. Chicago Press. Pp. xxiii+1040.

Peterson, R. C., & Thurstone, L. L. 1933. Motion pictures and the social attitudes of children. New York: Macmillan. Pp. xvii+75.

Pintner, R. 1933. A comparison of interests, abilities, and attitudes. *J. Abn. & Soc. Psychol.*, 27, 351-357.

PRATT, K. C., NELSON, A. K., & SUN, K. H. 1930. The behavior of the newborn infant. *Ohio State Univ. Contrib. Psychol.*, No. 10. Pp. xiii+237.

PYLE, W. H. 1928. The psychology of learning. (Rev. ed.) Baltimore, Md.: Warwick & York. Pp. ix+441.

REMMERS, H. H. [Ed.] 1934. Studies in attitudes. *Stud. Higher Educ.*, Purdue Univ., No. xxvi. Pp. 112.

RICE, S. A. 1926-27. Stereotypes: a source of error in judging human character. *J. Person. Res.*, **5**, 267-276.

————. 1930. Statistical studies of social attitudes and public opinion. In *Statistics in social studies*. Philadelphia: Univ. Pa. Press. Pp. 171-192.

ROGUIN, E. 1931 & 1932. Sociologie. (2 vols.) Lausanne: Charles Pach. Pp. iv+651; xxxix+789.

ROSS, E. A. 1908. Social psychology. New York: Macmillan. Pp. xvi+372.

SCHANCK, R. L. 1932. A study of a community and its groups and institutions conceived of as behaviors of individuals. *Psychol. Monog.*, No. 195. Pp. 133.

SHERIF, M. 1935. An experimental study of stereotypes. *J. Abn. & Soc. Psychol.* (to be published).

SHERMAN, M. 1932. Theories and measurement of attitudes. *Child Develop.*, **3**, 15-28.

SMITH, J. 1930. Social psychology. Boston: Badger. Pp. 468.

SPENCER, H. 1862. First principles. (Reprinted from 5th London ed.) New York: Burt. Pp. xv+483.

STECKELINGS, W. 1929. Die Schuldfrage im eigenen Urteil des Rechtbrechers. Paderborn: Schöningh. Pp. 187.

STONE, C. L. 1933. The personality factor in vocational guidance. *J. Abn. & Soc. Psychol.*, **28**, 274 f.

STRONG, E. K., JR. 1927. Vocational interest test. *Educ. Rec.*, **8**, 107-121.

SYMONDS, P. M. 1927. What is an attitude? *Psychol. Bull.*, **24**, 200 f.

————. 1928. The nature of conduct. New York: Macmillan. Pp. 346.

————. 1931. Diagnosing personality and conduct. New York: Century. Pp. xvi+602.

THOMAS, W. I. 1923. The unadjusted girl. Boston: Little, Brown. Pp. xvii+261.

THOMAS, W. I., & ZNANIECKI, F. 1918. The Polish peasant in Europe and America. Vol. 1. Boston: Badger. Pp. 526.

THURSTONE, L. L. 1927-28. Attitudes can be measured. *Amer. J. Sociol.*, **33**, 529-554.

————. 1928. An experimental study of nationality preferences. *J. Gen. Psychol.*, **1**, 405-425.

————. 1929. Theory of attitude measurement. *Psychol. Rev.*, **36**, 222-241.

————. 1932. The measurement of social attitudes. *J. Abn. & Soc. Psychol.*, **26**, 249-269.

THURSTONE, L. L., *et al.* Various scales for the measurement of attitudes. Chicago: Univ. Chicago Press.

THURSTONE, L. L., & CHAVE, E. J. 1929. The measurement of attitude. Chicago: Univ. Chicago Press. Pp. xii+97.

TITCHENER, E. B. 1909. Experimental psychology of the thought processes. New York: Macmillan. Pp. ix+318.

————. 1916. A text-book of psychology. (New ed.) New York: Macmillan. Pp. xvii+564.

UHRBROCK, R. S. 1933. Attitudes of 4500 factory workers. *Psychol. Bull.*, **30**, 733 f.

VETTER, G. B. 1930a. The study of social and political opinions. *J. Abn. & Soc. Psychol.*, **25**, 26-39.

————. 1930b. The measurement of social and political attitudes and the related personality factors. *J. Abn. & Soc. Psychol.*, **25**, 149-189.

VETTER, G. B., & GREEN, M. 1932. Personality and group factors in the making of atheists. *J. Abn. & Soc. Psychol.*, **27**, 179-194.

VOELKER, P. F. 1921. The function of ideal and attitudes in social education. *Teach. Coll. Contrib. Educ.*, No. 112. Pp. 126.

WANG, C. K. A. 1932. Suggested criteria for writing attitude statements. *J. Soc. Psychol.*, **3**, 367-373.

WARREN, H. C. 1922. Elements of human psychology. Boston: Houghton Mifflin. Pp. x+416.

————. [Ed.] 1934. Dictionary of psychology. Boston: Houghton Mifflin. Pp. ix+372.

WARREN, H. C., & CARMICHAEL, L. 1930. Elements of human psychology. Boston: Houghton Mifflin. Pp. ix+462.

WASHBURN, M. F. 1916. Movement and mental imagery. Boston: Houghton Mifflin. Pp. xv+252.

WOODWORTH, R. S. Dynamic psychology. New York: Columbia Univ. Press. Pp. 210.

YOUNG, K. [Ed.] 1931. Social attitudes. New York: Holt. Pp. 375.

ZELIGS, R., & HENDRICKSON, G. 1933. Racial attitudes of two hundred sixth-grade children. *Sociol. & Soc. Res.*, **18**, 26-36.

ZILLIG, M. 1928. Einstellung und Aussage. *Zsch. f. Psychol.*, **106**, 58-106.

THE PSYCHOLOGIST'S FRAME OF REFERENCE[1]

Reprinted from *Psychological Bulletin*, **37**, No. 1, January 1940, 1-28

For the first time in the forty-seven years of its history this Association has elected to assemble on the coast of the Pacific. This meeting at two great centers of learning and research is not only proof of the ocean-to-ocean sweep of our membership, of our influence and prosperity, but may be taken to symbolize as well the westward trek of culture in America; or to those who like epic perspective, it may signify the westward march of Mind from Asia, to Europe, to America. But whether we think in terms of historical symbolism or not, we can hardly deny, at a time when heavy darkness has descended over the European continent, that this Forty-seventh Annual Meeting finds the burden of scientific progress in psychology resting as never before upon the membership of this Association. Fortunate we are in assuming this burden to have the support of gifted émigrés who have come so recently to join their strength to ours.

With the responsibility for the preservation and eventual rehabilitation of world psychology falling upon our shoulders, we do well to examine our credentials. Are we American psychologists equipped for the versatile leadership demanded by our comprehensive discipline; are we prepared to develop the potentialities of all its parts? These are not rhetorical questions but questions of such immediate, practical import for our science that I propose from this unusual vantage point today to seek answers as definite and unequivocal as possible. By charting the course American psychology has taken in its recent past we can determine whether the signs we observe augur the wholesome growth of psychology under our leadership and the extension of its beneficial influences to humanity at large.

[1] Presidential address delivered at the Forty-seventh Annual Meeting of the American Psychological Association, Berkeley, California, September 7, 1939.

Fifty Years of Change

Since psychology is whatever competent psychological workers make of it, I am asking, first, what it is that competent psychologists in America have been making of our science in the past fifty years, and seek to answer the question by the well-known method of combing our professional journals.

Thirty colleagues rated fifty journals according to their significance for, and devotion to, the advancement of psychology as science. The fourteen journals at the top of the list were chosen for analysis. For every tenth year, beginning 1888 and ending 1938, the entire periodical literature of these fourteen journals was read and analyzed.[2] To be sure, only two journals extend as far back as the decade beginning 1888,[3] and some of them did not come into existence until 1938. Yet, if the sample is smaller for the earlier years, it is likewise more exhaustive, since virtually no periodicals were omitted from the earlier years.

The selected journals contained over sixteen hundred articles in all, each of which was read and fitted to a system of thirty-two rubrics. Since many of these rubrics, especially those pertaining to the theoretical predilections of the authors of the articles, required subjective judgment, for a generous sample of the material independent judgments were secured from two classifiers. Mr. Jerome Bruner was my collaborator, and our agreement for all our separate judgments was 91%. At a later date the results of our analysis will be published in detail (9). For my purposes this afternoon a few of the most representative results will serve.

First, we note the decline in "facultative" treatments of mental functions. Figure 1 reflects the diminution in the *deus ex machina* type of explanation. Owing to the fewness of cases in the earlier years, we combine 1888 and 1898, and find that 19% of all articles in these years lean for their interpretation upon instinct, the "power" of attention, synthetic apperceptive unity, and kindred concepts. In successive years the falling off is gradual but almost complete. Off-

---

[2] The journals were the *Psychological Review; Journal of Experimental Psychology; American Journal of Psychology; Journal of Abnormal and Social Psychology; Journal of General Psychology; Psychological Bulletin; Journal of Psychology; Pedagogical Seminary and Journal of Genetic Psychology; Journal of Social Psychology; Character and Personality; Journal of Educational Psychology; Psychometrika; Journal of Comparative Psychology; Journal of Applied Psychology.*

[3] The *Psychological Review,* founded 1888, and the *Pedagogical Seminary,* founded 1891.

setting it in part, however, is the rise of a modern facultative treatment, different in terminology, but kindred in spirit. Here we place some of the contributions, though by no means all, that deal with

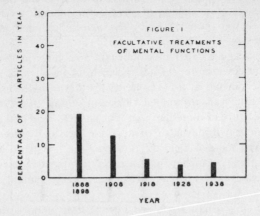

FIGURE I

FACULTATIVE TREATMENTS
OF MENTAL FUNCTIONS

factors, abilities, or the libido, as if they, too, were gods of a machine. On the whole, however, this latter tendency is not marked.

Another declining interest, so far as its explicit treatment in periodical literature is concerned, is the body-mind problem. Figure 2

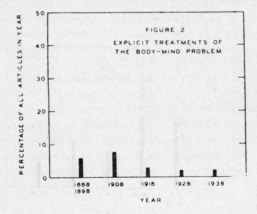

FIGURE 2

EXPLICIT TREATMENTS OF
THE BODY-MIND PROBLEM

shows the irregular decline. To a certain extent, however, this figure masks a significant shift in viewpoint. In the earlier literature solutions to the problem were boldly offered in monistic or dualistic terms; today the fashion is to deny the existence of the body-mind problem, the denial being generally effected with the aid of Vienna logic.

Figure 3 demonstrates the rise and fall of the unconscious. True, psychoanalytic journals are not included in our survey, but the point is here established that the principal periodicals written and read by our own Association reflect a loss of faith in the causal efficacy of the unconscious as well as of faculties in general.

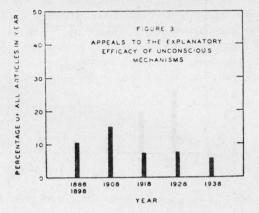

Another decreasing interest is in speculation concerning the true and essential nature of this or that mental *process*. The two parts of Figure 4 bring into contrast what might be called *process as entity*

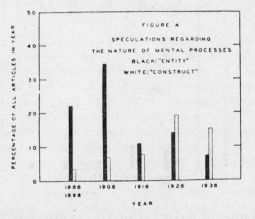

and *process as construct,* or the " realistic " view of the nature of process *versus* the " nominalistic " view. Nowadays we care less than formerly what the *nature* of " intelligence," " learning," " attention," or " drive " may be, but at the same time we care more about avoiding the hypostatization of mental processes. In the white bars are entered all articles dealing with what might broadly be called methodological formalism—methods for determining constructs from operations, postulational and geometric substitutes for mental entities, criticisms of " verbal magic," and the case for " intervening variables."

Turning from rational interpretation to experimental studies, in Figure 5 we encounter a distinct change in the manner of attacking the higher mental processes (excluding from this count perception, but including learning). In black we see a decline in studies based on language behavior, as involved in learning, reasoning, concept-

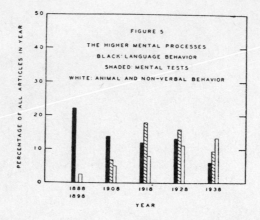

formation, reverie, or creative thinking. Every study of higher mental processes requiring the verbal coöperation of the subject, excepting those based on standard intelligence tests, is here included. Note how few there are in 1938. Shaded bars represent all studies of cognitive functions and abilities based on the application of mental tests. Even these have declined in recent years. White bars include maze learning in animals and men, conditioning experiments, and all other investigations of higher mental processes by means of non-verbal methods. It is clear that the distinctively human function of language has a decreasing appeal for psychologists, even when the language expression is in the form of standardized tests. Note that the only increase is in those studies of higher mental processes conducted with animal subjects or with human subjects who for the duration of the experiment are rendered totally speechless.

Interest in the single case has also lessened. Included in Figure 6 are articles directed toward the understanding of the individual event, based upon intensive studies of clinical cases, individual persons, or

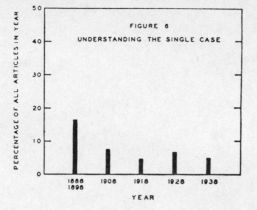

single historical events, stressing the setting of the case in its life-environment. Formerly the idiographic view of the single case was fairly popular; in recent years it has almost been ruled out of court. We seem now relatively uninterested in what the individual case can teach us, or in checking our scientific schemes against the obdurate concrete event.

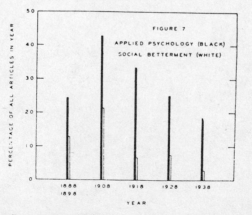

In Figure 7 we see a decline in the percentage of contributions dealing with applied psychology as well as of those concerned with social betterment. In view of the flourishing activity of the American Association for Applied Psychology and the Society for the Psychological Study of Social Issues, it is surprising to find a distinct falling off in articles applying psychology to life or pointing it in the interests of social amelioration. The conclusion to be drawn, I think. is not that our membership as a whole is less-interested in the usefulness of psychology, but that a certain professional cleavage is developing. Psychologists using the fourteen journals studied are, in their writings, becoming more and more remote from living issues and more abstract in the presentation of their subject matter. The consulting, applied, and socially-minded psychologists are turning to other, more specialized, journals not included within our survey. Thus, the indication is that " pure " and " applied " psychology are

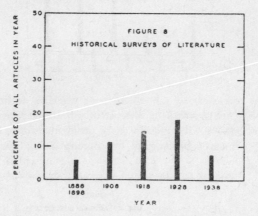

parting ways to some extent—an event which some will deplore and others welcome.

A decline of another sort is seen in the diminution of historical surveys. After steadily increasing their recognition and acknowledgment of antecedent studies, it looks now as if psychologists have started to declare their independence of the past. There are fewer historical reviews, as such, in our journals, and fewer historical preludes to experimental reports. Whether the fault lies with the authors who no longer feel respect for past work in their special lines of research, or with the editorial guillotine that decapitates articles to fit our crowded journals, I cannot say. But the fact remains that as research accumulates in our archives it is cited less frequently in our current publications.

Turning from negative to positive trends, we find, first, striking evidence of the increased use of statistical aids in the treatment of research data. Formerly, statements of central tendency were sufficient. Nowadays, measures of range, variability, correlation, and still more elaborate quantitative treatment of data are increasingly employed, until nearly half of all our periodical literature shows dependence upon them.

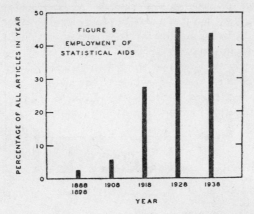

It is still too early to tell whether or not the decline in 1938 reflects a substantial growth of interest in more intensive work with fewer subjects, though there seem to be promises of this change not only among clinical psychologists but among animal psychologists as well.

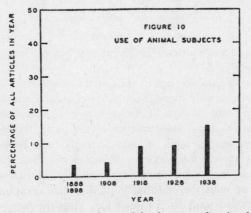

Another decidedly upward trend is the use of animal subjects in psychological research. In 1888 and 1898, taken together, only 3.5% of all studies employed animals—and this always with the intent of finding out how animals *as animals* behave; whereas last year over 15% of all articles were based upon investigations with animals and with no such modest expectation. Today it seems animals are not studied for their own sakes, but rather for what Fabre, the naturalist.

called the "universal psychology" revealed by all animals from
insects to *Homo sapiens.*

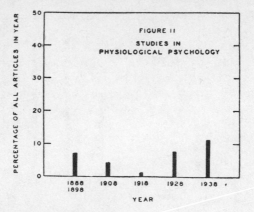

Another rise is seen in the growth of studies dealing specifically
with physiological functions.   Figure 11 shows the trend.   The
earlier studies for the most part sought physiological correlates of
conscious experience.   The reviving interest in physiological research,
accompanied by incomparably greater proficiency in such techniques
as extirpation and electrical recording, centers less often upon the

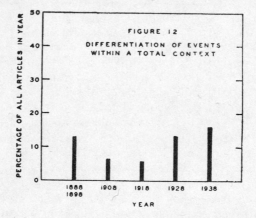

parallelism of bodily functions and experience, but studies bodily
functions directly in a manner that makes the line between psychophysiology and physiology increasingly difficult to draw.

Somewhat more elusive for classification is the growing tendency
to regard processes or events as differentiated within a total context.
Figure 12 shows a decline and rise in this point of view.   Most of

the earlier entries did mere lip-service to the proposition that all factors in the total situation must be considered. Only a few of them actually demonstrated the truth of this proposition as recent researches have done. The latter show unmistakably the influence of both modern neurology and Gestalt theory. Entries include studies of physical and mental growth, the figure-ground relationship, field theory, situational determination. In a variety of ways these investigations recognize the importance of dynamic segregation, of the determination of the part by the whole.

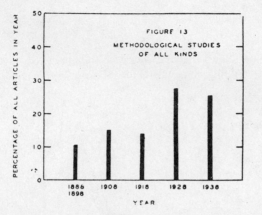

Next, though in a way the point is repetitious, I call your attention to the general upswing in methodological studies. Making no distinction as to what kind of methodology is under discussion, we see the trend in Figure 13. As a matter of fact, the earlier methodological articles dealt chiefly with the metaphysical nature of psychological data and asked how we should set about our studies of attention, intelligence, and thought, viewed as real processes. Later studies, on the other hand, are concerned primarily with getting rid of entities, giving the necessary arguments for constructs, intervening variables, rational learning curves, and the like. More specifically, the modern methodologists generally subscribe to some form of logical empiricism, increasingly to operationism.

Concerning operationism itself, the term, though new, has a special lure. Figure 14 shows its upward path. In 1928, close on the heels of Bridgman's book, one article mentioning operationism appeared. To bring the trend to date, the percentage for the first six months of 1939 has been added.

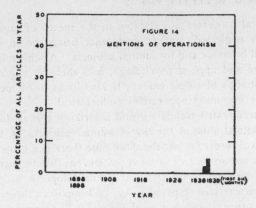

A close-up shows that the course of this magic concept is onward and upward, leading somewhere into the world of tomorrow.

1928   19381939 $\left(\begin{array}{c}\text{FIRST SIX}\\\text{MONTHS}\end{array}\right)$

Such are some of the waxing and waning fashions of the day. The story is incomplete, but even from the few points just plotted, we can draw a significant perspective. Reviewing the evidence, we find mental faculties and hypostasized psychic processes vanishing rapidly, though here and there still masquerading behind new terms. The body-mind problem, never solved, has been declared popularly null and void. Dualism evokes rejection responses of considerable vehemence. (Indeed, of all philosophical pollens, psychologists seem most allergic to this.) The appeal of the unconscious is dwindling.

Higher mental processes as exhibited in the speech of human beings are relatively neglected, marked preference being shown for studies of non-verbal behavior and for animal subjects. A schism is apparent between pure and applied psychology, and there is a growing disregard for studies of single cases. It also looks as if modern psychology were becoming appreciably unhistorical.

Among accelerated trends we find a striking rise in the employment of statistical aids, in the use of animal subjects, in the spread of physiological research. At the same time there is a growing recognition of the importance of context, which has led to many fruitful studies of dynamic segregation. Methodological studies have mounted, characterized especially by philosophical theorizing concerning the nature of psychological constructs. Operationism is the current watchword of an austere empiricism. Synoptic systems, such as those of McDougall and Stern, have given way to miniature systems, and embracing theories expounded in the grand manner have yielded to diminutive theories implemented with great precision. Immediate experience is rigidly excluded from most modern systems, and in its place surrogate operational functions are sought. Needless to say, all these trends have staunch and able advocates, but our task today is not to extol them—rather, to view them in perspective and to anticipate their long-range effects on our science.

PERSPECTIVE

The psychological system-builders of the Nineteenth and early Twentieth Centuries were filled with the lingering spirit of the Enlightenment which hated mystery and incompleteness. They wanted a synoptic view of man's mental life. If moral and metaphysical dogmatism were needed to round out their conception of the complete man, they became unblushing dogmatists. Yet even while their synoptic style flourished, the very experimental psychology which they helped to create was leading others into new paths. Their own students, in the very process of enhancing their experimental proficiency, came to admire not the work of their masters, but the self-discipline of mathematics and of the natural sciences. Willingly they exchanged what they deemed fruitless dialectics for what to them was unprejudiced empiricism. Nowadays, for one experimentalist to proclaim another " superior to controversy about fundamentals " is considered high tribute (8, p. 133).

There are with us still, of course, stubborn apostles of the Enlightenment who have not been pleased with this turn of events.

They complain that we are putting too little architectonic into our work; that, though not everyone should be a myth maker, we must have a few whose weighty influence will keep the rest of us keyed to the necessity of seeing larger significance in what we do. They say we have become a craft overstuffed with techniques and that, preoccupied with minutiae, we are in danger of losing perspective. They even say that Leipzig in labor brought forth a mere mouse (36, p. 429). But the modernist says à bas! with such nostalgia, and down, too, with synoptic systems, and down with the dated subjective categories derived from immediate experience that are invoked to sustain these systems. We will have no more of them!

Fierce and portentous is the modern attack upon immediate experience.[4] While it is commonly granted that the immediate experience of the investigator is the source of the subject matter of psychology, as of all other sciences, yet it is said that like the older sciences psychology should instantly supplant this direct experience by indirect objective formulations. Subjective immediatism must give way to a public outdoor attitude toward our knowledge. It is said that the very claim made by some psychologists that their work remains true to life, close to untrammeled common sense, is the very thing that disqualifies this work from being scientific (26, p. 178). There is no need for a curve of sensory intensity to feel like sensory intensity, for the obstruction method to feel like a desire, nor for a curve of conforming behavior to look like a crowd at a traffic intersection (19, p. 33).

So it comes about that after the initial take-off we, as psychological investigators, are permanently barred from the benefit and counsel of our ordinary perceptions, feelings, judgments, and intuitions. We are allowed to appeal to them neither for our method nor for our validations. So far as method is concerned, we are told that, because the subject is able to make his discriminations only after the alleged experience has departed, any inference of a subjectively unified experience on his part is both anachronistic and unnecessary (6). If the subject protests that it is evident to him that he had a rich and vivid experience that was not fully represented in his

---

4 A full explanation of this attack would have to include an account of many influences, among them (a) long frustration with the body-mind problem, (b) cumulative attacks upon the reliability of introspection, (c) imitative strivings after the "monism" of the natural sciences, (d) slight success in empirical studies of thinking, reasoning, volition, (e) correspondingly greater (felt) success with animal experimentation.

overt discriminations, he is firmly assured that what is vividly self-evident to him is no longer of interest to the scientific psychologist. It has been decided, to quote Boring, that " in any useful meaning of the term existence," " private experience does not exist " (7).

When it comes to *validating* his work, the modernist follows a logic all his own. He certainly *implies* that his findings overspread the problem initially formulated from experience—that thresholds of discrimination correspond to thresholds of consciousness,[5] that crossings of a grid correspond to desire, and that PGR deflections correspond to felt emotions. But should he return to the initial experience from which he started in order to validate or to apply these findings, he would probably be startled—even as the layman is startled—by the grotesque lack of fit. Fortunately for him, however, his creed forbids him to consult more than his skeletonized operations—the full-bodied experience he started with is never appealed to.

The consequences of the raid on immediate experience have already been shown in the graphs: disbelief in the existence or approachability of mental processes as such, a flight from linguistic functions, loss of interest in the single case, as well as in the historical background of psychology, and at the same time the development of a notable schism between the psychology constructed in a laboratory and the psychology constructed on the field of life.

An increasing number of investigators now pin their faith upon experimentation with animals. Our program tells us that 25% of the papers delivered at this year's meetings are based upon animal research. In 1914, twenty-five years ago, the corresponding percentage was 11.

A colleague, a good friend of mine, recently challenged me to name a single psychological problem not referable to rats for its solution. Considerably startled, I murmured something, I think, about the psychology of reading disability. But to my mind came flooding the historic problems of the aesthetic, humorous, religious, and cultural behavior of men. I thought how men build clavichords and cathedrals, how they write books, and how they laugh uproariously at Mickey Mouse; how they plan their lives five, ten, or twenty years ahead; how, by an elaborate metaphysic of their own contrivance, they deny the utility of their own experience, including the utility of the metaphysic that led them to this denial. I thought of poetry and puns, of propaganda and revolution, of stock markets and

---

[5] A point concerning which J. G. Miller's experiment has raised considerable doubt (23).

suicide, and of man's despairing hope for peace. I thought, too, of the elementary fact that human problem-solving, unlike that of the rat, is saturated through and through with verbal function, so that we have no way of knowing whether the delay, the volition, the symbolizing and categorizing typical of human learning are even faintly adumbrated by findings in animal learning.[6]

One should not prejudge this issue; but before we wander much farther down the road we are traveling might we not with profit hold a symposium for the purpose of discovering to what extent infrahuman analogues have given us power to predict, understand, and control human behavior? It is not, of course, a question of the parallels from anatomy and physiology obviously valuable for medical science, but of parallels in gross molar conduct applicable in a sphere where the culture and peculiar genius of humanity prevail. We need to ask ourselves point-blank whether the problems we frame with our rats are unquestionably of the same order as the problems we envisage for human kind; and further, if we succeed in solving a problem for rats, how we are to make sure the findings hold for man unless we repeat the whole investigation on man himself; and if we are forced to verify our principles by a separate study of man, whether we have the right to inveigh against the psychologist who prefers to study human manners and morals, since it is upon his work that the validation of our own will ultimately rest.

At the present time there can be little doubt that it is not altogether the demonstrated value of animal research that accounts for its vogue, but in large part its delightful suitability for the exercise

[6] In a valuable paper on the experimental analysis of instinctive behavior K. S. Lashley tells of the activity of the microstoma, a tiny marine worm, that, having no stinging cells of its own, captures and ingests hydras that have, until it is sated and has incorporated in itself the nettles it needs for its own protection. Regarding this remarkable performance Lashley has written: "Here, in the length of half a millimeter, are encompassed all of the major problems of dynamic psychology. There is a specific drive or appetite, satisfied only by a very indirect series of activities, with the satisfaction of the appetite dependent upon the concentration of nettles in the skin" (20, p. 446). One wonders whether the only major problems of dynamic psychology are those having to do with specific drive and its satisfaction through an indirect series of activities performed by an uncorticated organism. Does a cortex bring no major problems of its own? Are symbols, dreams, autism, irreality, guilt feelings, the ego ideal, of no essential significance? Does culture create no major problems for dynamic psychology? And has the microstoma, one wonders, that curious type of scientific motivation that requires it to view itself as a mechanism devoid of immediate experience and volition?

of objective and approved methods. By studying rats, not men, we gain status as scientists, for like the natural sciences we can, in this line of investigation, employ precision techniques and operational modes of communication. This desire for status on our part is understandable, but because of it we are in danger of losing sight of the true source of the eminence of the elder sciences. Their enviable glory does not consist in their fidelity to a set of conventional methods, but rather in the unexampled power they have given mankind in *predicting, understanding,* and *controlling* the course of nature for mankind's own benefit. As a mature science psychology, too, will find its justification, not in performing a ritual of method, but in contributing to humanity the power to achieve these ends.

PREDICTION

Considering, then, man's interest in his own well-being, let us ask how matters stand with psychological prediction. Is it not true' that apart from a narrow range of segmental reactions in the laboratory we psychologists can predict very little concerning human conduct? It is argued, of course, that sophistication in methodology will improve matters. Yet there are two grounds for doubting this claim. First, since the current methodological trend will not take direct experience as a model for its constructs nor return to it for a validation of its results, it seems unlikely that the utility of its predictions will be great. Or to state the point affirmatively, in order to predict events of pressing significance for human life one must *deal* with these events (not with some simplified surrogate or analogue), studying them at a suitable level of complexity and checking one's predictions by the actual lives men lead.

The second ground for misgiving lies in the fact that the modern methodologist, no less than his predecessors throughout the history of psychological science, fails to see the peculiar need in psychology for the prediction of the individual event. Of the two kinds of prediction appropriate to psychology—the actuarial and the individual— the former only, up to now, has received the attention it deserves.

Suppose we set out to discover the chances of John Brown to make good on parole, and use for the purpose an index of prediction based upon parole violations and parole successes of men with similar histories. We find that 72% of the men with John's antecedents make good, and many of us conclude that John, therefore, has a 72% chance of making good. There is an obvious error here. The fact that 72% of the men having the same antecedent record as John will make good is merely an actuarial statement. It tells us nothing about John. If we knew John sufficiently well, we might say not that he had a 72% chance of making good, but that he, as an individual, was almost certain to succeed or else to fail. Indeed, if we believe in determinism at all, his chances are either zero or else 100; he is bound to succeed or else to violate because the germs of his future are already contained in his attitudes, in the meaning to him of his antecedent life, and in the specific psychological environment that molds him. Even admitting the possibility of unforeseeable accidents, as scientific determinists we ought to strive for a prediction more accurate than the senseless 72% that is derived from a table of norms based on the antecedents of paroled men *en masse*. Or again, if seven in ten Americans go to the movies each week, it does not follow that I have seven in ten chances of attending. Only a knowledge of *my* attitudes, interests, and environmental situation will tell you my chances, and bring your prediction from a 70% actuarial statement to a 100% certain individual prediction.

The upshot of the matter is this: psychology will become *more* scientific, *i.e.* better able to make predictions, when it has learned to evaluate single trends in all their intrinsic complexity, when it has learned how to tell what will happen to *this* child's IQ if we change his environment in a certain way, whether *this* man will make a good executive, whither *this* social change is tending.

For certain purposes actuarial predictions have their uses. They are based on the type of law that transcends geographical-historical context. Yet in many cases we find that human conduct is so utterly modified by geographical-historical context, and by all concurrent internal trends accompanying the behavior in question, that laws ignoring context do not entirely meet our need.[7]

Our survey has shown that an increasing number of psychologists are becoming aware of the importance of context. The time is therefore ripe to seek more assiduously those laws that define the influence of ground upon figure, context upon judgment, traits upon behavior, frames of reference upon attitudes and activity, situational fields upon

[7] It does no good to object that everything in the universe supplies a context for everything else, that "if a man is ever to utter the whole truth about a natural event, he must not shut his mouth until he has expressed all nature" (7, p. 445). It is still a question of *what degree* of limitation upon the system chosen for study is most serviceable. Because some limitation is obviously required it does not follow that the most fruitful level to adopt is that of the most isolated possible motor automatism (the elementary discrimination).

performance. These contextual laws are stepping stones toward that form of synthetic understanding on the basis of which truly serviceable predictions concerning individual happenings are made.

One large section of our profession will claim success in the line of approach I have indicated. Clinical psychologists will say that their daily work requires all manner of individual predictions, and that guidance is based upon it. In principle they are right, but two admonitions are in order. First, clinicians need to check their judgments rigorously, for the validity of clinical predictions is rarely known. Further, they need to make explicit the basis on which their correct predictions are made. Urgently we need to know the way in which successful predictions in individual cases are arrived at. In the meantime psychologists in general might do worse than study the bases of correct predictions made by statesmen, psychiatrists, lawyers, and even head waiters, whose skill in forecasting important aspects of human behavior is greater than ours. If we can first learn from them, we may ultimately teach them and ourselves more. To raise our level of prediction above that achieved by common sense, even by superior common sense, should be our steadfast aim.

UNDERSTANDING

To the power of prediction science adds the capacity to understand what we observe. By understanding I mean the ability that human beings have to place details of information within a pattern of thought. Psychologists have long known that no fact apprehended ever stands alone, for it cannot be a fact until it is embedded within, and interpreted by, a context to which it is in some way related. With the advent of dynamic psychology it became common knowledge that what is accepted as fact depends very largely upon the individual's sense of the importance of fact, each individual carrying with him convictions concerning what is important for him.[8] Sometimes we call these convictions his values. Unless we can first comprehend our subject's value-context, we are unable to know the significance of his behavior as he performs it, for the simple reason that the behavior we perceive is instantly ordered to *our* own presuppositions without any regard to what *his* presuppositions may be. In other words, our frame, not his, supplies the context.

Let me give an illustration. Suppose a psychologist sets about to study learning. Suppose, too, he brings to his task a firm sense

[8] Especially instructive is A. N. Whitehead's discussion of the relation between matter-of-fact and the sense of importance of fact (35, Chap. 1).

of the importance of mechanical connectedness. He observes the subject's behavior, and since fact depends upon the sense of the importance of fact, he interprets this observed behavior in terms of his own presuppositions concerning mechanical connectedness. Now, the learning itself was achieved by an individual who had a very different sense of values. He was not learning in order to demonstrate mechanical connectedness to himself, but in order to acquire something important to him. Shall the psychologist understand this behavior with the aid of his own imperatives or strive to understand it in the light of the subject's imperatives? In the former case mechanical connectedness becomes the chief law of learning; in the latter case interest and importance become the chief law.[9]

Instead of attempting to understand the other organism's point of view and interpreting his activity in reference to this, it is our custom early in our investigations to disregard or even to disrupt his context of behavior, and, instead of comprehending his activity within his frame of importance, to interpret his behavior in terms of our own. Moreover, when we make rational reconstructions of our findings (constructs), we do so from the point of view of our presuppositions and communicate them to other scientists sharing these same presuppositions. In the course of this procedure the pattern of trends peculiar to the organism, what the organism is trying by himself to do, is almost completely lost to sight.

You will recognize that I have here been skirting the problem of *Verstehen* formulated and explored by German psychology; and you will admit that it is one of the leads from German psychology that has not been followed very far by Americans. Our own psychology would profit if we undertook to apply to it our genius for clarification. There are, of course, in America a few theoretical skirmishes with the problem (2, 17), and some native experiments that point the way, among them the investigations of Murray and his collaborators (25), L. B. Murphy (24), Allport, Walker, and

[9] To be sure, the organism has a way of insistently making its point of view apparent, trying, as it were, to tell the psychologist that the primary law of learning lies in this sense of importance. So the psychologist then postulates demands or drives to account for learning, but continues to view these within his (the psychologist's) own frame of importance. Our current conceptions of motivation are not framed from the subject's point of view. If they were, we should study less often mechanical retroaction, and more often the classificatory power that interest confers on memory; less often the effects of specific incentives or drives, and more often the mature interest systems in accordance with which human beings acquire their knowledge and skill.

Lathers (1), Estes (14), Cartwright and French (11).[10] In various ways all these experiments have shed light upon the process of understanding the contexts and imperatives that determine behavior from the subject's point of view.

Let us turn back for a moment from the subject's sense of importance to the experimenter's. To some extent it is inevitable that in striving for system each of us plan his experiment in his own way, select his instruments and subjects, and draw his interpretations in accordance with his own presuppositions, excluding what is not consistent with his frame of importance. Such natural pedantry is not necessarily an evil, for specialization must be allowed within our extensive subject matter. But it follows that, unless we have a diversity of presuppositions and interests in our science, we shall lose all those forms of experience that are automatically excluded when but one set of presuppositions is followed. Especially today variety is needed, for limited and miniature systems are in fashion, from which exclusions are exceedingly strict.

Our survey has shown that this is an age of interest in methodology. What it has not so clearly shown is that the purveyor of methods is necessarily asking you to accept his own frame of presuppositions. It is for this reason that it becomes necessary to scrutinize the consequences of any commitment of method. Even so harmless a methodological doctrine as operationism is fraught with unexpected entanglements.

In an age of turmoil, one hundred and seventy years ago, Voltaire made the demand: " If you would converse with me, you must first define your terms." In our present age of turmoil, operationism is making the same refreshing demand (31). It is a demand that appeals to all sensible men. Now, the best way to define a term is by the use of the typical instance or event. When we speak operationally we say, in effect, " I mean something which is illustrated by the

---

[10] The importance of this last-named experiment, soon to be published, lies in its demonstration that in judgments of personality the validity attained by each of two judges can be in excess of their reliability. That is, two investigators may have demonstrable correctness that exceeds their agreement with one another, because each understands different *aspects* of the subject's personality. It follows that when we pare down our acceptable data until only that portion remains upon which all investigators agree, we are left with less than our just scientific reward. What is needed is a method of combining demonstrably valid insights rather than a reduction of our data to the bare bones upon which all observers may objectively agree.

following actions." In this way, through the telling illustration, we communicate a prior understanding in ourselves in order to arouse a like understanding in others. Operationism thus may become a useful tool of understanding.

But when the operationist goes further and insists that "a concept is synonymous with the corresponding set of operations," can he mean what he says? If so, there must be an infinitude of discrete concepts. Think, for instance, of all the different operations that have gone into the study of learning. To prevent complete and senseless pluralism operations have to be grouped by classes, and there is ultimately no way of grouping them except by relational thought. The most austere operationist communicates not operations, but a prior concept, for operational symbolizing depends upon prior ideas of entities and relations that are symbolized. Even if we try to rely upon the "standard experiment," as Tolman proposes, to serve as the operation by which a concept is defined (32), it is only by virtue of some act of understanding that the equivalence of this experiment with others can be established.[11]

It is not to operationism's demand for illustrative definitions that objection can be made, but to the fact that its hidden metaphysical presuppositions of extreme nominalism beckon us away from the fundamental problem of how we know things together. Hyperaesthesia for our operations and anaesthesia for understanding make us lose our way in an infinitude of detail. Synoptic views become more and more difficult; an entropy of scientific energy sets in. Fearful lest we imply that we did something more than our experiments indicate, we are tempted to give up our search for useful generalizations and to disclaim responsibility for the wider application of our work.

Along this path lies skepticism which—as historians have noted—sends forth its pallid bloom at the end of eras of great intellectual

[11] Critics have pointed out that the agreements under the operational creed do not go deep, and that the unity of science is after all not just around the corner. Some advocates of operationism maintain that it readily includes both immediate experience and the introspective technique within its view, some think the opposite; some would admit purposive interpretations within operationism, others would exclude them; some think that field theory fits, some that it does not. And if, as some say, its sole objective is to separate the rational criteria of inquiry from the positive and experimental criteria, then there is but temporary gain, since we have to return to understanding in order to know-together the rational and empirical ingredients of the analysis.

advance. Permit me to quote two passages from a recent methodological book written by an able experimentalist:

Science after all is only one of the games played by the children of this world, and it may very well be that those who prefer other games are in their generation wiser. It must be remembered, however, that *science is a game* and those who play it have a right to insist that it be played according to rule. If some of the players, or the bystanders, try to change the rules, the game will go to pieces, or at least, it will not be the same game (26, p. 57).

And again:

Science is a vast and impressive tautology. Its laws are summaries of observations, its hypotheses involve arguments that are circular. Since its explanations are true only if they can be demonstrated empirically, they explain nothing that is not already known. The mystery which surrounds the life of man is as dark today as it was when man first came out of the jungle, and will be just as impenetrable when the last surviving scientist thinks his concluding thought or writes his final sentence (26, p. 154).

Such weariness is inevitable so long as we make the test of psychology one of fidelity to method rather than to understanding, prediction, and control. Methodism as the sole requirement of science means that all the faithful crowd onto a carpet of prayer, and with their logical shears cut more and more inches off the rug, permitting fewer and fewer aspirants to enjoy status. Two debilitating attitudes result: that of the playboy who likes his childish games, and that of the fatalist who sees no duty devolving upon a scientist other than that of formal ritual. The survival value of either attitude is zero, for both lead us, and all those who look to psychology for help, to believe that psychology has no essential relation to life, and that human events lie entirely beyond our control. Such a belief undermines the very civilization that has endowed psychology with its freedom, in return charging it with the contribution of useful knowledge.[12]

CONTROL

Until our deficiencies in prediction and understanding are repaired, it is unlikely that psychology can go far in meeting the third and

---

[12] Not infrequently the skeptic derides applied psychology. Outside the laboratory he lives a cultured and varied life of a free agent and useful citizen. Yet his methodical work in the laboratory overspreads very little of his daily experience and prevents integration in his life. Though he generally repudiates a dualism of mind and body, he welcomes the equally stultifying dualism of laboratory and life.

supreme criterion of validity for science—that of practical control of human affairs. The clinician is most active in this direction. He and other consultants, educators, and technicians are controlling human events, but whether more successfully than unaided common sense could do depends on evidence still to be supplied in conscientious records of success and failure.

Outside of the clinical field little control is attempted. The man of common sense approaching our treatises for help finds that a large portion of his daily conduct is not only left unexplained, but is not represented at all. From agencies of government, industry, education, and human welfare come daily appeals for assistance in their service to mankind. Psychology, as science—may I repeat?—can be justified only by giving mankind practical control over its destinies, not by squatting happily on a carpet of prayer [13]

Frame of Reference

Fortunately, currents engender countercurrents. The flow in psychology today is not altogether toward the shoals and reefs of formalism and of skepticism. Our evidence (Fig. 12) shows a strong revival of interest in the problems of context, which of necessity include the structure of the human personality and its activity within its social surroundings. To study highly integrated functions at levels where serviceable prediction and understanding result is, of course, a most difficult undertaking, requiring inventions of method not dreamed of today; requiring, also, the borrowing of many tools of precision and safeguards of measurement from the experimentalist's storehouse. It is characteristic of this new movement that its concepts have a realistic and humanistic flavor, for it is vital in this new work to believe that something real and substantial is under investigation.

An example of the trend is the growing interest in the *frame of reference*, a concept which I have appropriated for the title of this address. It is of recent origin and may for that reason be viewed with suspicion. Yet it is, I feel sure, the legitimate offspring of the flourishing principle of dynamic differentiation. It expresses the

[13] It seems only fair to add that there are signs of a growing demand among psychologists for significant and useful research. The demand is clearly apparent among social psychologists, and elsewhere as well. T. L. Kelley, speaking recently to mathematical psychologists, has urged them to invent and employ "measures of utility" in order that the factors they conjure into being may turn out not to be factors of just no importance at all (16).

importance of context; it repairs the ravages that result from viewing the behavior of other organisms exclusively within the investigator's frame of presuppositions; it aids in understanding. Its fruitfulness is seen in many experimental studies of the past five years, including those of Ansbacher (4), Cantril (10), Darley (12), Kornhauser (18), McGregor (22), Sells (28), Sherif (29), Stagner (30), Watson and Hartmann (34), and others.

Frame of reference has to do with any context whatever that exerts a demonstrable influence upon the individual's perceptions, judgments, feelings, or actions. Often the influence is—to use Köhler's term—" silent." Of the existence of frames the subject himself is only partially aware, and unless he is well warned the investigator too may overlook them entirely. At the present time it is especially the social and dynamic psychologists who are ardent on the trail, although much pertinent related work is found wherever there is research upon problems of equivalence, aspiration level, life space, constancy phenomena, and psychophysical judgment.

Many frames, of course, especially those encountered in psychophysics, are neutral and impersonal in type, providing simple spatial and temporal orientations. Others are personal and ego-involving.[14] The position of college buildings upon a campus is an impersonal spatial system that orients and directs our excursions to and from our classes; but our status within the collegiate hierarchy is of a more personal order, charged with intimate importance to ourselves, and determining affective attitudes of motivational significance. Dynamic and social psychologists are especially concerned with these personal, ego-involving frames, and are often able to show that what are sometimes thought to be neutral-perceptual judgments, even the judgments of scientists themselves, are not wholly determined by an objectively established frame, but are entangled deep in the web of personality.

The relation of frames to *attitudes* and to *traits* is a problem yet to be worked out. These concepts all refer in various gradations to complex and relatively persistent forms of mental organization. Their popularity, together with that of *trend, need, sentiment,* and other kindred concepts, gives support to McDougall's claim, expressed in one of his last papers, that the most indispensable doctrine in modern psychology is that of *tendency* (21). All are frankly class

[14] In making the distinction between personal and impersonal frames, T. A. Ryan (27) confines the former to certain self-referred systems of space, time, or meaning, neglecting to consider the emotional frames that are ego-involving.

concepts, and can be defended, I think, for the superior promise they hold in our triple task of predicting, understanding, and controlling behavior.

Class concepts though 'they are, they do not necessarily exclude considerations of cultural influence nor the situational field. It is especially those frames of reference adopted as the " wise prejudices " of our own station, class, and culture that reflect prevailing social norms. We are now making progress in the detailed study of conforming behavior, in the composition of ideological thought, and in the genesis and development of frames in childhood.[15] We are beginning to sort out that monstrously tangled heap our Councils have christened "personality and culture." Not yet, however, are we able to tell what makes a mauve decade mauve, or a skeptical age skeptical, or psychology in the 1880's soulful and in the 1930's soulless. Nor do we know the extent to which a man can shake himself free of the influence of his times, or even recreate them to his liking. Freud, we know, had something to do with Queen Victoria's downfall; but was he consequence or cause? Who can say?

Speaking on this very campus forty years ago, John Dewey, later to become the eighth president of our Association, made what for that time was a striking observation (13). Psychology, he held, cannot help but be politically conditioned. He had in mind, for example, the fact that doctrines of the fixedness of human nature flourish in an aristocracy and perish in a democracy. The privileges of the elite in ancient Greece, and the doctrines of the Church in mediaeval times, provided the setting for psychological theories of their day. Under modern conditions theories of statehood play a major role.[16]

The president of the *Deutsche Gesellschaft*, addressing that organization last year, praised typological studies that enabled psychology, in matters of heredity, race, and education, to pick out the national *Gegentypus* whose unwelcome qualities are individualism and intellectualism. In passing, he warned against using the mental tests that one of the great figures in psychology, William Stern, a

[15] Especially fascinating are the problems in this area. Consider, for example, the question which frames the child adopts from his playmates and which from his parents. Matters of politics and religion he ordinarily seems to refer to frames taken from parents, but standards of speech and clothing to frames acquired from his contemporaries. Why does he do so?

[16] In this connection the striking fusion of John Dewey's own psychological theories with his allegiance to democracy is well worth special study (cf. 3, Chap. 9).

Jew, had introduced, and said that he wondered not at all that some of his colleagues had been censured for pursuing a pre-revolutionary course of thought. At the same time he added:

Antagonistic foreign countries speak of coordination (*Gleichschaltung*) whenever conformity of science and politics is perceived. No, this conformity is certainly not based on coordination, but upon the fact that politics and science, now for the first time, strive after truth even in the basic questions of existence, over which heretofore darkness and error reigned (15, p. 14).

And what is the situation with us? Do we American psychologists lack politically determined attitudes? At first thought it would seem so, for are we not entirely free in our individual researches, and may we not hold any fantastic view that we choose? We may, and that proves the point for the political determinist, for only in a democracy can anything like a " socially detached intelligentsia " be realized. On the theory that democracy will ultimately gain by giving each thinker all the space he wants, we American psychologists are subsidized, encouraged, and defended. Each worker may elect, as he pleases, any section or subsection of psychology that he finds suited to his taste and abilities.

The desirability of keeping alive diversified investigation and a diversified sense of importance is the generous lesson that democracy teaches us. Now, if ever, must we learn it well and apply it to ourselves. If we rejoice, for example, that present-day psychology is— as Bills has pointed out (5) and as our survey has shown—increasingly *empirical, mechanistic, quantitative, nomothetic, analytic,* and *operational,* we should also beware of demanding slavish subservience to these presuppositions. Why not allow psychology as a science— for science is a broad and beneficent term—to be also *rational, teleological, qualitative, idiographic, synoptic,* and even *non-operational?* I mention these antitheses of virtue with deliberation, for the simple reason that great insights of psychology in the past—for example, those of Aristotle, Locke, Fechner, James, Freud—have stemmed from one or more of these unfashionable presuppositions.

My plea, therefore, is that we avoid authoritarianism, that we keep psychology from becoming a cult from which original and daring inquiry is ruled out by the application of one-sided tests of method; that we come to evaluate our science rather by its success in enhancing —above the levels achieved by common sense—our powers of *predicting, understanding,* and *controlling* human action. As an aid to progress I have tried especially to strengthen the case for research upon complex patterns of human mental organization, frames of reference, the subject's point of view, and the act of understanding.

If we but watch with amused humility our own personal frames affect our perceptions and our deeds, we will then enjoy and profit from our disagreements. Best of all, we shall be able to sink these disagreements into a common determination that the vast horizons of our science shall not prematurely close down, neither through bigotry, nor surrender to authoritarianism, nor through our failure to pay our way in the civilization that is sustaining us.

BIBLIOGRAPHY

1. ALLPORT, F. H., WALKER, L., & LATHERS, E. Written composition and characteristics of personality. *Arch. Psychol., N. Y.*, 1934, **26**, No. 173.
2. ALLPORT, G. W. Personality : a psychological interpretation. New York : Holt, 1937.
3. ALLPORT, G. W. The individual and social psychology of John Dewey. *In* Schlipp, P. A. (Ed.), *The Philosophy of John Dewey*. Evanston : Northwestern Univ. Press, 1939. Chap. 9.
4. ANSBACHER, H. Perception of number as affected by the monetary value of the objects. *Arch. Psychol., N. Y.*, 1937, **30**, No. 215.
5. BILLS, A. G. Changing views of psychology as a science. *Psychol. Rev.*, 1938, **45**, 377–394.
6 BORING, E. G. Temporal perception and operationism. *Amer. J. Psychol.*, 1936, **48**, 519–522.
7. BORING, E. G. A psychological function is the relation of successive differentiations of events in the organism. *Psychol. Rev.*, 1937, **44**, 445–461.
8. BORING, E. G. Review of R. S. Woodworth's *Experimental psychology*. *Amer. J. Psychol.*, 1939, **52**, 131–138.
9. BRUNER, J. S., & ALLPORT, G. W. Fifty years of change in American psychology. (Forthcoming in the *Psychol. Bull.*)
10. CANTRIL, H. The prediction of social events. *J. abnorm. soc. Psychol.*, 1938, **33**, 364–389.
11. CARTWRIGHT, D., & FRENCH, J. R. P. The reliability of life-history studies. *Character & Pers.*, 1939, **8**.
12. DARLEY, J. G. Changes in measured attitudes and adjustments *J. soc. Psychol.*, 1938, **9**, 189–199.
13. DEWEY, J. Psychology as philosophic method. Berkeley : Univ. Chronicle, 1899 ; reprinted as Consciousness and experience, in his *Influence of Darwin on Philosophy and Other Essays*. New York : Holt, 1910. Pp. 242–270.
14. ESTES, S. G. Judging personality from expressive behavior. *J. abnorm. soc. Psychol.*, 1938, **33**, 217–236.
15. JAENSCH, E. Wozu Psychologie? *Ber. XVIth Kongr. dtsch. Ges. Psychol.*, Leipzig, 1939, 7–30.
16. KELLEY, T. L. Mental factors of no importance. *J. educ. Psychol.*, 1938, **30**, 139–142.

17. KLEIN, D. B. Scientific understanding in psychology. *Psychol. Rev.*, 1932, 39, 552–569.
18. KORNHAUSER, A. W. Attitudes of economic groups. *Publ. Opin. Quart.*, 1938, 2, 260–268.
19. LASHLEY, K. S. The behavioristic interpretation of consciousness. *Psychol. Rev.*, 1923, 30, 237–272.
20. LASHLEY, K. S. Experimental analysis of instinctive behavior. *Psychol. Rev.*, 1938, 45, 445–471.
21. McDOUGALL, W. Tendencies as indispensable postulates of all psychology. *Proc. XIth int. Congr. Psychol.*, Paris, 1937, 157–170.
22. McGREGOR, D. The major determinants of the prediction of social events. *J. abnorm. soc. Psychol.*, 1938, 33, 179–204.
23. MILLER, J. G. Discrimination without awareness. *Amer. J. Psychol.*, 1939, 52, 562–578.
24. MURPHY, L. B. Social behavior and child personality: an exploratory study of some roots of sympathy. New York: Columbia Univ. Press, 1937.
25. MURRAY, H. A., *et al.* Explorations in personality. New York: Oxford Univ. Press, 1938.
26. PRATT, C. C. The logic of modern psychology. New York: Macmillan, 1939.
27. RYAN, T. A. Dynamic, physiognomic, and other neglected properties of perceived objects: a new approach to comprehending. *Amer. J. Psychol.*, 1938, 51, 629–650.
28. SELLS, S. B. The atmosphere effect: an experimental study of reasoning. *Arch. Psychol., N. Y.*, 1936, 29, No. 200.
29. SHERIF, M. The psychology of social norms. New York: Harper, 1936.
30. STAGNER, R. Measuring relationships among group opinions. *Publ. Opin. Quart.*, 1938, 2, 622–627.
31. STEVENS, S. S. Psychology and the science of science. *Psychol. Bull.*, 1939, 36, 221–263.
32. TOLMAN, E. C. Operational behaviorism and current trends in psychology. *Proc. 25th Anniv. Celeb. Inaug. Grad. Stud.*, Univ. So. Calif., Los Angeles, 1936, 89–103.
33. TOLMAN, E. C. Psychology versus immediate experience. *Phil. Sci.*, 1938, 2, 356–380.
34. WATSON, W. S., & HARTMANN, G. W. Rigidity of a basic attitudinal frame. *J. abnorm. soc. Psychol.*, 1939, 34, 314–336.
35. WHITEHEAD, A. N. Modes of thought. New York: Macmillan, 1938.
36. ZANGWILL, O. L. Review of R. S. Woodworth's *Experimental psychology*. *Brit. J. Psychol.*, 1939, 29, 429–431.

THE FUNCTIONAL AUTONOMY OF MOTIVES

Reprinted from *The American Journal of Psychology*, 1937, **50**, 141-156.

For fifty years this JOURNAL has served both as a rich repository for research and as a remarkably sensitive record of the psychological temper of the times. These two services are of great historical value. Since there is no reason to doubt that *The American Journal* will continue to hold its position of leadership in the future, one wonders what new currents of psychological interest its pages will reflect in the coming half-century. With what problems will psychologists be chiefly concerned? What discoveries will they make? What types of scientific formulation will they prefer?

To predict at least one of these trends accurately requires no clairvoyance. On all sides we see the rising tide of interest in problems of personality. Up to a few years ago the somewhat segregated field of clinical psychology alone was concerned; but now theoretical and experimental psychology are likewise deeply affected. As never before the traditional portrait of the "generalized human mind" is being tested against the living models from which it is derived. As compared with particular minds it is found to lack locus, self-consciousness, organic character, and reciprocal interpenetration of parts, all of which are essential to personality. Unless I am greatly mistaken the coming half-century will see many attempts to replace the abstract datum (mind-in-general) with the concrete datum (mind-in-particular), even at the peril of a revolutionary upset in the conception of psychology as *science*.

Some of the best known definitions of psychology formulated in the past fifty years have given explicit recognition to the individuality of mind—that is, to its dependence upon the person. But these definitions have not as yet noticeably affected the abstractive tendency of psychological research—not even that of their authors. Wundt, James, and Titchener serve as examples. The first wrote: "*It* [psychology] *investigates the total content of experience in its relations to the subject.*" The second: "*Psychology is the science of finite individual minds;*" and the third:

"Psychology is the study of experience considered as dependent on some person." None of these authors developed his account of mental life to accord with his definition. It is as though some vague sense of propriety guided them in framing their definitions; they *knew* that mind (as a psychological datum) exists only in finite and in personal forms. Yet their historical positions—the spirit of the times in which they worked —prevented them from following their own definitions to the end. Had any one of them done so, the psychology of personality would have had early and illustrious sponsorship.

In line with what I regard as a certain development in the psychology of the future I venture to submit a paper dealing, I think, with the one issue that above all others divides the study of mind-in-general from the study of mind-in-particular. Motivation is the special theme, but the principle involved reaches into every nook and cranny of the evolving science of personality.[1]

Two Kinds of Dynamic Psychology

Any type of psychology that treats *motives*, thereby endeavoring to answer the question as to *why* men behave as they do, is called a *dynamic psychology*. By its very nature it cannot be merely a descriptive psychology, content to depict the *what* and the *how* of human behavior. The boldness of dynamic psychology in striking for causes stands in marked contrast to the timid, "more scientific," view that seeks nothing else than the establishment of a mathematical function for the relation between some artificially simple stimulus and some equally artificial and simple response. If the psychology of personality is to be more than a matter of coefficients of correlation it too must be a dynamic psychology, and seek first and foremost a sound and adequate theory of the nature of human dispositions.

The type of dynamic psychology almost universally held, though sufficient from the point of view of the *abstract* motives of the generalized mind, fails to provide a foundation solid enough to bear the weight of any *single* full-bodied personality. The reason is that prevailing dynamic doctrines refer every mature motive of personality to underlying original instincts, wishes, or needs, shared *by all men*. Thus, the concert artist's devotion to his music is sometimes 'explained' as an extension of his self-assertive instinct, of the need for sentience, or as a symptom of some repressed striving of the libido. In McDougall's

---

[1] What follows is drawn in part from Chapter VII of my forthcoming book, *Personality: A Psychological Interpretation*, 1937.

hormic psychology, for example, it is explicitly stated that only the instincts or propensities can be prime movers. Though capable of extension (on both the receptive and executive sides), they are always few in number, common in all men, and established at birth. The enthusiastic collector of bric-a-brac derives his enthusiasm from the parental instinct; so too does the kindly old philanthropist, as well as the mother of a brood. It does not matter how different these three interests may seem to be, they derive their energy from the same source. The principle is that a very few basic motives suffice for explaining the endless varieties of human interests. The psychoanalyst holds the same over-simplified theory. The number of human interests that he regards as so many canalizations of the one basic sexual instinct is past computation.

The authors of this type of dynamic psychology are concerning themselves only with mind-in-general. They seek a classification of the common and basic motives by which to explain both normal or neurotic behavior of *any* individual case. (This is true even though they may regard their own list as heuristic or even as fictional.) The plan really does not work. The very fact that the lists are so different in their composition suggests—what to a naïve observer is plain enough—that motives are almost infinitely varied among men, not only in form but in substance. Not four wishes, nor eighteen propensities, nor any and all combinations of these, even with their extensions and variations, seem adequate to account for the endless variety of goals sought by an endless variety of mortals. Paradoxically enough, in many personalities the few simplified needs or instincts alleged to be the *common* ground for all motivation, turn out to be completely lacking.

The second type of dynamic psychology, the one here defended, regards adult motives as infinitely varied, and as self-sustaining, *contemporary* systems, growing out of antecedent systems, but functionally independent of them. Just as a child gradually repudiates his dependence on his parents, develops a will of his own, becomes self-active and self-determining, and outlives his parents, so it is with motives. Each motive has a definite point of origin which may possibly lie in instincts, or, more likely, in the organic tensions of infancy. Chronologically speaking, all adult purposes can be traced back to these seed-forms in infancy, but as the individual matures the tie is broken. Whatever bond remains, is historical, not functional.

Such a theory is obviously opposed to psychoanalysis and to all other genetic accounts that assume inflexibility in the root purposes and drives of life. (Freud says that the structure of the Id *never* changes!) The theory declines to admit that the energies of adult personality are infantile or archaic in nature. Motivation is *always* contemporary. The life of modern Athens is *continuous* with the life of the ancient city, but it in no sense *depends* upon its present "go." The life of a tree is continuous with that of its seed, but the seed no longer sustains and nourishes the full grown tree. Earlier purposes lead into later purposes, and are abandoned in their f'vor.

William James taught a curious doctrine that has been a matter for incredulous amusement ever since, the doctrine of the *transitoriness of instincts*. According to this theory—not so quaint as sometimes thought —an instinct appears but once in a lifetime, whereupon it promptly disappears through its transformation into habits. If there *are* instincts this is no doubt of their fate, for no instinct can retain its motivational force unimpaired after it has been absorbed and recast under the transforming influence of learning. Such is the reasoning of James, and such is the logic of functional autonomy. The psychology of personality must be a psychology of *post-instinctive* behavior.

Woodworth has spoken of the transformation of "mechanisms" into "drives."[2] A mechanism Woodworth defines as any course of behavior that brings about an adjustment. A *drive* is any neural process that releases mechanisms especially concerned with consummatory reactions. In the course of learning, many preparatory mechanisms must be developed in order to lead to the consummation of an original purpose. These mechanisms are the effective cause of activity in each succeeding mechanism, furnishing the drive for each stage following in the series. Originally all these mechanisms were merely instrumental, only links in the long chain of processes involved in the achievement of an *instinctive* purpose; with time and development, with integration and elaboration, many of these mechanisms become activated directly, setting up a state of desire and tension for activities and objects no longer connected with the original impulse. Activities and objects that earlier in the game were *means* to an end, now become *ends* in themselves.[3]

---

[2] R. S. Woodworth, *Dynamic Psychology*, 1918. Equivalent assertions are those of W. Stern concerning the transformation of "phenomotives" into "genomotives" (*Allgemeine Psychologie*, 1935, 569), and of E. C. Tolman regarding the "strangle hold" that "means-objects" acquire by "setting up in their own right" (Psychology versus immediate experience, *Phil. Sci.*, 2, 1935, 370).

[3] "The fundamental drive towards a certain end may be hunger, sex, pugnacity or what not, but once the activity is started, the means to the end becomes an object of interest on

Although Woodworth's choice of quasi-neurological terminology is not the best, his doctrine, or one like it is indispensable in accounting for the infinite number of effective motives possible in human life, and for their severance from the rudimentary desires of infancy. Further discussion of the operation of the principle and a critique of Woodworth's position will be more to the point after a review of the evidence in favor of the principle.

EVIDENCE FOR FUNCTIONAL AUTONOMY

We begin in a common sense way. An ex-sailor has a craving for the sea, a musician longs to return to his instrument after an enforced absence, a city-dweller yearns for his native hills, and a miser continues to amass his useless horde. Now, the sailor may have first acquired his love for the sea as an incident in his struggle to earn a living. The sea was merely a conditioned stimulus associated with satisfaction of his 'nutritional craving.' But now the ex-sailor is perhaps a wealthy banker; the original motive is destroyed; and yet the hunger for the sea persists unabated, even increases in intensity as it becomes more remote from the 'nutritional segment.' The musician may first have been stung by a rebuke or by a slur on his inferior performances into mastering his instrument, but now he is safely beyond the power of these taunts; there is no need to compensate further; now he loves his instrument more than anything else in the world. Once indeed the city dweller may have associated the hills around his mountain home with nutritional and erotogenic satisfactions, but these satisfactions he now finds in his city home, *not* in the mountains; whence then comes all his hill-hunger? The miser perhaps learned his habits of thrift in dire necessity, or perhaps his thrift was a symptom of sexual perversion (as Freud would claim), and yet the miserliness persists, and even becomes stronger with the years, even after the necessity or the roots of the neurosis have been relieved.

Workmanship is a good example of functional autonomy. A good workman feels compelled to do clean-cut jobs even though his security, or the praise of others, no longer depends upon high standards. In fact, in a day of jerry-building his workman-like standards may be to his economic disadvantage. Even so he cannot do a slipshod job. Workmanship is not an instinct, but so firm is the hold it may acquire on

---

its own account" (Woodworth, *op. cit.*, 201). "The primal forces of hunger, fear, sex, and the rest, continue in force, but do not by any means, even with their combinations, account for the sum total of drives activating the experienced individual" (*ibid.*, 104).

a man that it is little wonder Veblen mistook it for one. A business man, long since secure economically, works himself into ill-health, and sometimes even back into poverty, for the sake of carrying on his plans. What was once an instrumental technique becomes a master-motive.

Neither necessity nor reason can make one contented permanently on a lonely island or on an isolated farm after one is adapted to active, energetic city life. The acquired habits seem sufficient to urge one to a frenzied existence, even though reason and health demand the simpler life.

The pursuit of literature, the development of good taste in clothes, the use of cosmetics, the acquiring of an automobile, strolls in the public park, or a winter in Miami—all may first serve, let us say, the interests of sex. But every one of these instrumental activities may become an interest in itself, held for a life time, long after the erotic motive has been laid away in lavender. People often find that they have lost allegiance to their original aims because of their deliberate preference for the many ways of achieving them.

The maternal sentiment offers a final illustration. Many young mothers bear their children unwillingly, dismayed at the thought of the drudgery of the future. At first they may be indifferent to, or even hate, their offspring; the 'parental instinct' seems wholly lacking. The only motives that hold such a mother to child-tending may be fear of what her critical neighbors will say, fear of the law, a habit of doing any job well, or perhaps a dim hope that the child will provide security for her in her old age. However gross these motives, they are sufficient to hold her to her work, until through the practice of devotion her burden becomes a joy. As her love for the child develops, her earlier practical motives are forgotten. In later years not one of these original motives may operate. The child may be incompetent, criminal, a disgrace to her, and far from serving as a staff for her declining years, he may continue to drain her resources and vitality. The neighbors may criticize her for indulging the child, the law may exonerate her from allegiance; she certainly feels no pride in such a child; yet she sticks to him. The tenacity of the maternal sentiment under such adversity is proverbial.

Such examples from everyday experience could be multiplied *ad infinitum*. The evidence, however, appears in sharper outline when it is taken from experimental and clinical studies. In each of the following instances some new function emerges as an independently structured unit from preceding functions. The activity of these new units does not depend upon the continued activity of the units from which they developed.

(*1*) *The circular reflex*. Everyone has observed the almost endless repetition of acts by a child. The good-natured parent who picks up a spoon repeatedly thrown down by a baby wearies of this occupation long before the infant does. Such repetitive behavior, found likewise in early vocalization (babbling), and in other early forms of play, is commonly ascribed to the mechanism of the circular reflex.[4] It is an elementary instance of functional autonomy; for any situation where the consummation of an act provides adequate stimulation for the repetition of the *same* act does not require any backward tracing of motives. The act is self-perpetuating until it is inhibited by new activities or fatigue.

(*2*) *Conative perseveration*. Many experiments show that incompleted tasks set up tensions that tend to keep the individual at work until they are resolved. No hypothesis of self-assertion, rivalry, or any other basic need, is required. The completion of the task itself has become a quasi-need with dynamic force of its own. It has been shown, for example, that interrupted tasks are better remembered than completed ta;ks,[5] that an individual interrupted in a task will, even in the face of considerable opposition return to that task,[6] that even trivial tasks undertaken in a casual way become almost haunting in character until they are completed.[7]

Conative perseveration of this order is stronger if an empty interval of time follows the period of work, showing that *left to itself*, without the inhibiting effect of other duties or activities, the motive grows stronger and stronger. The experiment of Kendig proves this point, as well as that of C. E. Smith.[8] The latter investigator demonstrated that there is more success in removing a conditioned fear if the de-conditioning process is commenced immediately. After a twenty-four hour delay the fear has become set, and is more difficult to eradicate. Hence the sound advice to drivers of automobiles or airplanes

---

[4] E. B. Holt, *Animal Drive and the Learning Process*, 1931, esp. Chaps. VII and VIII.
[5] B. Zeigarnik, Über das Behalten von erledigten und unerledigten Handlungen, *Psychol. Forsch.*, 9, 1927, 1–86.
[6] M. Ovsiankina, Die Wiederaufnahme unterbrochener Handlungen, *ibid.*, 11, 1928, 302–379.
[7] I. Kendig, Studies in perseveration, *J. Psychol.*, 3, 1936, 223–264.
[8] C. E. Smith, Change in the apparent resistance of the skin as a function of certain physiological and psychological factors, A thesis deposited in the Harvard College Library, 1934.

who have been involved in an accident, that they drive again immediately to conquer the shock of the accident, lest the fear become set into a permanent phobia. The rule seems to be that unless specifically inhibited all emotional shocks, given time to set, tend to take on a compulsive autonomous character.

(3) *Conditioned reflexes not requiring reënforcement.* The pure conditioned reflex readily dies out unless the secondary stimulus is occasionally reënforced by the primary stimulus. The dog does not continue to salivate whenever it hears a bell unless sometimes at least an edible offering accompanies the bell. But there are innumerable instances in human life where a single association, *never* reënforced, results in the establishment of a life-long dynamic system. An experience associated only once with a bereavement, an accident, or a battle, may become the center of a permanent phobia or complex, not in the least dependent on a recurrence of the original shock.

(4) *Counterparts in animal behavior.* Though the validity of a principle in human psychology never depends upon its having a counterpart in animal psychology, still it is of interest to find functional autonomy in the lower organisms. For example, rats, who will first learn a certain habit only under the incentive of some specific tension, as hunger, will, after learning, often perform the habit even when fed to repletion.[9]

Another experiment shows that rats trained to follow a long and difficult path, will for a time persist in using this path, even though a short easy path to the goal is offered and even after the easier path has been learned.[10] Among rats as among human beings, old and useless habits have considerable power in their own right.

Olson studied the persistence of artificially induced scratching habits in rats. Collodion applied to the ears of the animal set up removing and cleaning movements. Four days later the application was repeated. From that time on the animals showed significantly greater number of cleaning movements than control animals. A month after the beginning of the experiment when the ears of the rats as studied by the microscope showed no further trace of irritation, the number of movements was still very great. Whether the induced habit spasm was permanently retained the experimenter does not say.[11]

---

[9] J. D. Dodgson, Relative values of reward and punishment in habit formation, *Psychobiol.*, 1, 1917, 231-276. This work has already been interpreted by K. S. Lashley as favoring Woodworth's dynamic theory as opposed to Freud's (Contributions of Freudism to psychology: III. Physiological analysis of the libido, *Psychol. Rev.*, 31, 1924, 192-202).

[10] H. C. Gilhousen, Fixation of excess distance patterns in the white rat, *J. Comp. Psychol.*, 16, 1933, 1-23.

[11] W. C. Olson, *The Measurement of Nervous Habits in Normal Children*, 1929, 62-65.

(5) *Rhythm.* A rat whose activity bears a definite relation to his habits of feeding (being greatest just preceding a period of feeding and midway between two such periods) will, even when starved, display the same periodicity and activity. The acquired rhythm persists without dependence on the original periodic stimulation of feeding.[12]

Even a mollusc whose habits of burrowing in the sand and reappearing depend upon the movements of the tide, will, when removed from the beach to the laboratory, continue for several days in the same rhythm without the tide. Likewise certain animals, with nocturnal rhythms advantageous in avoiding enemies, obtaining food, or preventing excessive evaporation from the body, may exhibit such rhythms even when kept in a laboratory with constant conditions of illumination, humidity, and temperature.[13]

There are likewise instances where acquired rhythms in human life have taken on a dynamic character. Compulsive neurotics enter upon fugues or debauches, apparently not because of specific stimulation, but because "the time has come." A dipsomaniac, in confinement and deprived for months of his alcohol, describes the fierceness of the recurrent appetite (obviously acquired) as follows.

> Those craving paroxysms occur at regular intervals, three weeks apart, lasting for several days. They are not weak, nambypamby things for scoffers to laugh at. If not assuaged with liquor they become spells of physical and mental illness. My mouth drools saliva, my stomach and intestines seem cramped, and I become bilious, nauseated, and in a shaky nervous funk.[14]

In such states of drug addiction, as likewise in states of hunger, lust, fatigue, there is to be sure a physical craving, but the rhythms of the craving are partially acquired, and are always accentuated by the mental habits associated with it. For instance, eating in our civilized way of life takes place not because physical hunger naturally occurs three times a day, but because of habitual rhythms of expectancy. The habit of smoking is much more than a matter of craving for the specific narcotic effects of tobacco; it is a craving for the motor ritual and periodic distraction as well.

(6) *Neuroses.* Why are acquired tics, stammering, sexual perversions, phobias, and anxiety so stubborn and so often incurable? Even psychoanalysis, with its deepest of depth-probing, seldom succeeds in

---

[12] C. P. Richter, A behavioristic study of the activity of the rat, *Comp. Psychol. Monog.,* 1, 1922, (no. 2), 1-55.
[13] S. C. Crawford, The habits and characteristics of nocturnal animals, *Quart. Rev. Biol.,* 9, 1934, 201-214.
[14] Inmate Ward Eight, *Beyond the Door of Delusion,* 1932, 281.

effecting *complete* cures in such cases, even though the patient may feel relieved or at least reconciled to his difficulties after treatment. The reason seems to be that what are usually called 'symptoms' are in reality something more. They have set themselves up in their own right as independent systems of motivation. Merely disclosing their roots does not change their independent activity.[15]

(7) *The relation between ability and interest.* Psychometric studies have shown that the relation between ability and interest is always positive, often markedly so. A person likes to do what he can do well. Over and over again it has been demonstrated that the skill learned for some external reason, turns into an interest, and is self-propelling, even though the original reason for pursuing it has been lost. A student who at first undertakes a field of study in college because it is prescribed, because it pleases his parents, or because it comes at a convenient hour, often ends by finding himself absorbed, perhaps for life, in the subject itself. He is not happy without it. The original motives are entirely lost. What was a means to an end has become an end in itself.

Furthermore, there is the case of genius. A skill takes possession of the man. No primitive motivation is needed to account for his persistent, absorbed activity. It just *is* the alpha and omega of life to him. It is impossible to think of Pasteur's concern for health, food, sleep, or family, as the root of his devotion to his work. For long periods of time he was oblivious of them all, losing himself in the white heat of research for which he had been trained and in which he had *acquired* a compelling and absorbing interest.

A much more modest instance is the finding of industrial research that when special incentives are offered and work speeded up as a consequence, and then these special incentives removed, *the work continues at the speeded rate*. The habit of working at a faster tempo persists without external support.

(8) *Sentiments vs. instincts.* Every time an alleged instinct can by rigid analysis be demonstrated not to be innate but acquired, there is in this demonstration evidence for functional autonomy. It is true enough that maternal conduct, gregariousness, curiosity, workman-

---

[15] The case of W. E. Leonard, *The Locomotive God*, 1927, is instructive in this regard. An intense phobia was not relieved by tracing its history backward to the start of life. Even though he could explain why he was once frightened for a very good reason (by a locomotive), the author is quite unable to explain why now he is frightened *for no particular reason*. Such neuroses, and psychotic delusional systems as well, often acquire a "strangle hold," and the task of dislodging them is usually more than therapeutic skill is equal to.

ship, and the like, have the tenacity and compelling power that instincts are supposed to have. If they are not instincts, then they must be autonomous sentiments with as much dynamic character as has been attributed to instincts. It is not necessary here to review all the arguments in favor of regarding such alleged instincts as acquired sentiments.

(9) *The dynamic character of personal values.* When an interest-system has once been formed it not only creates a tensional condition that may be readily aroused, leading to overt conduct in some way satisfying to the interest, but it also acts as a silent agent for selecting and directing any behavior related to it. Take the case of people with strongly marked esthetic interests. Experiments with the word-association test have shown that such people respond more quickly to stimulus-words connected with this interest than to words relating to interests they lack.[16] Likewise, in scanning a newspaper they will observe and remember more items pertaining to art; they also take a greater interest in clothes than do non-esthetic people; and when they are asked to rate the virtues of others, they place esthetic qualities high. In short the existence of a well-established acquired interest exerts a directive and determining effect on conduct just as is to be expected of any dynamic system. The evidence can be duplicated for many interests other than the esthetic.[17]

CRITIQUE OF FUNCTIONAL AUTONOMY

Objections to the principle of autonomy may be expected from two sides. Behaviorists will continue to prefer their conception of organic drive with its capacity for manifold conditioning by ever receding stimuli. Whereas purposivists will be unwilling to accept a pluralistic principle that seems to leave motives so largely at the mercy of learning.

The behaviorist is well satisfied with motivation in terms of organic drive and conditioning because he feels that he somehow has secure anchorage in physiological structure. (The closer he approaches physiological structure the happier the behaviorist is.) But the truth of the matter is that the neural physiology of organic drive and conditioning is no better established, and no easier to imagine, than is the neural physiology of the type of complex autonomous units of motivation here described.

---

[16] H. Cantril, General and specific attitudes, *Psychol. Monog.*, 42, 1932, (no. 192), 1-109.
[17] H. Cantril and G. W. Allport, Recent applications of the *study of values*, *J. Abnorm. & Soc. Psychol.*, 28, 1933, 259-273.

Two behavioristic principles will be said to account adequately for the instances of functional autonomy previously cited, viz., the circular reflex and cross-conditioning. The former concept, acceptable enough when applied to infant behavior, merely says that the more activity a muscle engages in, the more activity of the same sort does it engender through a self-sustaining circuit.[18] This is, to be sure, a clear instance of autonomy, albeit on a primitive level, oversimplified so far as adult conduct is concerned. The doctrine of cross-conditioning refers to subtle recession of stimuli, and to the intricate possibility of cross-connections in conditioning. For instance, such ubiquitous external stimuli as humidity, daylight, gravitation, may feed collaterally into open channels of activity, arousing mysteriously and unexpectedly a form of conduct to which they have unconsciously been conditioned. For example, the angler whose fishing expeditions have been accompanied by sun, wind, or a balmy June day, may feel a desire to go fishing whenever the barometer, the thermometer, or the calendar in his city home tells him that these conditions prevail.[19] Innumerable such crossed stimuli are said to account for the arousal of earlier patterns of activity.

Such a theory inherits, first of all, the well-known difficulties resident in the principle of conditioning whenever it is made the sole explanation of human behavior. Further, though the reflex circle and cross-conditioning may in fact exist, they are really rather trivial principles. They leave the formation of interest and its occasional arousal almost entirely to chance factors of stimulation. They give no picture at all of the spontaneous and variable aspects of traits, interests, or sentiments. These dispositions are regarded as purely *reactive* in nature; the stimulus is all-important. The truth is that dispositions *sort out* stimuli congenial to them, and this activity does not in the least resemble the rigidity of reflex response.[20]

A variant on the doctrine of cross-conditioning is the principle of redintegration.[21] This concept admits the existence of highly integrated dispositions of a neuropsychic order. These dispositions can be aroused *as a whole* by any stimulus previously associated with their

---

[18] E. B. Holt, *op. cit.*, 38.
[19] *Ibid.*, 224.
[20] The basic fact that complex "higher" centers have the power of inhibiting, selecting, and initiating the activity of simpler segmental responses is a fact too well established to need elaboration here. It constitutes the very foundation of the psychophysiological theories advanced by Sherrington, Herrick, Dodge, Köhler, Troland, and many others.
[21] Cf. H. L. Hollingworth, *Psychology of the Functional Neuroses*, 1920.

functioning. In this theory likewise, the disposition is regarded as a rather passive affair, waiting for reactivation by some portion of the original stimulus. Here again the variability of the disposition and its urge-like quality are not accounted for. The stimulus is thought merely to reinstate a complex determining tendency. Nothing is said about how the stimuli themselves are *selected*, why a motive once aroused becomes insistent, surmounting obstacles, skillfully subordinating conflicting impulses, and inhibiting irrelevant trains of thought.

In certain respects the principle of autonomy stands midway between the behavioristic view and the thoroughgoing purposive psychology of the hormic order. It agrees with the former in emphasizing the acquisition of motives, in avoiding an a priori and unchanging set of original urges, and in recognizing (as limited principles) the operation of the circular response and cross-conditioning. It agrees with the hormic psychologist, however, in finding that striving-from-within is a far more essential characteristic of motive than stimulation-from-without. It agrees likewise in distrusting the emphasis upon stomach contractions and other "excess and deficit stimuli" as "causes" of mature behavior. Such segmental sources of energy even when conditioned cannot possibly account for the "go" of conduct. But functional autonomy does not rely as does hormic theory upon modified instinct, which after all is as archaic a principle as the conditioning of autonomic segmental tensions, but upon the capacity of human beings to replenish their energy through a plurality of constantly changing systems of a dynamic order.

The hormic psychologist, however, will not accept the autonomy of new motivational systems. If mechanisms can turn into drives, he asks, why is it that habits and skills as they become exercised to the point of perfection do not acquire an ever increasing driving force?[22] The mechanisms of walking, speaking, or dressing, cannot be said to furnish their own motive-power. One walks, speaks, or dresses in order to satisfy a motive entirely external to these learned skills.[23]

The criticism is sufficiently cogent to call into question Woodworth's form of stating the principle, viz., "mechanisms may become drives." It is not an adequate statement of the case.

Looking at the issue more closely it seems to be neither the perfected

---

[22] W. McDougall, Motives in the light of recent discussion, *Mind*, 29, 1920, 277-293.

[23] Though this objection is usually valid, it is not always so, for there are cases where the liking for walks, for talking for the sake of talking, or for dressing, playing games, etc., seems to be a self-sustaining motivational system.

talent nor the automatic habit that has driving power, but the imperfect talent and the habit-in-the-making. The child who is *just learning* to speak, to walk, or to dress is, in fact, likely to engage in these activities for their own sake, precisely as does the adult who has an *unfinished* task in hand. He remembers it, returns to it, and suffers a feeling of frustration if he is prevented from engaging in it. Motives are always a kind of striving for some form of completion; they are unresolved tension, and demand a "closure" to activity under way. (Latent motives are dispositions that are easily thrown by a stimulus or by a train of associations into this state of active tension.) The active motive subsides when its goal is reached, or in the case of a motor skill, when it has become at last automatic. The novice in automobile driving has an unquestionable impulse to master the skill. Once acquired the ability sinks to the level of an *instrumental* disposition and is aroused only in the service of some other *driving* (unfulfilled) motive.

Now, in the case of the permanent interests of personality, the situation is the same. A man whose motive is to acquire learning, or to perfect his craft, can never be satisfied that he has reached the end of his quest, for his problems are never completely solved, his skill is never perfect. Lasting interests are recurrent sources of discontent, and from their incompleteness they derive their forward impetus. Art, science, religion, love, are never perfected. Motor skills, however, are often perfected, and beyond that stage they seldom provide their own motive power. It is, then, only mechanisms-on-the-make (in process of perfecting) that serve as drives. With this emendation, Woodworth's view is corrected, and McDougall's objection is met.[24]

IMPLICATIONS OF FUNCTIONAL AUTONOMY

The principle of functional autonomy accounts, as no other principle of dynamic psychology is able to do, for the concrete impulses that lie at the root of personal behavior. It is thus the first step in establishing a basis for the more realistic study of unique and individual forms for personality. "But how—" the traditionalists may cry, "how are we ever to have a *science* of unique events? Science must generalize." So it must, but it is a manifest error to assume that a general principle of motivation must involve the postulation of abstract or general motives. What the objectors forget is that *a general law may be a law that tells*

---

[24] This theory embraces very easily the work of K. Lewin and his associates upon the nature of "quasi-needs." The urgency of these needs is greatest just before a goal is reached, after which time the motive subsides completely.

how uniqueness comes about. The principle of functional autonomy is general enough to meet the needs of science, but particularized enough in its operation to account for the uniqueness of personal conduct. Its specific advantages stand out in the following summary.

(*1*) It clears the way for a completely dynamic psychology of *traits*, *attitudes*, *interests*, and *sentiments*, which can now be regarded as the ultimate and true dispositions of the mature personality.

(*2*) It avoids the absurdity of regarding the energy of life now, in the *present*, as somehow consisting of early archaic forms (instincts, prepotent reflexes, or the never-changing Id). Learning brings new systems of interests into existence just as it does new abilities and skills. At each stage of development these interests are always contemporary; whatever drives, drives *now*.

(*3*) It dethrones the stimulus. A motive is no longer regarded as a mechanical reflex or as a matter of redintegration, depending entirely upon the capricious operation of a conditioned stimulus. In a very real sense dispositions *select* the stimuli to which they respond, even though *some* stimulus is required for their arousal.

(*4*) It readily admits the validity of all other established principles of growth. Functional autonomy recognizes the products of differentiation, integration, maturation, exercise, imitation, suggestion, conditioning, trauma, and all other processes of development; and allows, as they do not, considered by themselves, for the preservation of these products in significant motivational patterns.

(*5*) It places in proper perspective the problems of the origin of conduct by removing the fetish of the genetic method. Not that the historical view of behavior is unimportant for a complete understanding of personality, but so far as *motives* are concerned the cross-sectional dynamic analysis is more significant. Motives being always contemporary should be studied in their present structure. Failure to do so is probably the chief reason why psychoanalysis meets so many defeats, as do all other therapeutic schemes relying too exclusively upon uncovering the motives of early childhood.

(*6*) It accounts for the force of delusions, shell-shock, phobias, and all manner of compulsive and maladaptive behavior. One would expect such unrealistic modes of adjustment to be given up as they are shown to be poor ways of confronting the environment. Insight and the law of effect should both remove them—but too often they have acquired a strangle hold in their own right.

(*7*) At last we can account adequately for socialized and civilized behavior. The principle supplies the correction necessary to the faulty logic of *bellum òmnium contra omnes*. Starting life, as a completely selfish being, the child would indeed remain entirely wolfish and piggish throughout his days unless genuine transformations of motives took place. Motives being completely alterable, the dogma of Egoism turns out to be a callow and superficial philosophy of behavior, or else a useless redundancy.

(*8*) It explains likewise why a person often *becomes* what at first he merely *pretends* to be—the smiling professional hostess who grows fond of her once irksome rôle and is unhappy when deprived of it; the man who for so long has counterfeited the appearance of self-confidence and optimism that he is always driven to assume it; the prisoner who comes to love his shackles. Such *personae*, as Jung observes, are often transformed into the real self. The mask becomes the *anima*.

(*9*) The drive behind genius is explained. Gifted people demand the exercise of their talents, even when no other reward lies ahead. In lesser degree the various hobbies, the artistic, or the intellectual interests of any person show the same significant autonomy.

(*10*) In brief, the principle of functional autonomy is a declaration of independence for the psychology of personality. Though in itself a general law, at the same time it helps to account, not for the abstract motivation of an impersonal and therefore non-existent mind-in-general, but for the concrete, viable motives of each and every mind-in-particular.

MOTIVATION IN PERSONALITY: REPLY TO MR. BERTOCCI

Reprinted from *Psychological Review*, **47**, No. 6, November 1940, 533-554.

I. INTRODUCTION

Mr. Bertocci has written an accurate and challenging critique of my views regarding the nature of motivation in human personality (4). Because he has read my work sympathetically and checked his understanding of my position with care his criticisms are helpful and relevant. Where on rare occasion misunderstanding still remains, it is I and not my critic who must take the blame.

It will be noted that Mr. Bertocci shapes his attack essentially from the McDougallian point of view. When McDougall died shortly after the publication of my book I gave up hope of ever benefiting from his fierce but friendly criticisms. Mr. Bertocci has now rescued me from disappointment and has laid upon me with the same hefty cudgels that McDougall would have used, and for good measure has employed a few additional cudgels of his own.

His attack, as I see it, must be met on seven fronts, *viz.*, (1) the argument for hormic purposivism, (2) the sufficiency of instinct, (3) the necessity in science for employing universal dimensions, (4) the 'mystery' of ontogenetic emergence, (5) the nature of functional autonomy, (6) adequate accounting for continuity in personality, and (7) the place of sentiments in the structure of personality. Each of these lines of attack calls for extensive defense and counter-offense, but since space is limited and since some of the disputed issues are by their very nature insoluble, I shall try to content myself with the briefest possible rebuttal.

II. PURPOSE *versus* MECHANISM

Mr. Bertocci accuses me of wobbling between the principle of purpose and the principle of mechanism. Specifically he does not like the emergent step implied in my contrast between the apparently mechanistic 'push' in infancy and the apparently teleological 'pull' in maturity. In later pages I shall attempt to meet his objections to emergence, but for the moment confine myself to one or two general comments on the nature of purpose and of mechanism.

In modern times it seems to me that the former sharp antagonism between these two principles of explanation has been somewhat overcome. Mechanistic reflexology has certainly been vanquished; and in recent times its adherents seem to have been re-aligning themselves either with the operational creed which is frankly sceptical of the principle of causation, or else with the organismic position that re-defines both purpose and mechanism, reconciling them within the new concepts of *structure* and *system*. From this latter point of view—to which I subscribe—it seems unnecessary to ask whether reflex irritability defines and limits goal-seeking responses, or whether goal-seeking is an initial property to which reflex irritability merely holds various 'keys.' The modern tendency is to deal with systemic properties in nature, conceived as neither mechanistic nor purposive but as *organismic*. Just as modern physics has redefined the meaning of 'contact' in such a way that 'push' and 'pull' give place to the concept of interacting molecular systems, so too psychology largely under the influence of Gestalt theory is dealing these days with patterned events, contexts that constrain, structural wholes.[1]

When I remarked to Mr. Bertocci in personal correspondence which he quotes that I saw no difficulty in embracing a principle of 'push' in infancy and of 'pull' in maturity, I did not intend to commit myself to so extreme a paradox as he has made of it. Whether the system that we call gravitation 'pushes' or 'pulls' at my feet it is, as Eddington has shown, impossible to say. Similarly the pattern of hunger behavior in an infant is marked by a sequence of events that may be viewed as either mechanistic or purposive, but preferably as

[1] For evidence of the rise of this tendency in contemporary psychology see J. S. Bruner and G. W. Allport (6).

systemic and self-regulating.   Yet—and this is the important point—as compared with the corresponding events in adulthood this infantile hunger-system lacks foresight, respect for taboo, epicurean embellishments, idiosyncrasy of taste and all other ideational features.   I think, therefore, that we may truly say that the infant is, *relative to the adult*, 'pushed' by immediate, simple, vegetative and proximate features in his hunger system.   The adult is to a greater degree 'pulled' by the delayed, ideational, non-proximate features in his system of hunger-behavior.   Push and pull are therefore relative terms, signifying respectively the presence of less or more of the personalized and planful components in a system of events and the presence of a slight and limited environmental stimulus field, or the presence of a richly extended and diversified stimulus field.

Were I *forced* to choose between mechanism and purposivism as an ultimate principle of motivation, I should unhesitatingly choose—as I think my book amply indicates—purposivism.   Yet I think it entirely proper to see in infancy *less* evidence of purposive behavior than in adulthood.   Infant behavior, I submit, conforms more closely to the alleged characteristics of drive-impelled conduct.   Adult behavior with its widened consciousness of goals, and with its lavish use of symbols and all higher mental operations, on the other hand, shows the working of a type of motivation that can only be expressed in terms of *interest, attitude, value, desire, will*—terms quite inappropriate to infancy.

Bertocci, I believe, agrees with me concerning the barrenness for psychology of the postulate of an initial *Hormé*.   Neither of us is disposed to deny it metaphysical status, but we both want it broken up into particular manifestations—he into McDougallian propensities; I into individualized motivational systems.   His complaint is that in accepting an *élan* and in denying instincts I am guilty of metaphysical abstraction with a vengeance.   My reply is that to me individualized motivational systems seem just as saturated with *élan*, ego-involvement, urge, or *Hormé* as do the alleged instincts; but as expressions of *élan*, they are variable, personal, and empirically discovered rather than universal, external, and *a priori*.

III. The Sufficiency of Instincts

And so we come to the instinct controversy. Let it be remembered that only instincts in McDougall's sense are here the issue, for Bertocci does not rest his case on such innate sensory-motor co-ordinations as have been empirically established. The principal difficulty with McDougall's set channels of purpose is precisely this: They never can be discovered empirically. Two assumptions make them fatally elusive: (*a*) the contention that "propensities are but loosely geared to goals,"—this contention making it possible always to interpret any case as fitting the formula; and (*b*) the reliance on maturation of purposes, another proposition unverifiable. It is recognized that some course of learning invariably precedes alleged maturation. It would be impossible, I think, ever to demonstrate that sympathy matures as a 'non-specific innate tendency,' because two or three years of individualizing personal experience precede its overt manifestations. Since purposes never ripen in an experiential vacuum I think it is wiser to order the phenomenon of the growth of motives to the psychology of progressive mental organization—in other words, to the psychology of learning. My critic, on the other hand, prefers to believe that learning can best be subordinated to the doctrine of fixed motives which throughout life predetermine 'in a general way' the direction of active response. Later I shall give other reasons for thinking that learning rather than inheritance is the leading category in the psychology of motivation.

To another of my objections—that the assumption of universal instincts is not a parsimonious procedure—Mr. Bertocci rightly, but not altogether relevantly, retorts that it is the scientist and not nature that shows a partiality for parsimony. (Certainly in my ascribing 'an infinite variety of motives to an infinite variety of mortals' I myself am in no danger of saddling nature with the canon of parsimony.) But the point is that instincts explain *too much*. Even Mc-

Dougall admits that people can be found who seem to lack one or more of the 18 primary propensities. If this is so, then to regard the 18 (or any other number) as 'normal' and the exceptions as 'abnormal' is clearly an extravagant convention. In nature, we must assume, there are no exceptions; every case is completely and adequately determined by law. If then, certain purposes seem to be absent in some people, why should we suppose they were ever meant to be there? Only if purposes can empirically be shown to be present are we obliged to account for them. In the psychology of personality we need a law of motivation that will have no exceptions. Even a formula of considerable subsumptive power is not enough, for unlike other branches of science, the psychology of personality is bound to account for *individuality*. Instincts being universal in their reference lack individualizing power.

Before expanding this last remark I should like to call attention to one promising feature of Mr. Bertocci's position. He admits that in the course of development a person's abilities and individual temperament, as well as the exigencies of his peculiar environment, have an individualizing effect on his purposes so that his goals are not exact duplicates of other people's goals. He admits likewise that "all actual, existential goal-seeking, as opposed to the conceptual description of it, is specific and individual. One never seeks food in general or recognition in general, but his actual seeking is always undergoing particular psycho-physiological processes in relation to particular food, people, and so on." These admissions seem to show that Mr. Bertocci is impressed by precisely what impresses me—by the concrete and individual character of 'actual, existential goal-seeking.' Am I wrong in believing that in the passage just quoted he admits a contradiction between the impressively concrete, unique, and personal character of goal-seeking, and the 'conceptual description' of it that he is defending?

IV. Necessity for Universal Dimensions

While admitting—in the passage just quoted and in others—that uniqueness is the mark of personality, that "life exists in individual forms," Bertocci, like other of my critics, insists that "to accept uniqueness as alone ultimate is to destroy the possibility of rational knowledge of any sort. Uniqueness can be felt, lived through, but not expressed or understood in relation to other common factors." He writes also: "My understanding can assimilate unique individuality only by noting the extent to which it is similar to and different from other individuals known to me." In these passages Bertocci is stating the traditional view of psychological science that the data of human nature must be treated nomothetically (in terms of general dimensions) and that scientific understanding of these data proceeds through inference (associative comparison).

Readers of my book (2) will perhaps recall that I endorse the use of nomothetic procedures (*e.g.*, Ch. 15 on 'Common Traits') and admit the importance of inference in the process of understanding people (Ch. 19, 'Inference and Intuition'). Certainly I would subscribe to Mr. Bertocci's statement that "psychology would do well to search for whatever universality may be found in human motivation." But unlike Bertocci and my other critics I am unwilling to stop here. I believe there is—*in addition* to these nomothetic and inferential procedures common to all science—something quite special about the psychology of personality that marks it off from all other branches of science, namely, its obligation to deal with integrated individuality. In order to fulfill this special obligation I submit that the psychology of personality needs *not only* the customary procedures and habits of thought employed by nomothetic and inferential science, but needs to develop likewise new idiographic methods and intuitive skills.[2] "A complete study of the individual," I have written, "will embrace both approaches."

Freud, Adler, Spearman, McDougall, Murray, Kretsch-

---

[2] A particularly effective argument for this point has been made by D. L. Watson (8).

mer, Thurstone, Guilford, and others have produced nomothetic dimensions to which personalities are to be ordered.
But consider the differences, and even the contradictions,
between these dimensional schemes! Think too of the lists
of 'primary motives' in textbooks of psychology. I doubt
that there is justification for Bertocci's statement that we
know some of the 'inevitable components of human motivation.' Even where agreement seems to be reached—Bertocci
suggests hunger, sex, fear, anger—the biological capacities
mentioned have nothing much to do with the personal level
of conduct, and they illuminate little if at all the concrete
needs and specifiable desires of actual individuals.

The question is this: Can we not, even while we make use
of many maps prepared by many nomothetists, get still closer
to the structure of personality by fixing our attention upon
individual lives? So to fix our attention requires, of course,
a certain re-centering of our theories; (I suggest, for example,
the theory of traits and the principle of functional autonomy).
Required also are new and different methods of study (greater
use, among other techniques, of *intra-individual* statistics,
case studies, matching, interviews, expressive and stylistic
procedures, and the like). McDougall's map of the propensities is suggestive—so too are all other maps. They serve
to call attention to *probable* emotional foci in certain lives.
I say 'probable,' not because Providence has endowed all men
with eighteen channels of purpose; but because "similarly
constructed individuals living in similar environments influenced by similar culture, *would* develop similar goals and
employ similar modes of obtaining them."

This last quotation (from page 113 of my book) offends
my critic deeply. He accuses me of placing too much weight
on culture, of overlooking instincts which alone can be 'the
basic cause of culture and its similarity in the first place.'
My reply is that the universal features in cultural practices
all over the earth appear to be too few in number to argue
from them to common instinctive causation. Of course, universal features in the bodily structure of *Homo Sapiens* lie at
the root of certain bodily needs; but there is not one of these

needs which is not strangely revised and transformed at the psychological level before it becomes an actual, integrated motivational system. (I have just been reading a well-attested account of orthodox Jews who in Nazi concentration camps suffered inanition and not infrequently death by refusing to violate the food restrictions of their religion.) It is for this reason that I think of biological needs or tissue change as offering a wholly inadequate, sub-personal, picture of psychological motivation.

As I pointed out in the preceding section this personalizing of motives, different in each life, seems to be admitted by my critic. He writes "The statement: 'men hunger for food,' is a highly abstract description of the concrete unique hunger-pangs and the concrete, unique food seeking which are actually involved." Such admissions, it seems to me, prepare the way for a more concrete theory of motivation which will account for the fact that systems of desires are well integrated, and that the object of desire is by no means arbitrary and detachable—as the cathexis theory holds—but is rather a firm part of the system itself.

To summarize: As a first approximation I have no objection to the use of a conceptual schedule of two drives, four wishes, eighteen propensities, or twenty-five needs in approaching the motives of men. Such maps are useful in calling attention to the sort of things that people (physically similar in structure) exposed to roughly similar environments and cultures commonly desire. But this type of nomothetic procedure runs its course on a plane of abstraction that is not within reach of actual personalities. A full-bodied psychology of personality (as opposed to a general psychology of motives) must do a better job. A law of motivation that accounts for the individual organizations of desires is in order. Although I am aware of the argument made by Bertocci and others that "we cannot give up the search for the common pattern underlying various purposes simply because our predecessors and contemporaries disagree about the number and kinds of irreducible unlearned motives," yet I am a bit pessimistic. Within 2000 years of self-conscious psychologizing

no stencil to fit human desires has yet been found, because, I
suspect, there is none to find.   May it not be that the 'irreducible unlearned motives' of men are—excepting in early
infancy—a scientific will of the wisp?

To the instinctivist it seems that 'the extension, variation,
condensation of propensities' can account for all variety that
is needed.   To this view I reply that Procrustes had a similar
ambition for his bed.   Of course cases can be sheared to fit.
But unless academic psychologists concern themselves with
the problem of the integral individuality of the motivational
pattern (as some clinical psychologists do) I fear they will
forever be wrangling about the relative merits of their respec-
tive Procrustean couches.   All stencils fit concrete cases only
with the loosest approximation.   They seldom help the clinician or the average man in understanding the structure of
the individual life.

V. The Principle of Ontogenetic Emergence

Mr. Bertocci asks, "Can a need of given limitations be the
father of a need which is totally different?"   He thinks it
cannot; I think it can.   He believes that it would abrogate
continuity in personality to have 'outright novelties' emerge;
he holds that learning is not a process of adding in number to
the purposive tendencies resident in the original nature of
man, and he regards it as all very mysterious how any new
purposes can ever evolve.   He concludes: "As the situation
now stands, we can appeal to the mysterious concept of ontogenetic emergent evolution to account for the appearance of
new needs and consequent pleasures.   Or we can appeal to an
instinct-theory which attempts to delineate what these basic
drives (and consequent pleasures) are in the first place, and
then show how they are modified by ability and environment
to constitute the uniqueness and the continuity of the individual personality."   To me it seems that personal interests
undergo marked and essential change in the course of life:
that when we become men we put away for the most part
the desires of childhood.   It is not merely the 'object cathexis' that is altered; it is the basic structure of motivation.

Mr. Bertocci himself thinks of human personality as 'always in a state of transition,' but he regards the transition as applying to skills and abilities rather than to the 'general ends implicit in its very being.' Just why *transition* should characterize the *Rüstungsdispositionen* and not the *Richtungsdispositionen* is not evident to me. So far as the directional dispositions are concerned I incline toward Wundt's view expressed in his almost forgotten principle of the 'heterogeny of ends.' Primitive man—to cite his somewhat florid example—entered a cave to take refuge from a storm, and finding there a wild dog likewise taking shelter, he emerged from the cave with a desire and plan for domesticating the dog. New purposes have their seeds in old purposes, but the satisfactions they yield are so unexpected, so unpredictable, that only some such principle as the 'heterogeny of ends,' or 'functional autonomy' seems to cover the obvious facts.

My critic argues—and I am glad to agree with him—that the logic of learning must apply to both skills and motives equally. The dispute then comes to a head in the question whether learning creates *novel* skills and purposes or mere variations on the *old*. Since Mr. Bertocci does not favor the emergence of new purposes (although he has written, "novelties in human motivation are the empirical facts that break the back of any mechanical theory of instinct"), he is forced to deny the creation of novel abilities (although he has admitted that human personality is 'always in a state of transition'). "No psychologist," he says, "talks about the outright creation of a new ability within the lifetime of a given individual. A 'new' ability would be a particular, environmentally provoked, development of a given ability. What fact alters the use of this same logic when we come to motivation?" I agree that the same logic must prevail, but I doubt that every psychologist would look upon new skills as mere variations on the old. Is the dextrous piano playing of Horowitz 'a particular, environmentally provoked, development' of his infantile grasp reflex (or some other 'given' ability)? Is the oratory of a Demosthenes essentially a modification of his infant babble? And what functional continuity with some 'given' ability can be demonstrated in the case of skills employed in surgery, aviation, or writing verse? If skills can change until they are wholly unrecognizable and no longer dependent functionally on their seed-forms, so too can motives. I am glad Mr. Bertocci admits that the same logic must apply to both. (In making this admission I think he is on sounder ground than some critics who seem to hold that while learning may transform skills it somehow passes motivation by, leaving it preserved in the waterglass of infancy. Just why learning should reintegrate patterns of skill and not of motives no one has yet explained.)

The emergent step regarded by my critic as most outrageous is my apparent shift (in discussing the ontogenetic course of development) from a mechanistic to a purposive view of motives. "Why begin with the psychological (purposive) level of description at the age of two or three?" he asks, and adds, "the hormist starts with the psychic level of purposive striving and maintains it throughout." I think I have met this objection in my denial that I would regard 'push' and 'pull' as essentially opposed principles. They are merely convenient terms for expressing the fact that the infant seems to be a more vegetative creature than the adult. Bertocci regards it as inconceivable that sophisticated purposes should emerge from vegetative urges. It is black magic, he thinks, to hold that out of the young infant's demand for only the physical comfort its mother can give, should eventually grow a craving for the 'social, æsthetic, and mental' comfort of her companionship. This proposition does not seem magical to me, but on the contrary about as simple and straightforward a statement of empirical fact as we are likely to find in the realm of motivation.

We do need, I admit, a psychology of learning that will explain how transformations come about from the pre-social or vegetative drives to social, æsthetic, and spiritual desires. This particular problem has not, I believe, been adequately considered. Although I cannot discuss it here, I would call attention to two helpful principles in learning, both of them strangely neglected not only by motivationists but by psychologists in general. (1) Sheer familiarity seems to engender positive valuing (demand) on the part of an organism. Ask a child if he thinks American children are nicer than the children of any other nationality. He will reply yes. If you ask why, the child with naive insight will probably say, "Because I *know* American children and don't know the others." Even an infant, through sheer habituation, without human companionship, develops free locomotion and play in a strange room after 8-10 trials: another sign of the affective value of familiar situations. Let psychologists explore the dynamic effects of an accustomed situation, if they would discover one reason why motivation becomes transformed, why habits become 'drives.' (2) The psychology of learning has not, I think, given adequate recognition to the dynamic character of the task-attitude. Let a task be accepted for any reason at all, and the attitude engendered seems to furnish its own drive until accomplishment is reached. If it is objected that this perseverative principle depends upon ego-involvement, I shall agree; but the important point is that while the ego is set upon completing an enterprise it has temporarily adopted, this enterprise itself helps to reconstitute the demands and desires of the ego. For example, a young man in college studies his psychology hard in order to reward his immature ego with a pat on the back from his professor. The subject gradually gets under his skin, and high grades come to mean less to him than the solution of intellectual puzzles. Finally, through years of study he equips himself to become a researcher, a teacher, or, perhaps a clinician. All along the line the ego is served, but in the process it is also redefined and reconstructed. The study of psychology serves the *élan*, but the tasks imposed in the course of study create ever new demands and satisfactions on the part of this *élan*. To generalize the illustration, the progressive acceptance of adaptive tasks throughout one's lifetime results inevitably in continuous change in the motivational demands at successive stages in the individual's development. The following section amplifies this proposition which, I submit, represents a second neglected principle of motive-learning.

VI. The Nature of Functional Autonomy

The principle of functional autonomy holds (1) that all motives are contemporary, that whatever drives must drive now; that the 'go' of a motive is not bound functionally to its historical origins or to early goals, but to present goals only; (2) that the character of motives alters so radically from infancy to maturity that we may speak of adult motives as *supplanting* the motives of infancy; (3) that the maturity of personality is measured by the degree of functional autonomy its motives have achieved; even though in every personality there are archaisms (infantilisms, regressions, reflex responses), still the cultivated and socialized individual shows maturity to the extent he has overcome early forms of motivation; (4) that the differentiating course of learning (reflecting ever more diversified environmental influence), acting upon divergent temperaments and abilities, creates individualized motives. The dynamic structure of every personality is unique, although similarities due to species, culture, stages of development, climate, may produce certain resemblances that justify—so long as they are admitted to be approximations— the use of universal dimensions for the purposes of comparing individuals in reference to a norm, or for the purpose of constructing convenient 'types' according to the special interests of the investigator. While not denying the possible existence of instincts in infancy—or even the persistence of some instinctive (or reflex) forms of activity throughout life—still the principle of functional autonomy regards the *developed* personality as essentially a post-instinctive phenomenon.

Bertocci believes that the instinct doctrine is sufficiently flexible to account for the known modifiability of motives. He thinks that my arguments would be valid if "according to instinct theory the present motive had somehow to reach back into the non-existent past for its 'go,'" or if "we supposed that propensities were constant streams of energy, piped in fixed ways through the individual." But he concludes that I labor under too substantive a conception of propensitive action, and that McDougallian propensities are so 'generic' and so 'loosely geared,' that they escape my criticisms.

I can only reply that McDougall's account of propensities seems to me highly substantive. To quote one illustrative passage,

Thus a man's efforts to attain success in the practice of his profession may be sustained by tendencies springing from *several propensities; at one moment one of these, at another some tendency of a very different source, playing the predominant part.* . . . And he is fortunate and happy in so far as these *several powerful motives,* tendencies springing from *several distinct and very different propensities,* cooperate harmoniously and successfully. . . . (7, pp. 132 f.) (Italics mine.)

From this passage and many like it it seems to me that McDougall does regard purposes as fixed and constant streams of energy.

Bertocci believes that what I call functionally autonomous motives are only *proximate*—"the means which the ultimate motives have found in their struggle for satisfaction." What I see as the growing independence of a motive from its source he views as a mere transfer of instrumentality from one ultimate motive to another: "Mechanisms which served one master well may in time serve another master even better (or worse)." Or, "in McDougall's terminology, the sentiment which was once a focus for the expression of given instincts may become quite different in aim and in character as it becomes the new means of expression for other propensities." Now, if interests and sentiments can be passed around from propensity to propensity (instead of constituting, as I maintain, ultimate facts of motivational structure) it is fair for me to ask what psychological cement holds a sentiment together? I had supposed that according to McDougall's theory a sentiment is anchored to one or more instincts. If this is so, how can it be detached and passed around—unless indeed it has some organization of its own? If the sentiment is detachable from the propensity must it not have some degree of functional autonomy? If so, Bertocci has admitted my point, even though he may choose to hold to instincts as an *additional* factor in motivation.

The next issue raised by my critic betrays a defect in my previous exposition: "Why don't all old mechanisms become self-sufficient drives? Why does the ex-sailor have a present hankering for the sea but not for his captain, his boat, and a multitude of other objects of early instrumental value?" I reply, the functional autonomy which a motive may demonstrate was never intended to indicate autonomy of the Self, or ego. Mechanisms do not become drives unless in so doing they produce some satisfaction for the *person* (though not necessarily for an innate purpose planted by Original Nature within that person). I can readily endorse Bertocci's statement that functionally autonomous motives do not form themselves in a person unless they "serve the present status of his 'drive development.'" I regret ever implying (to some readers) that motives fly off at a tangent and have no bedrock anchorage in the satisfaction of the ego. In spite of my stress upon the importance of self-esteem, my assumption of a 'will-to-live,' and, more specifically, my discussion (Ch. VII) of the 'extension of the self' my exposition seems to have been faulty. Motives, I contend, may be autonomous in respect to their origins but never in respect to the ego.

When are we to tell whether a motive is to be regarded as functionally autonomous of its origins? Bertocci as well as other critics has raised this question. The reply, I think, is that the plasticity of the organism under conditions of learning is such that in any given case of a mature individual *unless proof to the contrary is forthcoming all motivational systems that can be empirically identified should be regarded as autonomous of their origins.* It is obvious that on occasion infantile structures persist and serve a somewhat neurotic function in the adult personality. It is obvious too that sneezing, sleep, elimination, and like bodily functions persist throughout life with relatively little personalizing. Furthermore, if one *wishes* to take the biological functions of feeding, anger, sex, fear, stripped of all their individual variability and regard them as abstract categories of motivation—they too may be regarded as unchanging potentialities. But most *concrete* motivational systems, I submit, are individually integrated with unique emotional patterning and peculiar object attachments. As such they differ from person to person and from one period of an individual's life to the other.

Bertocci criticizes me for using the phrase 'permanent interests of personality.' In my sphere of discourse this phrase is intended merely to convey the undisputed fact that in the course of life, sometimes earlier, sometimes later, an interest (sentiment, value, trait) may become essentially fixed in its organization, remaining in that form because it produces adequate satisfactions for the person who in adulthood finds himself in a fairly stable environment and in possession of the basic psychological systems that are to serve as his *modi vivendi*. The standardization of a personality at thirty, and in some respects earlier, seems to be a fact, and I think, therefore, that no paradox is involved between the principle of functional autonomy and the assumption of 'permanent interests.'

A final word about habits. Like James, Dewey, Woodworth and the behaviorists, I place relatively more stress upon the driving power of habits than do Bertocci and McDougall. But it is not that I believe each one to be a self-sufficient dynamo. Habits may remain instrumental or they may turn into interests. While 'on the make' most habits seem to *be* interests. After a time they either slip into a state of mere instrumentality, or else, as Dewey points out, become integrated into new motivational systems that are forming. It is not, I think, particularly pertinent for Bertocci to ask what habits are 'on the make' *for*. As I have indicated previously conative perseveration as represented in task attitudes—*e.g.*, learning to drive a car—is a dynamic condition simply because it is accepted by the individual as 'something to be done.' Tasks once accepted are always ego-involved, but for many reasons and in many ways. It is not necessarily their 'instinctive' appeal that makes them accepted. They may be accepted because of suggestion, previous habits of obedience, simple association with the routine of living, or any other mode of involvement in the developing ego.

Bertocci tears to pieces some of my illustrations of functional autonomy. But I am not dismayed. He asks how we are to know that the ex-sailor did not find other satisfactions than the nutritional at sea; so that today, although the need for making a living is no longer present, he is still in love with the sea for the satisfaction it brings to his instincts of submissiveness, self-assertion, curiosity or gregariousness. We are not to know that this is *not* the case, neither are we to know that it *is*. In this particular illustration I am, of course, assuming that the sentiment is a motive in its own right. I cannot prove it. When Masefield wrote, "I must go down to the sea in ships," he too felt that he was expressing an ultimate, not merely a proximate, motive. It seems to me, as I have previously indicated, that it is more reasonable to take a motive at its face value, to assume that it is pretty much what it seems to be, *unless* proof is adduced that instincts are actually at the basis of the motive, or that it is sustained by some infantile fixation. These demonstrations, I submit, are rarely forthcoming.

VII. Continuity within Personality

Bertocci's remaining objection to functional autonomy is that it fails to account for unity and continuity within personality. My critic fears that without a hormic base the doctrine of functional autonomy may come to stand for an assembly of separate and self-active faculties, thought to govern behavior all by themselves without interference. I hope I have met this objection by admitting that all motives imply some form of ego-satisfaction. I agree with Bertocci's statement that "the constancy of a trait is determined not by its own self-sufficient energy, but by its capacity to satisfy the total needs of the psychophysiological organism." Let me add, however, that to my way of thinking, these 'needs' are not instincts, nor any other de-personalized desires, but rather whatever integral demands the individual organism happens to have. To be sure no motive ultimately runs itself; it serves the organism. But the organism is, after all, but a living system of interdependent motives. Hence it comes about that evolving motives reconstitute the ego even while dependent upon it for their viability.

The view presented by the hormist differs. The ego is not reconstituted. It remains forever the same. The picture is one of an eternal *élan*, running its course in pre-established channels, thereby guaranteeing the essential fixity of the individual life. One consequence of this view is the necessary belief that instincts, which are common to the species, serve as identical cores in all personalities, so that all personalities are at bottom the same. My preference is for a more individual view of personality. Its identity is its own, guaranteed not by unchanging purposes, but by *sui generis* motivational systems, some more or less permanent (especially in adulthood, when the subjective sense of unity is at its maximum). Its identity is guaranteed likewise by individual threads of memory, habits of expectation, recurrent plans, hopes, and ideas of future goals. These and other psychological processes discussed in Chapter 13 of my book seem to me to provide adequately for all the unity any life possesses. It is, as this chapter points out, easy to over-state the degree of integration in personality. I fear that the hormist by putting his stress on permanent instincts does in fact overstate the case. In so far, however, as he puts his stress on the 'sentiment of self-regard' (as McDougall sometimes does), he seems to be moving in the direction of functional autonomy, for this sentiment can most reasonably be viewed as constantly in the process of restructuration.

VIII. Sentiments *versus* Traits

The final section of Bertocci's critique should be considered along with another of his recent papers (5). He states his willingness to accord a prominent place to both *traits* and *attitudes* in social psychology, and proceeds to work out a plan for co-ordinating these concepts with *sentiment* and *instinct* as defined by McDougall. His plan briefly is this: Let instincts be acknowledged as *ultimate* prime movers, the mainsprings of energy behind all behavior; but let it be admitted that unique organizations of instinctive energy take place in the course of each life-history so that we may for many purposes of analysis be content with a *proximate* picture of motivation, in terms of sentiments, attitudes, and traits.

Among the proximate motives the most dynamic are the *sentiments* which are compelling organizations of love and hate. It is characteristic of the sentiments that they beget lively emotions (not merely an attitudinal feeling of favor or disfavor), and that their symbol-attachments are personalized or personified (wife, mother, country, God, Hitler, sin, etc.).

Attitudes are less dynamic, representing mere postures of feeling—for or against. They are secondary in importance. Though like the sentiments in being *proximate* motives, they stand farther down a dynamic continuum, being less driving and more *directive* in character (less energizing and more instrumental); they are not laden with emotion but only with feeling. "In sum, then, sentiments are aroused (we are driven) when the objects of the environment are seen as imminent, effective (or enduring) friends or foes, through personalization or ego-involvement, while attitudes are aroused (we are favorably or unfavorably disposed toward) by the multiplicity of objects and ideas which are neither of great promise or portent (less personalized, less ego-involvement)" (5, p. 252).

Finally, in his system Bertocci introduces *traits*, representing 'a stage of development beyond the sentiment, though influenced by sentimental organization.' A trait would be 'the manner in which many past expressions of propensities have transformed the individual' and be 'uniquely expressive of their form of adjustment rather than of the environment.' In short, traits are needed because sentiments do not adequately represent the persistent and continuously functioning characteristics of the individual's adaptive and expressive history. Dominant, greedy, courteous, ruthless, grave, pessimistic *manners* of conducting oneself are 'residues' of past expressions of propensities and must be admitted as a development beyond sentiments, having no specific objects of attachment, but representing still 'one of the levels at which the hormic energy organizes itself in the life of a given individual.'

In reply to this ingenious scheme for structuring the personality I may say that with one of its principal features I fully agree, and that is with the view that attitude, trait, and sentiment are all indispensable concepts. I agree likewise in giving sentiment an especially prominent place in the psychology of personality for it is with hierarchical and lasting organizations that we have here to deal. But whether the *term* sentiment is always to be used is not so clear. In one passage in my book I wrote, "After the level of infancy is passed primitive segmental drive rapidly recedes in importance, being supplanted by the more sophisticated type of motives characteristic of the mature personality, and commonly represented by such terms as *interest, sentiment, value, trait, ambition, attitude, taste,* and *inclination.* Obviously none of these motives are found full-fledged in the newborn child" (2, pp. 113f.). Thus it seems there are many terms available for expressing the dynamic unit we have in mind. Because no other generic term was available I have designated this *class* of structural units as *traits.* Perhaps my choice was not the wisest, but from my point of view a sentiment is one form of trait. All the units listed in the above quotation have essentially the properties of traits as set forth in Chapters XI and XII of *Personality.* Although the principal properties are the same, yet there are slight differences so that in some contexts *value* fits best, in some contexts *interest,* in some *sentiment,* in others one has no alternative but to use the simple term *trait.* This last term, then, is used by me generically as referring to several kinds of motivational units differing only slightly from one another; or else it is used to designate a motivational integer for which no other special term is available (*e.g.,* 'stylistic traits').

Bertocci's suggestion that sentiments have more 'driving' power than attitudes is partly acceptable to me. General usage would seem to favor this suggestion. Difficulty arises, however, in cases where the motivational complex is well integrated and contains both sentimental and attitudinal features. In such a case I believe it does violence to the organized character of the motive to insist upon the distinction he proposes. For example, a young man is heart and soul bent upon becoming a doctor. As I see it this goal may represent a simple, integral fact of motivation in his personality. It would falsify this organization to dissolve it into a component sentiment (*e.g.*, love for suffering humanity), an attitude (*e.g.*, liking for materia medica), and a trait (*e.g.*, a friendly manner). It is much better in this case to scrap all these three terms and speak only of an *ambition*. (In the generic sense, of course, the *ambition* is itself a *trait*.)

We need diversity and flexibility in our terminology respecting motives. Sometimes we may speak more appropriately of *sentiment*, sometimes of *attitude*, or of *trait*. (There are borderlines where all three seem equally appropriate, as when we speak with propriety of a sentiment, attitude, *or* trait of *patriotism*.) Or we may, if the case requires, employ such terms as *value, frame of reference, ambition, taste, inclination, interest*. For careful thinking in the sphere of motivation these terms should all be distinguished from one another. Elsewhere I have attempted to contribute something toward this clarification of terminology, but do not need to repeat my thoughts on the subject here. (See 1, pp. 806–810; 2, pp. 290–295; 3, pp. 23–25.)

Although these distinctions are not unimportant, what matters most to me is that *all of these units of motivational structure be regarded as dynamic, unique, personal, and ultimate*. Hence I cannot accept Mr. Bertocci's proposal to regard them as merely 'proximate' factors in motivation. He has given his arguments for wishing to stand by McDougall's propensities as 'ultimate' causes. I have given my reasons for not wishing to do so. Respecting the immediate structural components we agree quite well. If only he would not insist upon viewing these components (which are all that can be established empirically) as proximate! To my way of thinking they offer as *ultimate* a representation of human motivation as psychological knowledge today warrants.

REFERENCES

1. ALLPORT, G. W. *Attitudes.* Ch. 17 in *A Handbook of Social Psychology* (C. Murchison, ed.). Worcester: Clark Univ. Press, 1935.

2. ———. *Personality: a psychological interpretation.* New York: Henry Holt, 1937. Pp. xiv + 588.

3. ———. The psychologist's frame of reference. *Psychol. Bull.*, 1940, **37**, 1–28.

4. BERTOCCI, P. A. A critique of G. W. Allport's theory of motivation. PSYCHOL. REV., 1940, **47**, 501–532.

5. ———. Sentiments and attitudes. *J. soc. Psychol.*, 1940, **11**, 245–257.

6. BRUNER, J. S., & ALLPORT, G. W. Fifty years of change in American psychology. *Psychol. Bull.* (In press.)

7. McDOUGALL, W. *The energies of men.* New York: Scribner's, 1932. Pp. ix + 395.

8. WATSON, D. L. On the role of insight in the study of mankind. *Psychoan. Rev.*, 1938, **25**, 358–371.

THE EGO IN CONTEMPORARY PSYCHOLOGY [1]

Reprinted from *Psychological Review*, **50**, No. 5, September 1943, 451-478.

I. INTRODUCTION

One of the oddest events in the history of modern psychology is the manner in which the ego (or self) became sidetracked and lost to view. I say it is odd, because the existence of one's own self is the one fact of which every mortal person—every psychologist included—is perfectly convinced. An onlooker might say, "Psychologists are funny fellows. They have before them, at the heart of their science, a fact of perfect certainty, the one warrant for the being of all other things, and yet they pay no attention to it. Why don't they begin with their own egos, or with our egos—with something we all know about? If they did so we might understand them better. And, what is more, they might understand us better."

Back in the 1880's, of course, it was good form for James, Royce, Dewey and their contemporaries to speak freely of the ego, the self, or even the soul. The soul, to be sure, was giving way under Wundt's onslaughts, and everyone was finding it exhilarating to shake off the alleged 'theological domination,' and to emerge unfettered and positivistic into the era of the New Psychology. They forgot that their predecessors had not endorsed the soul because of their theological leanings, but rather, because associationism did not recognize or explain to their satisfaction the *coherence, unity,* and *purposiveness* which they thought prevailed in mental life. Granted that the 'soul' also failed to explain these properties, it at least called attention to their existence.

After the expulsion of the soul, these unifying properties of mental life were occasionally referred to under the designa-

[1] President's address to the 14th Annual Meeting of the Eastern Psychological Association, Hunter College, April 30, 1943.

tion of 'self.' For a time, thanks to James, Calkins, Prince, and the French psychopathologists, 'self' was a reasonably popular concept. But gradually it too fell into disuse.

The total eclipse of soul and the partial eclipse of self were due in part, as I have just said, to the rise of positivism in psychology. Positivism, we all know, is a scientific program for moral re-armament, whose imperatives include absolute monism, absolute objectivity, and absolute reductionism—in short, absolute chastity. From this ascetic point of view, subjective certainties are suspect, selves seem a bit indecent, and any hint of metaphysics (that is, of non-positivistic metaphysics) savors of laxness. As Gardner Murphy pointed out to this Association one year ago there was no prestige to be gained from a psychology of the self (39).

But for all its sumptuary control, positivism had one undisputed merit: it engendered a wholesome dislike for question-begging explanations. Much of the older psychology, it showed, suffered from a tendency to labor over words as if words were the essence of things. Thanks to positivism faculty psychology, resting as it did on verbal realism, became discredited, and dialectics fell into disrepute. Much of self-psychology, we must now admit, dwelt on the unenlightening plane of dialectics. Its statements were often redundant or circular. In the manner of Gertrude Stein it sometimes asserted that a self is a self is a self. Not being, by nature, especially lyrical, psychologists failed to see any deeper significance in this exalted formula. Quite understandably they refused to admit such a stammering self to the gray citadel of their laboratories.

But when a concept becomes taboo it is probable that the taboo will irradiate to cover a whole range of problems associated with the concept. Something of this sort seems to have happened. It is not only the soul and the self that suffered ostracism, but along with them a vast array of problems having to do with the coherence and unity of mental life, with pride, ambition, and status, with values, ideals, and outlook on the future. The eclipse, of course, has not been total, but it has been considerable.

As if to compensate for the neglect of these interests within the field of psychology proper, psychoanalysis rose upon the horizon emitting a spectacular, if sporadic, light. Small wonder that the world at large turned to psychoanalysis for guidance in dynamic psychology. There was precious little other guidance to be had. I am inclined to believe history will declare that psychoanalysis marked an inter-regnum in psychology between the time when it lost its soul, shortly after the Franco-Prussian War, and the time when it found it again, shortly after World War II.

Until psychoanalysis becomes finally fused into a broader and more adequate psychology, it may take pride in having preserved and advanced the study of certain functions of the self that positivistic psychology had consigned to oblivion. It may take credit too for preserving one term, more or less cognate with 'self,' from the dark taboo of which I have spoken. 'Ego' has featured prominently in psychoanalytic literature from its beginning. This term I am now appropriating to signify the recentering that is taking place in psychological theory.

But it is not from psychoanalysis alone that we draw our threads. The position of the ego in contemporary psychology is determined by certain other historical trends as well.

II. Main Conceptions of the Ego

Among the different conceptions of the ego found in psychological literature the following are certainly the most important:

1. *The ego as knower.*—The nominative form of the word ego implies that some subject is busily engaged as Brentano would say in 'intending' his relations to the universe. The problem of the knower or 'Pure Ego' has been of little interest to psychologists since James gave it his lengthy *coup de grâce* in the *Principles.* It is enough, says James in effect, to admit that knowing goes on. A separate knowing-ego is not a necessary assumption. For phenomenologists (4, 42) and personalists (*e.g.*, 37), of course, the problem of the subject-object relationship remains uppermost. But for the

most part, since the time of Brentano and James, psychologists have passed the problem by.[2] For our purposes, we need only record this first usage, and note its relative rarity.

2. *The ego as object of knowledge.*—Some investigators have set themselves the problem of the nature of our experience of the self (**2, 22, 33**). This approach, limited as it is to the deliverances of introspection, has not been particularly rewarding. It yields relatively unenlightening localizations for the ego which is felt to lie 'between the eyes,' or to consist of 'motions in the head,' or to be situated 'between right and left,' 'between up and down,' 'between behind and before.' Following this line of investigation Horowitz came upon such a diversity of results (reports locating the ego in the head, heart, chest, face, brain, genitals) that he concludes "the localization of the self as it is reported in the literature quoted, in the responses on our questionnaire, in informal discussion, in the investigation of children, is not the basic phenomenon one might hope for to ease an analysis of the structure of the self and personality" (**22**, p. 386).

There seem to be only two facts upon which there is general agreement. (1) Infants, all writers concur, do not recognize themselves as individuals; they behave in what Piaget calls an 'undifferentiated absolute' composed of self and environment. Only gradually and with difficulty does a segregated ego evolve. (2) The ego of which we are aware is variable in its dimensions. Sometimes it includes less than the body and sometimes more. In a semi-doze we lose all sense of our egos though we may be conscious enough of impersonal items. Our feet perhaps are suddenly perceived as strange objects not belonging to us. In pathological conditions, we know, remarkable experiences of depersonalization take place (**7, 10**). Conversely, we sometimes think of a tool we are using as parts of our extended ego-system, and at

[2] Private correspondence with Koffka concerning his own usage of the term brought out the interesting fact that in writing his chapters on the ego he had never thought of ego in the rôle of the knower (**28**). "To be quite frank, I never put this question to myself." He adds, "That my solution will be similar to Brentano's I doubt. At the moment it seems to me that it will be found in the theory of Ego subsystems, more particularly in the relation of the Self-system to other Ego-systems."

times we regard our children, our lodge, or our ancestors as an intimate part of our extended selves.   It is agreed that in this manner the ego-systems of which we are aware contract and expand in a most variable fashion (33).

3. *The ego as primitive selfishness.*—A century ago Max Stirner wrote *Der Einzige und Sein Eigenthum* (49), a volume in which he developed the thesis that man is by nature unalterably egoistic.   In 1918 the French biologist Felix Le Dantec handled the same theme more brilliantly in his *L'egoïsme: seule base de toute société* (29).   Unquenchable egoism is the foundation of the social edifice, says Le Dantec, and hypocrisy is its keystone.   Psychologists are partial to such hard-headed realism, and have themselves gone far in unveiling the hypocrisy in man's nature.   Projections, rationalizations, defense mechanisms have been exposed for what they are—the whitewashing of ego-centric motivation.   During this century psychologists have joined with historians, biographers, novelists in the fashionable sport of debunking human motives.

4. *The ego as dominance-drive.*—Related to this view of primitive egoism, we find many investigations that deal with dominance feelings, with ascendance, with pecking orders, with euphoria.   From this point of approach the ego is that portion of the personality that demands status and recognition.   The negative states of anxiety, insecurity, defensiveness, resistance are just as truly indicators that whenever the ego is debased there arise impulses for its defense and restoration to status.

5. *Ego as a passive organization of mental processes.*—Psychoanalysis, we all know, has contributed much to the interpretation of human nature in terms of egoism.   Its whole theory of motivation is based upon the assumption of hedonistic self-interest.   But in psychoanalysis egoism, oddly enough, is not ascribed to the ego, but to the urges arising from the id.   For Freud the ego proper is a passive percipient, devoid of dynamic power, 'a coherent organization of mental processes' that is aware of the warring forces of the id, superego, and external environment (16).   The ego, having no

dynamic power, tries as well as it can to conciliate and to steer the warring forces, but when it fails, as it often does, it breaks out in anxiety. The ego is born of restraint of the instinctual impulses, and it continually needs strengthening. But even when through the analytic process it is strengthened, it is still essentially nothing more than a passive victim-spectator of the drama of conflict.

Dissatisfied with Freud's denial of dynamic power to the ego, we know that later psychoanalytic writers, French (14) and Hendrick (20) among them, have ascribed more *momentum* to the ego. It is the agent that plans, that strives to master as well as to conciliate the conflicts. One analyst, Heinz Hartmann, departing considerably from Freud, holds that "adaptation to reality—which includes mastery of it—proceeds to a large extent from the ego and in particular from that part of the ego which is free from conflict; and it is directed by the organized structure of ego-functions (such as intelligence, perception, etc.) which exist in their own right and have an independent effect upon the solution of conflicts" (18, p. 214). To such writers the ego-ideal is no longer, as it was with Freud, a passive reflection of the superego, which in turn is conceived as a mere legacy of the parent. The ego through its ideals reaches into the future, becomes an executive, a planner, a fighter.

6. *Ego as a 'fighter for ends.'*—We are brought then, by some of the more modern psychoanalysts to a position not unlike that of McDougall, or of James in his more teleological moments. For McDougall self-regard was the master and controlling sentiment in whose interest all other sentiments function (34, p. 383). The phrase 'fighter for ends' I borrow from James (25, I, p. 141), who at times was intensely dynamic and personalistic in his conception of the self.

The purposive view of the ego may be linked to Koffka's postulate that there is ever active "a force which propels the ego upwards" (28, p. 670). The position is represented too in those dynamic psychologies that recognize the subservience of the biological drives to one central drive of ego-satisfaction. One of the most forceful expressions of this point of view is to be found in Goldstein's *Human nature in the light of psychopathology.*[3]

7. *The ego as a behavioral system.*—In spite of his postulation of "a force which propels the ego upwards," Koffka's position is characteristically somewhat less dynamic than that just described. The ego, he says, is only one segregated system within an homogeneous field. Much behavior occurs with no reference to the ego. Not all perception, not all action, not all emotion, not all consciousness, are related to an ego-system. The ego varies widely in its boundaries from time to time, and under certain circumstances acts as a system which determines the course of events as does any other dynamic system according to the theory of Gestalt. But much of the time behavior is free from the influence of an ego-system.

More influential because of its experimental fruitfulness is Lewin's treatment of the subject (31, p. 181). Although he seldom uses the term ego he too allows for a central subsystem within the person. Not all behavior is ego-linked, but many kinds of experimentally obtained results cannot be accounted for without referring to the special types of tension that exist whenever the ego is 'engaged.' The shifting aspiration level is, most obviously, a phenomenon of ego-tensions. Satiation, substitution, encapsulation, resistance, irreality, power-field are among the Lewinian concepts whose characteristics represent various properties of ego-tensions.[4]

It is clear that Lewin, no less than Koffka, wishes to avoid thinking of the ego as a single entity, and prefers to regard it

---

[3] "On the basis of our discussion I believe we are in no way forced to assume the existence of special drives. . . . They are special reactions in special situations, and represent the various forms by which the organism as a whole expresses itself. . . . The traditional view assumes various drives which come into the foreground under certain conditions. We assume only one drive, the drive of self-actualization, but are compelled to concede that under certain conditions the tendency to actualize one potentiality is so strong that the organism is governed by it" (17, pp. 144 f).

[4] A particularly suggestive contribution of Lewin pertains to the difference between nationalities in terms of the relative ease with which the ego becomes 'engaged.' Thus the American is less defensive, less touchy, less reticent than the German, due to the fact that the barriers of the German's ego lie near the 'surface.' He protects himself against familiarity and intrusion; whereas the American leads a much more 'public' life and protects only the 'core' of his personal life from public gaze (32).

as the variable set of forces that are aroused whenever the person enters into some novel and perhaps dangerous relation to his environment.

8. *Ego as the subjective organization of culture.*—In recent years, as everyone knows, there has been a drawing together of psychology, psychoanalysis and social anthropology. The resulting commensalism has produced a new conception of the ego. The picture of the selfish and unsocialized ego bequeathed us by Stirner and Le Dantec has been broadened. Sherif, for example, points out that although the ego is a 'genetic psychological formation,' yet it is acquired by the child under the ceaseless impact of influence by parents, teachers, and associates, with the result that we must say that the ego "is chiefly made up of social values" (48, p. 179). Since the process of segregating the ego in childhood is achieved largely by giving the child a name, a status, a code of behavior, a social sense of guilt, and social standards for making his judgments—Sherif concludes that the ego is nothing but the social part of man (48, p. 186). This author's position is extreme, for if the ego is nothing but 'the social in man,' one wonders what to call all the anti-social impulses and the solitary strivings that are normally called *egoistic?* Cantril's view is similar to, but less extreme than, Sherif's. Cantril admits that "a person's ego and, consequently, the way in which he regards himself, are by no means always entirely bound by the surrounding culture" (5, p. 44). But yet what an individual regards as himself is undeniably, in large part, socially determined. When his nation's flag is torn down *he* is insulted; when disparaging remarks are made of his parents, *he* is involved; when his political candidate loses a contest, *he* has been defeated.

By stressing the cultural content of the ego, these authors in effect eradicate the artificial Freudian distinction between ego and superego. They also rescue the ego from the anti-social solipsism of Stirner and Le Dantec and make of it a socialized agent ready to enter as an integrated unit into the complex relations of social life.

From this historical glance I have omitted many writers

who have made their contribution to the literature of the ego. But, nevertheless, I believe, I have mentioned the chief ways in which, up to now, the ego has been conceived, viz., (1) as knower, (2) as object of knowledge, (3) as primordial selfishness, (4) as dominator, (5) as a passive organizer and rationalizer, (6) as a fighter for ends, (7) as one segregated behavioral system among others, (8) as a subjective patterning of cultural values.

The question immediately arises as to whether these eight uses of the term ego have anything in common, or whether, as is often the case, a single term is allowed to obscure entirely different problems. Is the ego as knower the same ego that seeks status? Is the me that is known also a fighter for ends? Has the ego system proposed by Koffka any kinship with Freud's ego who attempts through insight to reclaim the id?

These are questions that cannot yet be answered. We cannot say whether these eight conceptions reflect irreconcilable theories, whether they shade imperceptibly into one another, or whether they are all ultimately to be subordinated under one inclusive theory of the ego.

In favor of the last possibility I should like to point to recent experimental studies which, if I mistake not, lend support to several of these conceptions simultaneously. The experiments result in one common finding, namely, that ego-involvement, or its absence, makes a critical difference in human behavior. When a person reacts in a neutral, impersonal, routine atmosphere, his behavior is one thing. But when he is behaving personally, perhaps excitedly, seriously committed to a task, he behaves quite differently. In the first condition his ego is not engaged; in the second condition it is. And it is my belief that in most of the experiments I shall report one finds that the ego is acting in several, if not all, of the eight capacities I have listed. In other words, *ego-involvement* is, as the phrase implies, a condition of total participation of the self—as knower, as organizer, as observer, as status seeker, and as socialized being. But now for the experimental evidence.

III. Experimental Evidence

1. *Generality and specificity.*—A few years ago I found myself involved in a controversy in the field of personality. Certain experimenters claimed that their findings demonstrated a situational specificity in human conduct. For example, a child, honest in one situation, would not be found honest in another (19); a person confident of one judgment would not be confident of another (53). Whole books were written in defense of specificity (50). Other investigators, by other methods, found a person honest in one situation to be honest in another (35); a person confident in one judgment to be confident in another (26); and whole books were written in defense of generality (1). It was a pleasant battle while it lasted. An arbitrator arose, a peacemaker by temperament— Gardner Murphy was his name—and he proposed a compromise. "Honesty," he suggested, "is either a general characteristic or a set of specific habits, depending on your interest and your emphasis" (38, p. 385). Murphy was right, but it was not until recently that the deciding interest and critical emphasis became clear at least to me. For my own belated insight I am indebted to an experiment by Klein and Schoenfeld (27).

These investigators gave to a group of subjects a series of mental tests under two experimental conditions. In the first, the atmosphere was neutral, dull, *non ego-involved*. The workers were merely laboratory subjects going through routine motions. After each of the six tests they were required to rate the degree of confidence they felt in the accuracy of their performances. Between the six tests there was little consistency in these certainty ratings. After an interval of time, a second equivalent set of tests was administered and the atmosphere was markedly changed. The subjects were placed under greater strain, were told to try hard since the results of these 'intelligence' tests would be entered on their college records. The shift in atmosphere was effective. The confidence ratings became markedly consistent. A student who felt assured in one test felt assured in the other five;

whereas a student who lacked confidence in one of his performances generally lacked confidence in the other performances. The authors conclude that confidence is a personality trait when the ego is involved, but that it is specific to each situation when the subject has no deep interest at stake.

This experiment supplies the hypothesis needed to settle a long-standing controversy. When there is ego-involvement there are general traits; when there is no ego-involvement there are no general traits.

From an entirely different source comes evidence of the same type. In connection with its polling investigations the Office of Public Opinion Research has found that *intensity* of feeling goes with *consistency* of opinion (**6**, Ch. 3). For example, in the pre-Pearl Harbor era it was found that those who felt most intensely in favor of aid to Britain were, by and large, those who endorsed all sorts and varieties of interventionist propositions. On the other hand, those who were lukewarm in their support of aid to Britain were far more inconsistent and specific in their answers. Sometimes they gave interventionist, and sometimes isolationist, replies. The measure obtained between the intensity scale and the generality of the attitude was a coefficient of correlation of +.63.

2. *Judgment.*—Eli Marks worked on judgments of skin-color among Negroes. He found it, in part, to be a function of the objective scale but, in part also, a function of an egocentric scale. A Negro of medium coloration is likely to be judged dark by a Negro of lighter complexion, and as light by a Negro of darker complexion (**36**). For decades psychophysicists have dealt with judgments of hue as a function of wave length, but Marks makes clear that judgments of hue may be also a function of one's sense of social status. Wave length is perceived by the sensitized retina, but it is perceived no less by the sensitized ego.

In the field of simple predictive judgment, it was found in the public opinion polls of 1940 that of the people who were strong Willkie supporters, 71 per cent predicted that he would win the election; of those who were weak Willkie supporters, only 47 per cent made this prediction (6). Assuming as we must that intensity of an attitude indicates ego-involvement, we find here a clear quantitative demonstration that a 24 per cent difference in the number of predictions exists when the ego-regions of the presonality are engaged. Admittedly, the ego's wish is only one factor in predictive judgments, but if conditions are right it can become the crucial factor as it did in these 24 per cent.

Polling research has uncovered yet another important fact concerning judgment. If you ask respondents to tell you to your face what they think about our allies, the British, or about some minority group in this country, or even about their own educational level, you obtain one set of results; but if you ask them to write their answers to the same questions privately and deposit them in a padlocked ballot box, on the average your results will be significantly different (6, Ch. 5). Now this difference between open and secret expressions of opinion seems to exist only when the answers might jeopardize the respondent's sense of status or affect his prestige in the interviewer's eyes. The discrepancy is great enough to warrant the use of secret balloting whenever questions are of a type that might expose the person to humiliation.

Judgments concerning one's self are remarkably interesting things to study. We know, for example, how inaccurate people are in rating their own economic status. Nearly all prefer to overlook the objective evidence and to identify themselves with the great middle class (6). We know something about the distortions that result when people report their own traits. Frenkel-Brunswik found the self-protective devices so powerful that her subjects would omit, justify, or completely reverse the facts, in their accounts of their own deficiencies (13). Although it is trite to point out what all psychologists know so well, that lack of objectivity is the rule when our egos are involved, yet it is not trite to remark that very little work has been done on the extent and nature of the distortion, nor upon the curious and momentous question why it is that some personalities attain objectivity even in the face of extreme ego-involvement.   Insight, it would seem, grows more and more difficult to achieve as the inner regions of the personality are approached.   And yet some individuals accomplish remarkable feats of self-objectification.   Why do they succeed and others fail?

3. *Memory.*—Thanks to Bartlett we know how cultural schemata alter our memory traces (3).   Here, of course, is an example of the silent influence of an ethnocentric frame.   But within any given culture striking memory-efforts can be traced to egocentric frames as well.

Edwards has demonstrated that if memory material fails to fit comfortably into an ego-involved frame, it contorts itself until it does so.   Using three groups of students, each with a different attitude toward the New Deal (favorable, neutral, or opposed) he first read them a 10-minute passage concerning the relations of the New Deal to communism. The subjects knew they were to be tested for the accuracy of their retention.

Immediately after the reading, a multiple choice recognition test consisting of 46 items was given to the subjects.   Half or 23 of the items on the test were answered in the passage in a manner favorable to the New Deal, the other 23 were answered in a manner unfavorable.   The items on the test offered opportunities for rationalization of one's answer, if the correct answer was opposed to one's attitude.   The subjects were re-tested after an interval of 21 days.

Analysis of variance of the data showed that rationalization was directly associated with the degree of conflict between the correct answer and the attitudinal frames of reference of our subjects.   In general the results show—as do many other studies—that it is almost impossible to expect objectivity and accuracy in perception, learning, remembering, thinking, etc., when ego-involved frames of reference are stimulated (9, p. 234).

Here one might cite also the memory experiments of Zillig which show how members of the male sex recall fewer aphorisms favorable to women than to men (58).   Or, the Watson and Hartmann study concerning the distortions that occur in memory for theological arguments depending upon the subject's previous commitment to atheism or to theism (56). Or, Wallen's ingenious demonstration that after an interval of time subjects recall ratings of their own personalities in a

manner that makes them compatible with their own pre-
conceived opinions of themselves (54).

In a recent investigation Levine and Murphy demonstrated that pro-Communist sympathizers memorize pro-
Communist textual material more easily than they do anti-
Communist textual material (30).   What is more, they forget
the antipathetic text more rapidly and more completely than
the sympathetic text.   In anti-Communists the effects are
exactly reversed.   It was a brilliant stroke for these authors
to demonstrate in one experiment that both learning and
forgetting are functions of the political identifications of the
ego.

4. *Frame of reference.*—Some of the studies I have mentioned have been conducted in relation to what their authors
have called a 'frame of reference.'   Now, a frame of reference
seems to signify *any spatial-temporal or cultural orientation,
that relates many of an individual's attitudes, habits and judgments to one another, and influences the formation of new
judgments, attitudes, and habits.*   A general orientation favorable to the New Deal will, according to Edwards, determine
our specific remembrance of items from speeches concerning
the New Deal (8).   A general orientation regarding various
other subjects, Sells has shown (47), will affect our logical
reasoning in all matters pertaining to them.

Now it is important to note that not all frames are ego-
involved.   If I locate 9th Avenue or East 12th Street readily
it is because I have a geographic frame in mind for New York
City.   In my case this spatial orientation is not at all ego-
involved.   The point I am making is that research on the
problem of frames of reference is not necessarily research on
the problem of ego-involvement.   Many cultural frames having to do with language, etiquette, or dress, determine our
perceptions, our memory, our conduct, but their influence is
not felt as personally relevant.   Margaret Mead has expressed her anthropological astonishment at the odd custom
Americans have of appearing at her lectures with clothes on;
but to most of us this quaint folkway causes no ego-concern,
at least as long as it is operative.

But an interesting discovery has come to light in these days of war and violence. Certain cultural frames which were previously indifferent have suddenly become acutely personal. Probably no one in Alsace felt concerned about the bilingual frame of reference until the Nazis decreed that only German should be spoken, and that only Germanized names and inscriptions should appear on the tombstones. Bilinguality had always been taken for granted, but when this familiar, habitual frame was suppressed and placed under attack, then it became of central importance, and people reacted as to a personal insult. Many of us have recently discovered that hitherto indifferent frames of reference, such as the Constitutional guarantees we enjoy, previously taken for granted, have suddenly become ego-involved, and now in jeopardy are defended as if they were parts of our physical bodies. Suppose we in this room were forbidden to speak the English language. How enraged we would become. What had always been a mere ethnocentric frame would immediately become ego-involved.

Ethnocentric and egocentric frames both affect our conduct, and, as I have just pointed out, under certain conditions the ethnocentric frame is experienced also as an egocentric frame. But I think it is a mistake to confuse the concept of the ego with that of the socius (or cultural portion of our personalities) as Sherif has done. Under normal social conditions only a relatively small portion of our culture is ego-involved.

5. *Learning.*—The longest and most difficult chapter in psychology, no one will deny, is the chapter on learning. The latest Yearbook of the National Society for the Study of Education is devoted entirely to this subject (41). One searches its 463 pages in vain for any mention of the ego, and almost in vain for any recognition of the importance of *interest.* True, one finds occasional remarks to the effect that "the teacher who neglects the simple but powerful word of praise does so at her pedagogical peril" (41, p. 118), but the potential significance of such remarks for learning theory seems lost to view.

Clinical, educational, and industrial psychologists know that the first rule of all applied psychology is that every child and every adult needs some experience of success and social approval. John E. Anderson advises the teacher to go far out of her way if necessary to find an area in which these feelings can be engendered, and he adds

Success in one area may more than compensate for failure in many areas; some accomplishment furnishes an integrating center about which the personality may be integrated (41, p. 349).

Note especially Anderson's statement that "success in one area may more than compensate for failure in many areas." Only in terms of ego-psychology can we account for such fluid compensation. Mental health and happiness, it seems, does not depend upon the satisfaction of *this* drive or *that* drive, it depends rather upon the *person* finding *some* area of success *somewhere*. The *ego* must be satisfied, not the hunger drive, nor the sex drive, nor the maternal drive, however temporarily insistent these segmental tensions may be.

Now most theories of learning lean heavily upon the assumption of multiple drives. A segmental tension exists, the organism behaves, the tension is relieved, and the response set. In this sequence it is often assumed that all drives are equally potent for learning. The satisfaction of any drive, through the principle of reward or confirming reaction, is held to bring about an equal degree of learning. If this is so, how can we account for the fact that praise is found almost uniformly to be the leading incentive in school, in factory, and in ordinary life? If we are to hold to the theory of multiple drives at all, we must at least admit that the ego-drive (or pride, or desire for approval—call it what we will) takes precedence over all other drives.

. Not only does human learning proceed best when the incentive of praise and recognition is used, but the individual's *capacity* for learning actually seems to expand under this condition. Every psychometrist knows that in order to obtain a valid I.Q. the subject must be encouraged. Terman's instructions on this point are well known.

Nothing contributes more to a satisfactory *rapport* than praise of the child's efforts. . . . In general, the poorer the response, the better satisfied one should appear to be with it. . . . Exclamations like fine! splendid! etc., should be used lavishly (52, p. 125).

In other words, to maximize the child's intelligence we must maximize his ego. For psychological theory this is really a momentous fact. Intelligence is the ego's tool for solving its own problems. It is manifestly unfair to estimate intelligence on the basis of performance in which the individual himself has no interest. For this reason, through the device of praise, the subject must be encouraged to make the test-items into ego-involved problems which he can attack with maximally motivated effort. Intelligence is the individual's capacity to solve problems of importance to himself.

There is one unfavorable condition for learning that must be admitted lest we oversimplify the issue. Too intense an ego-involvement may be disruptive. Its normal integrative value may be actually undetermined when eagerness or self-consciousness reach a degree of intensity that lead to embarrassment or over-anxiousness. No one learns or performs well if his autonomic nervous system is in a turmoil. We need a rule that will help us determine the optimum degree of ego-involvement required for enhancing efficiency of learning and performance.[5]

One word about the law of effect. Its principal shortcoming, I think, stems from the assumption that rewarded *responses* tend to recur. Many experiments, in fact, show that rewarded responses do not blindly recur whenever an appropriate stimulus returns. Hoppe (21) points out that people normally do not strive again for a goal successfully achieved. What they do is to raise their aspirations to a point where they clearly risk failure. A student who makes an A record in a course in college, shows no tendency to repeat that course. He prefers to take new risks in the same

---

[5] One formulation of the needed rule is suggested by French: "So long as the tension does not exceed the available energy of the integrative mechanisms, so long will the integrative capacity of the goal-directed striving increase with increasing tension. But as soon as the tension of the need begins to exceed the available energy of the integrating mechanism, the effect of increasing tension will be the opposite" (15, p. 245).

general area. And an experiment by Rosenzweig indicates that it is definitely infantile to choose to repeat successful acts (46). For example, a puzzle once solved, even if accompanied by a burst of elation, no longer attracts the mature individual. He wants new worlds to conquer. Reward may bring merely satiation and boredom.

The fallacy, I repeat, lies in our speaking of rewarding a *response*. The law of effect would be truer if it held simply that a *person*, being rewarded, employs his past successes in whatever way he thinks is likely to bring him satisfaction in the *future*. Israeli has shown that, excepting for certain psychopaths, people are much more interested in their futures than in their pasts (24). Since this is so, an individual's past performances often mean little or nothing to him. Only if the ego would be served thereby, does he engage in a repetition of the successful act. More often he chooses to vary and refine his behavior so that he may feel that he himself is growing toward new successes in the future.

The relation between success and repetition, I suspect, is much closer in the case of non ego-involved behavior than in the case of ego-involved behavior. Over and over again I use the same motor combinations in typewriting, in driving my car, in dealing with tradesmen. They are reasonably successful acts; why should I change them? But I do not repeat successful research work, do not repeat a gratifying conversation with a friend, nor do I re-state the same goal in an aspiration-level experiment. Ego-involved tasks often demand changing goals and new responses. Rewarded behavior, it would seem, becomes stereotyped only in lower animals, or in such human activities of a routine nature that fail to engage the ego.

To summarize this brief discussion, it would seem that in order to employ the law of effect with human learning we must view it as secondary to the principle of ego-involvement. The law of effect, like cue reduction, conditioning, bond-formation, and most other popular principles of learning, have been worked out for the most part on animal subjects or on human beings deprived for the duration of the experiment, of their egos. The principles may be good ones, but I submit that when the ego is engaged they operate in a contingent fashion. Learning theory of the future, let us hope, will not remain so peripheral to the ego.

6. *Motivation.*—You may be thinking, "But, we've always known that one must be motivated in order to secure a response. Are you talking about anything more than the importance of motivation?" Yes. I am saying that there are two forms of motivation, one ego-involved and one not, and I am attempting by repeated citations from experiments to show the differences that-exist between them.

Take, for example, the work of Huntley and Wolff on judgments based upon records of expressive behavior (23, 57). These investigators working independently instructed their subjects to make judgments concerning the personalities of many people from their handwritings, from their recorded voices, from photographs of hands, and from their style of story telling. The subjects were motivated in a routine manner as is any laboratory subject. But, suddenly, in the midst of the series they were confronted with samples of their own expressive behavior which had been recorded without their knowledge. In the large majority of cases the subjects did not consciously recognize their own records and continued innocently with their characterizations. But something had happened. The characterizations began to take a different form. Even though a judge was wholly unaware that a certain expression was his own, he gave it a much more favorable rating than he gave similar expressive records taken from other subjects. Occasionally he gave it a vehemently unfavorable rating, but practically never did he give it an indifferent rating. Other people's records might arouse no affect, but not his. Whenever a subject became half-conscious, as it were, that a record might possibly be his, his judgments were still more intensely partisan; but when he fully recognized his own record then his social sense of modesty prevailed, and his judgments returned to the noncommital level.

In these experiments we have a particularly neat demonstration of the fact that ego-involved systems may operate in a wholly silent manner, affecting judgments in a most extreme way without the subject knowing the reason. The experiments also prove that the limen of ego-involvement is lower than the limen for self-recognition, an interesting finding which warns us once more that conscious report and introspection will never be a sufficient method for exploring the operations of the ego-system. But the important point for our present purposes, is to note that routine motivation to perform a task is one thing, and that ego-charged motivation is quite another. Routine motives yield one set of results, ego-motives a different set.

When is motivation ego-involved and when is it not? A partial answer seems to lie in the degree of frustration involved. As we have already noted many customary frames of reference are not felt to be personally relevant, and do not behave like egocentric frames, until their continuance is threatened (as in wartime). Many drives, too, run their course without engaging the ego unless they are interfered with. But serious frustration may instigate the clamor, the jealousy, the possessiveness, often characteristic of ego-involvement. And yet frustration by no means always produces this effect, especially if one has compensated for drive-frustration by success in other realms. And then, to complicate the situation further, we cannot say that ego-involvement is absent when there is no frustration. Many smooth-running instances of goal-seeking behavior are obviously ego-involved. A mother feels just as closely identified with her child when it is in good health as when her maternal care meets with frustration. A business man is as much absorbed in his enterprise in times of prosperity as he is in times of adversity. Let us say, then, that frustration of goal-seeking behavior or any kind of threat to the individual, is very likely to engage the ego-system; but that normally this ego-system is made up of the ordinary values which spell out the significance of life to the individual.

7. *The level of aspiration.*—The history of ten years' research on this Lewinian problem is too intricate to trace

here, but unless I am mistaken every investigation has directly or indirectly confirmed Hoppe's initial claim that the subject behaves in such a manner as to maintain his self-esteem at the highest possible level (21). Of course, many investigators have not used the conception of the ego at all. Yet whatever results are found they all seem to point to the essential inescapability of Hoppe's original hypothesis. Frank (11) for example, found that subjects in whom 'self competition, and consciousness of social pressure' were present, had D-scores three to seven times as large as did subjects who had no such sense of personal involvement in the situation.[6] Frank also found that subjects who are ego-involved do not change their estimates with every little variation in their performance. They try and try again before trimming their aspirations to fit their capacities; subjects not ego-involved on the other hand, quickly yield to the immediate realities of the situation, and lower their aspiration level (12). We know too that competitiveness, surely a symptom of ego-involvement, usually produces a rise and greater consistency in the aspiration level (43). But we cannot say that competitiveness always has this effect because subjects who dread competition will lower their level of aspiration consistently in order to avoid the risk of humiliation (11). In short, it seems always to be the ego-demand of the individual subject that determines the behavior of the aspiration level. Some subjects are adventurous, some cautious; their egos demand different types of satisfaction, and it is this fact that is repeatedly reflected in the results of the experiments. It is worth pointing out that historically the aspiration level may well be regarded as the door by which the ego re-entered the cloisters of academic psychology.

8. *Industrial psychology.*—Most of us, I suppose, have been impressed in recent years by the demonstrations of Roethlisberger and Dickson (44), of Watson (55), and others, that employees in industry are not 'economic men' so much as they are 'ego men.' What they want, above all else, is

---

[6] D-scores, of course, indicate the discrepancy between performance and the goal that the individual wishes or expects to achieve.

credit for work done, interesting tasks, appreciation, approval, congenial relations with their employers and fellow workers. These satisfactions they want even more than high wages or job security. Now, the employer's estimate of the worker's wants correlates just about zero with the worker's own report of his wants (55, p. 119). The employer thinks that wages and security are the dominant desires, whereas in reality the ego-satisfactions are primary. What a different outlook there would be on our economic life if we took firm hold on the issues of status and self-respect in industry, and re-planned our industrial society in a manner that would rescue the worker's ego from oblivion.

IV. THE NATURE OF THE EGO

In the experiments I have cited, and in many others of analogous nature, it turns out that one group of subjects (those who are personally aroused and committed to a task) behave in ways quite unlike other subjects (who are not so committed). In some instances there are measurable quantitative differences as great as 50 or 60 per cent, sometimes much more. In other instances there are qualitative changes that elude measurement. In short, we are here confronted with some parameter that makes a vast difference in our experimental results.

We have seen that under conditions of ego-involvement the whole personality manifests greater consistency in behavior, reveals not specificity in conduct but generality and congruence. In the field of judgment, we have seen how ego-involvement results in significant distortions of the ordinary psychophysical scales. In memory, we find that retention is characteristically superior (though at times repressions also may be more likely to occur, and rationalizations may creep into ego-involved memory). In intelligence, we note that ego-involvement is indispensable if we would obtain optimum performance. In learning theory, reforms seem indicated to make room for the demonstrable influence of the ego upon the acquisition of skill and knowledge. In motivation, the craving for recognition, status, and personal appreciation turns out to be supreme, so much so that our conceptions of procedure and policy in industrial relations, in education, and in psychotherapy, are profoundly affected. And these are only a few of the operational criteria by which we may demonstrate the existence of the ego.

Its admittance to good standing in contemporary psychology has been advocated by several psychologists besides myself. Koffka, Lewin, and the psychoanalysts have done so; as has Murray who makes a distinction between 'peripheralist' psychology and 'centralist' psychology (40). The thesis set forth in Roger's recent book *Counseling and psychotherapy* (45) seems to me especially clear evidence that the ego is coming into its own. Rogers, in effect, asks counselors to sit back and with little more than an occasionally well-placed *m-hm*, to encourage the patient himself to restructure and re-plan his life. The patient's ego takes command. It's about time it should.

Although we have given an adequate operational demonstration of the ego, we have not yet faced the difficult problem of definition. Earlier we saw that eight conceptions seem to prevail. But whenever we encounter ego-involvement the ego in several of its historical senses seems to be active. Furthermore, these historical conceptions seem to have much in common.

For one thing, it seems clear that all of the conceptions are less embracing than 'personality.' All writers seem agreed that the ego is only one portion, one region, or as the Freudians say, one 'institution,' of the personality. Many skills, habits, memories are components of personality but seldom, if ever, become ego-involved. Writers seem also agreed that the ego is non-existent in early childhood, evolving gradually as the child comes to mark himself off from his environment and from other human beings. They seem also to agree in viewing the ego as the portion of the personality that is in proximate relation to the external world. It senses the threats, the opportunities, and the survival significance of both outer and inner events. It is that portion of the personality, so to speak, that meets the world head-on. It is the contact-region of the personality. For that reason it is also the conflict-region. Yet it is coextensive with neither consciousness nor with unconsciousness, for much that we are conscious of is indifferent to our egos, and many unconscious stimuli silently but effectively engage them.

There is also agreement that the subjective sense of the ego varies greatly from time to time, now contracting to include less than the body, now expanding to include more. Its content keeps changing, for at certain moments the ego seems preoccupied with one activity and soon thereafter with a wholly different activity. This shifting scene however does not mean that there is no stable and recurring structure. On the contrary, if you know a person well enough, you find that you are able to predict with marked success what items will and what items will not be linked to his ego. By many writers the ego is represented as a layered structure. Certainly there are *degrees* of ego-involvement. A person may be intensely partisan or moderately partisan.

There seems to be one other property of the ego, less often discussed, namely its customary preoccupation with the future. Israeli, it will be remembered, reports that among his subjects over ninety per cent expressed themselves more interested in their futures than in their pasts (24). This finding is worth stressing, for as a rule, psychologists are more interested in a person's past than in his future. In other words, the psychologist and his subject customarily face in different directions, and that is unfortunate.

V. PSYCHOLOGY DURING THE WAR AND AFTER

You and I are ego-involved in the course of the war and in the outcome of the future peace. Likewise, for different reasons, we are involved in the development and progress of psychology as a science and as a profession. Now it is typical of the generalizing tendency in the ego that matters having a high degree of personal relevance do not ordinarily remain apart. They tend to become fused into an integrated plan of action. Thus, in order to help win the war approximately a thousand psychologists have transferred their professional activity to camps, factories, or government offices. And most of those who have remained in colleges have rearranged their lives in such a way as to blend their war interests with their professional activity.

Although it is too early to evaluate the work we all are doing, I wonder if you have the same impression I have concerning the utility of our previous training in psychology. It is my guess that insofar as our war work deals with sensory, perceptual, and psychometric problems, the transfer value of our previous psychological training is very high. But insofar as our war work deals with problems of morale, public opinion, national character, scapegoating, ideology, guidance, rehabilitation—any of the areas where the major hates, fears, and hopes of men are concerned—the transfer value of our previous training is much less. In other words, the psychology that treats the non-ego involved functions of the human organism has developed to a point of immediate utility, whereas the psychology of the 'central' regions of personality has not. I make this statement with full appreciation of the admirable work of our colleagues in OSS, in OWI, FBIS, and in other similar bureaus. But most of them, I think, would agree that the psychology available for application to their problems has shown itself to be both meagre and inept.

It might be argued that, being a young science, psychology has moved, as it were, from the surface inward. Given time we shall have as much to contribute to an understanding of the central layers as of the surface. But is it merely a matter of time? Is it not rather that the sumptuary regulations of our science have been unhealthy for the ego?

Everywhere we encounter the paradox: As a group, psychologists are liberal, internationally minded, and devoted to the welfare of the common man. They believe in providing a soil where the infinite varieties of the human ego may freely grow. At the same time their assumptions, their methods, their theories have not been well suited to the attainment of their objectives.

For the past ten years we have become increasingly aware of this paradox. As evidence, there is the mounting tide of experiments of the type I have reviewed. As further evidence, there is the widespread recasting of our activities in wartime and the notable turning of psychologists' interests to the formulation of conditions for a lasting peace (**51**). In all this work there is a somewhat novel co-operative spirit. The coming Inter-Society Constitutional Convention is one instance of what I have in mind. As never before we seem to desire to have our productions fit together. Ego-satisfactions, we are discovering, are not necessarily competitive. One is reminded here of the experiments of Helen Lewis (unpublished) which have demonstrated that *your* tensions may be resolved by *my* work and *my* tensions may be resolved by *your* work, provided only that we regard ourselves as co-operating members in a common undertaking.

The admittance of the ego to good standing in psychology does not mean a re-importation of the *deus ex machina* of pre-Wundtian psychology. It does mean, however, a recognition of the fact that our predecessors who regarded psychology as the science of the soul, were not wrong in setting the problems of unity and personal relevance before us. What they called the soul, we may now, with good conscience, call the ego. In so doing, no clocks need to be set backward. Dialectics has already given way to experiment and to the clinic, and to still newer methods for studying the common man in his normal social setting.

But disregarding the problems of method, which are beyond the scope of my paper, we may safely predict that ego-psychology in the twentieth century will flourish increasingly. For only with its aid can psychologists reconcile the human nature that they study and the human nature that they serve.

REFERENCES

1. ALLPORT, G. W. *Personality: a psychological interpretation.* New York: Henry Holt, 1937.
2. AMEN, E. W. An experimental study of the self in psychology. *Psychol. Monogr.*, 1926, 35, No. 165.
3. BARTLETT, F. C. *Remembering: a study in experimental and social psychology.* Cambridge, England: University Press, 1932.
4. BETH, M. Zur Psychologie des Ich. *Arch. f. d. ges. Psychol.*, 1933, 88, 323-376.

5. CANTRIL, H.   *The psychology of social movements.*   New York: John Wiley & Sons, 1941.
6. ——.   *Gauging public opinion.*   Princeton: University Press, 1943.
7. DELGADO, H.   Psicologia y psicopatologia de la conscientia del yo.   *An. Inst. Psicol.*, Univ. Buenos Aires, 1938, **2**, 135–176.
8. EDWARDS, A. L.   Political frames of reference as a factor influencing recognition.   *J. abnorm. (soc.) Psychol.*, 1941, **36**, 34–50.
9. ——.   Rationalization in recognition as a result of a political frame of reference.   *J. abnorm. (soc.) Psychol.*, 1941, **36**, 224–235.
10. FEDERN, P.   Narzissmus im Ichfüge.   *Int. Z. f. Psychoanal.*, 1927, **13**, 420–438.
11. FRANK, J. D.   Individual differences in certain aspects of the level of aspiration.   *Amer. J. Psychol.*, 1935, **47**, 119–128.
12. ——.   Some psychological determinants of the level of aspiration.   *Amer. J. Psychol.*, 1935, **47**, 285–293.
13. FRENKEL-BRUNSWIK, E.   Mechanisms of self-deception.   *J. soc. Psychol.*, 1939, **10**, 409–420.
14. FRENCH, R. M.   Some psychoanalytic applications of the psychological field concept.   *Psychoanal. Quart.*, 1942, **11**, 17–32.
15. ——.   Goal, mechanisms and integrative field.   *Psychosom. Med.*, 1941, **3**, 226–252.
16. FREUD, S.   *The ego and the id.*   (Transl. by J. Rivière.)   London: Hogarth Press, 1927.
17. GOLDSTEIN, K.   *Human nature in the light of psychopathology.*   Cambridge: Harvard University Press, 1940.
18. HARTMANN, H.   Ich-psychologie und Anpassungsproblem.   *Int. J. Psychoanal.*, 1940, **21**, 214–216.
19. HARTHSORNE, H., & MAY, M.   *Studies in deceit.*   New York: Macmillan, 1928.
20. HENDRICK, I.   Instinct and the ego during infancy.   *Psychoanal. Quart.*, 1942, **11**, 33–58.
21. HOPPE, F.   Erfolg und Miserfolg.   *Psychol. Forsch.*, 1930, **14**, 1–62.
22. HOROWITZ, E. L.   Spatial localization of the self.   *J. soc. Psychol.*, 1935, **6**, 379–387.
23. HUNTLEY, C. W.   Judgments of self based upon records of expressive behavior.   *J. abnorm. (soc.) Psychol.*, 1940, **35**, 398–427.
24. ISRAELI, N.   The social psychology of time.   *J. abnorm. (soc.) Psychol.*, 1932, **27**, 209–213.
25. JAMES, W.   *Principles of psychology.*   2 vols. New York: Henry Holt, 1890.
26. JOHNSON, D. M.   Confidence and speed in two-category judgment.   *Arch. Psychol.*, 1939, No. 241.
27. KLEIN, G. S., & SCHOENFELD, N.   The influence of ego-involvement on confidence.   *J. abnorm. (soc.) Psychol.*, 1941, **36**, 249–258.
28. KOFFKA, K.   *Principles of Gestalt psychology.*   New York: Harcourt, Brace, 1935.
29. LE DANTEC, F.   *L'egoïsme, seule base de toute société.*   Paris: Flammarion, 1916.
30. LEVINE, J. M., & MURPHY, G.   The learning and forgetting of controversial material.   *J. abnorm. (soc.) Psychol.* (to be published).
31. LEWIN, K.   *Principles of topological psychology.*   New York: McGraw-Hill, 1936.
32. ——.   Some social-psychological differences between the United States and Germany.   *Character & Pers.*, 1936, **4**, 265–293.
33. LUNDHOLM, H.   Reflections upon the nature of the psychological self.   PSYCHOL. REV., 1940, **47**, 110–126.
34. McDOUGALL, W.   *The energies of men.*   New York: Scribners, 1933.
35. MacKINNON, D. W.   Violation of prohibitions.   In *Explorations in personality*, H. A. Murray, Ed.   New York: Oxford University Press.   1938, pp. 491–501.
36. MARKS, E.   Skin color judgments of Negro college students.   *J. abnorm. (soc.) Psychol.*, 1943, **38**, 370–376.

37. Moore, J. S.   The problem of the self.   *Phil. Rev.*, 1933, 42, 487–499.
38. Murphy, G., & Jensen, F.   *Approaches to personality.*   New York: Coward-McCann, 1932.
39. Murphy, G.   Psychology and the post-war world.   Psychol. Rev., 1942, 49, 298–318.
40. Murray, H. A.   *Explorations in personality.*   New York: Oxford University Press, 1938.
41. National Society for the Study of Education.   *The psychology of learning.*   Forty-first Yearbook, Pt. 2.   Bloomington: Publ. School Pub. Co., 1942.
42. Oesterreich, T. K.   *Phenomenologie des Ich im ihren Grundprobleme.*   Leipzig: J. A. Barth, 1910.
43. Preston, M. G., & Bayton, J. A.   Differential effect of a social variable upon three levels of aspiration.   *J. exp. Psychol.*, 1941, 29, 351–369.
44. Roethlisberger, F. J., & Dickson, W. J.   *Management and the worker.*   Cambridge; Harvard University Press, 1939.
45. Rogers, C. R.   *Counseling and psychotherapy.*   Boston: Houghton Mifflin, 1942.
46. Rosenzweig, S.   Preferences in the repetition of successful and unsuccessful activities as a function of age and personality.   *J. genet. Psychol.*, 1933, 42, 423–441.
47. Sells, S. B.   The atmosphere effect: an experimental study of reasoning.   *Arch. Psychol.*, 1936, No. 200.
48. Sherif, M.   *The psychology of social norms.*   New York: Harper & Bros., 1936.
49. Stirner, M.   *The ego and his own.*   (Transl. by S. T. Byington.)   London: A. C. Fifield, 1912.
50. Symonds, P. M.   *The nature of conduct.*   New York: Macmillan, 1928.
51. Symposium.   Psychological considerations in making the peace.   *J. abnorm. (soc.) Psychol.*, 1943, 38, 131–224.
52. Terman, L. M.   *The measurement of intelligence.*   Boston: Houghton Mifflin, 1916.
53. Trow, W. C.   The psychology of confidence.   *Arch. Psychol.*, 1923, No. 67.
54. Wallen, R.   Ego-involvement as a determinant of selective forgetting.   *J. abnorm. (soc.) Psychol.*, 1942, 37, 20–39.
55. Watson, G.   Work satisfaction.   In *Industrial conflict: a psychological interpretation* (Ed. by G. W. Hartmann).   New York: Cordon Press, 1939, chapter 6.
56. Watson, W. S., & Hartmann, G. W.   Rigidity of a basic attitudinal frame.   *J. abnorm. (soc.) Psychol.*, 1939, 34, 314–336.
57. Wolff, W.   Selbstbeurteilung und Fremdbeurteilung im wissentlichen und unwissentlichen Versuch.   *Psychol. Forsch.*, 1932, 16, 251–329.
58. Zillig, M.   Einstellung und Aussage.   *Z. f. Psychol.*, 1928, 106, 58–106.

THE PSYCHOLOGY OF PARTICIPATION[1]

Reprinted from *Psychological Review*, **53**, No. 3, May 1945, 117-132.

John Dewey has shown that psychological theories are profoundly affected by the political and social climate prevailing in any given time and place. For example, an aristocracy produces no psychology of individual differences, for the individual is unimportant unless he happens to belong to the higher classes (11). Dualistic psychology, he points out, flourishes best when one group holds a monopoly of social power and wishes to do the thinking and planning while others remain the docile, unthinking, instruments of execution (12, p. 72). And apologists for the status quo, he adds, are the ones who most readily declare human nature to be unalterable. "The ultimate refuge of the standpatter in every field, education, religion, politics, industrial and domestic life, has been the notion of an alleged fixed structure of mind" (13, p. 273). It was no accident that psychological hedonism

flourished as a justification for Nineteenth Century laissez-faire, or that reflexology blended with dialectical materialism dominated Russian psychology after 1917. All of us watched with dismay the abrupt perversion of German psychological science after 1933 (34). With such evidence before us can we doubt that American psychology too bears its own peculiar stamp of political and social dependency?

It is not my purpose to examine the thesis that social and economic determinism has been decisive in the history of psychology, nor the countercontention that the facts about human nature must be true regardless of any politicoethical frame that we may hold. Dewey boldly declares democracy and sound psychology to be forever coextensive; it is impossible to have one without the other. He would frankly banish all psychological postulates that are not democratically oriented (4, esp. pp. 281, 283, 290).

Alluring as this whole problem is, let us limit our consideration to one distinctive, culturally-conditioned feature of American psychology.

I. AMERICAN PSYCHOLOGY PREDOMINANTLY A MOTOR PSYCHOLOGY

It will take but a moment's reflection for us to agree that the genius of American psychology lies in its stress upon action—or in slightly dated terminology,

---

[1] The Chairman's address to the Society for the Psychological Study of Social Issues, delivered September 16, 1944, at Columbia University. Dr. G. R. Schmeidler has kindly assisted in the preparation of this paper.

Author's note.—Were it customary for the Chairman of this Society to dedicate his address I should offer my remarks in honor of John Dewey. He more than any other scholar, past or present, has set forth as a psychological problem the common man's need to participate in his own destiny. Furthermore, as a torch-bearer of democracy he has illuminated the region where the problems of participation must inevitably find their solution.

upon the motor phase of the reflex arc. Of all schools of psychological thought that we might name only behaviorism, in both its muscle-twitch and operational versions, is primarily American. Functionalism is American (rather than German or British) chiefly in its motor emphasis. Capacity psychology and mental testing in America deal primarily with accomplishment, activity, performance. The individual differences that are said to be a typical American interest have to do chiefly with measurable operations. We seldom record, for example, an individual's unique and subjective pattern of thought-life.

Of the many potential lines of development laid down in James's *Principles* over 50 years ago, the threads that were picked up were the radical motor elements, leading in the hands of Holt, Washburn, and Langfeld to a *motor theory of consciousness;* in the hands of Dewey to a psychology of *conduct, adjustment,* and *habit.* James himself established *pragmatism,* a doctrine that invites attention almost exclusively to the motor consequences of mental life. When James waxed ethical, as he frequently did, his moral advice was generally, "If you really care about something, you should *do* something about it." Even Josiah Royce whose thought is often said to be the opposite of James's, agreed (like a good American) with his emphasis on *action.* Loyalty, said Royce, "is complete only in motor terms, never in merely sentimental terms. It is useless to call my feelings loyal unless my muscles somehow express this loyalty. . . . Nobody can be effectively loyal unless he is highly trained on the motor side" (30, pp. 239, 241).

Returning on every ship from Europe (until ten years ago) were fresh young American *Doktoranden.* Their intellectual luggage was filled with European theories and concepts. But when un-

packed at our motor-minded laboratories, these importations looked alien and were promptly subjected to a strenuous course in Americanization. *Feelings of innervation,* for example, were promptly dubbed outlandish. *Innervation* would do, but feelings were *de trop. Ideo-motor* theory arrived, and though given a hospitable welcome by James, made little headway. *Ideas,* as the sovereign source of movement, smacked too much of the divine rights of Herbart. When ideas were offered to American psychologists, they commonly replied, "Keep them: stimulus and response will do quite nicely, thank you." *Empathy* arrived in a portmanteau packed in Munich. It was embedded in a whole self-psychology and in an epistemology of *Wissen von fremden Ichen.* Everything went into the ash can save only a greatly oversimplified version of what Lipps originally intended. *Motor mimicry* was all we wanted. What would we be doing with a "mental act that held a guarantee of the objectivity of our knowledge"?

Importations in the psychology of thought were so roughly handled that they scarcely survived at all. What was *unanschaulich* in Würzburg became *anschaulich* in Cornell. To think without images seemed mildly treasonable; but to think *with* them gradually became unpatriotic. Better to think with our larynx, hands and viscera, or better still in recent years with our action currents. To explain volition in Würzburg an impalpable decision factor, a *Bewusstheit,* was needed. But it all became so much simpler in Berkeley—a mere matter of rat-vibrissæ quivering with VTE at a choice point in a maze.

Other transformations were equally drastic. Of the countless dimensions for the study of personality proposed by Stern, the IQ alone was picked up. Wertheimer died perplexed by the selective attention Americans were paying to the visible, tangible portions of his work (21). The entire *Geisteswissenschaft* is known in this country chiefly through an absurd little pencil and paper test leading to the inevitable profile. Small wonder that Spranger exclaimed, "Die grösste Gefahr Deutschland's ist die Amerikanizierung" (*Cf.* 32, p. 199).

One might think that phenomenology, since it derives from *Akt* psychology, might take hold in this country. But *mental* acts are not popular; it is *motor* acts that count. Or one might suppose Americans would take to *Intentionality*, a concept dealing with the orientation of the subject toward an object from which one might predict his future action. But such a concept is still too subjective. It is hard for us to even understand what it means. *Attitude* we will admit—if it can be operationally defined—but intentionality is just too Central European.

In short, we as Americans have motorized psychology. Our theories of human nature transform meditative functions into active functions. The process clearly reflects the demand of our culture that inner life issue quickly and visibly into tangible success: that closures be reached both overtly and swiftly.

Do I seem to deplore the one-sidedness of our approach? I do not mean to. Quite the contrary: it is our way of going at things. Our preference for action, for objectivity, has carried us to new levels of attainment, and will carry us still further. In the future European models will be followed even less than formerly. What we produce must be indigenous within our culture and must harmonize with our active orientation. It is especially true in social psychology, I think, that our derivations from Europe are virtually at an end. What may have been valid in Wundt, Durkheim, Le Bon, Tarde, Pareto, will in the postwar era find better expression in the fresher, behavioral approach of America. *It will do so, that is, if our psychology of social action expands to give fuller play to the activities of the total organism than has been customary in the past.* Even though subjective categories do not appeal, we need to find better ways of linking our psychology of action to the central regions of personality. Up to now little progress has been made in this direction.

II. MOTOR ACTIVITY AND HIGHER MENTAL PROCESSES

True, American psychologists have to their credit the discovery that motor activity plays a pivotal role in higher mental functions. Take as an example, *learning:* we have repeatedly insisted that learning is 'not passive absorption but an active response!' In the classic experiment by Gates, learning scores jumped 100 per cent when four-fifths of the subject's time was devoted to recitation rather than to passive reading (18). Haggard and Rose, recently reviewing many learning studies, including those that have to do with the simple conditioning of reflexes, report that in all cases learning seems to be facilitated if the subject himself overtly takes part, perhaps by turning the switch that rings the conditioning bell, or by drawing a line to accompany the apparent movement of the autokinetic phenomenon, or even by clenching the fist while memorizing nonsense syllables. These authors generalize these studies under a *Law of Active Participation,* ". . . when an individual assumes an active role in a learning situation (*a*) he tends to acquire the response-to-be-learned more rapidly, and (*b*) these response-patterns tend to be more stably formed, than when he remains passive" (20, p. 56).

How to permit such helpful motor activity to go on in a classroom where 50 pupils are busy learning, is a large-sized pedagogical problem. "The chief source of the 'problem of discipline' in schools," says Dewey, "is that the teacher has often to spend a larger part of the time in suppressing the bodily activities" of the children (14, p. 165). The situation is wholly abnormal in that the teacher tries to divorce bodily activity from the perception of meaning; and yet perception of meaning is incomplete without full manipulation and adequate bodily movement.

Memory for material learned in school and college is notoriously poor, so poor that educators are forced to console themselves with the wistful adage which holds education to be "what you have left when you have forgotten all you learned in school." Perhaps a few studious attitudes, a few analytical habits are left; but should *content* disappear from the mind as rapidly as it does? We know that content acquired through personal manipulation does not seem to evaporate so rapidly.

I recently asked 250 college students to write down three vivid memories of their school work in the 8th grade. Afterward I had them indicate whether the memories involved their own active participation in the events recorded. Were they reciting, producing, talking, playing, arguing, or were they passively listening, watching, not overtly involved? Three-quarters of the memories were for situations in which the subject himself was actively participating, even though the percentage of time actually spent in participation in the average 8th grade room must be small.

We may mention also the problem of *voluntary control*. Although America has contributed little enough to the psychology of volition, what it has contributed is typical—namely the finding of Bair (8) and others, that a large amount of excessive, and apparently futile, motor involvement is necessary before one can gain control voluntarily over a limited muscular segment of the body. We know that a considerable overflow of effort is needed before fine skills can be differentiated, and before the individual can develop any satisfactory degree of self-determination.

In the realm of modern *therapy* self-propelled activity plays an increasing part, as the 'Rogers technique' becomes more and more widely applied (29). Analogously, the Kenny treatment for infantile paralysis requires the patient to take more and more responsibility and to be more and more active, otherwise, it is discovered, the suggestions given by the therapeutist will not accomplish their purpose (10). Angyal refers to the universal experience of psychiatrists that healthy ideas can be easily conveyed to the patient on the intellectual level without the slightest benefit accruing. The difficulty is to induce a state in which the idea "permeates the personality and influences the behavior" (7, p. 326). In this war we have learned the importance of reconditioning at the front, that is, of allowing the patient himself quickly to work out his *own* relations with the terrifying environment that shocked him.

Facing the problem of *reëducation* in Germany, Lewin points to the impossibility of ideological conversion until requisite experience is available. "To understand what is being talked about," he says, "the individual has to have a basis in experience." No amount of verbal defining will convey the meaning of such concepts as 'his Majesty's loyal opposition' or 'fair play.' To most Germans loyalty is identified with obedience; the only alternative to blind obedience is lawless individualism and laissez-faire (24).

One of the chief problems confronting the AMG to-day is to keep the inhabitants of liberated countries active in shaping their own destiny (5). Handouts beget apathy, and apathy prevents an interest in one's own future. How much better it was for Parisians to retake their own city than for the Allies to have done all the work, handing over the finished product. In his excellent new book *Mental hygiene,* Klein expresses the point: "Without action there is no shift from the wish to the deed. There is motive, but no purpose. There is yearning without striving; hence the potential self-improvement dies stillborn" (22, p. 319). To be sure, we must not over-simplify the problem of rescue and emergency relief for Europe's dazed and demoralized citizens. Yet the only rule to follow, so far as it is at all practicable, is to allow them to participate fully in their own rescue and rehabilitation.

III. ACTIVITY *Vesus* PARTICIPATION

Facts of this sort prove to us that people have to be active in order to learn, in order to store up efficient memories, to build voluntary control, to be cured when they are ill, restored when they are faint.

But implied in much American work is the proposition that one activity is as good as any other activity. It is *random* movement, according to much of our learning theory, that brings the organism to an eventual solution. And according to one experimentalist, "If the body muscles are tense, the brain reacts much more quickly and intensely, if they are relaxed, it may react weakly or not at all" (9, p. 23). The implication seems to be that tenseness of any kind makes for mental alertness. Activity as such is approved.

Random movement theories of learning, muscular tension theories of efficiency, speed theories of intelligence, and motor theories of consciousness do not make a distinction that seems to me vital, namely, the distinction between mere *activity* as such and true, personal *participation*.

Before we examine this distinction as it affects psychological theory and practice, I should like to point out that the self-same distinction occurs in the economic and social life of the common man.

Take, for example, Citizen Sam, who moves and has his being in the great activity wheel of New York City. Let us say that he spends his hours of unconsciousness somewhere in the badlands of the Bronx. He wakens to grab the morning's milk left at the door by an agent of a vast Dairy and Distributing system whose corporate manœuvers, so vital to his health, never consciously concern him. After paying hasty respects to his landlady, he dashes into the transportation system whose mechanical and civic mysteries he does not comprehend. At the factory he becomes a cog for the day in a set of systems far beyond his ken. To him (as to everybody else) the company he works for is an abstraction; he plays an unwitting part in the 'creation of surpluses' (whatever they are), and though he doesn't know it his furious activity at his machine is regulated by the 'law of supply and demand,' and by 'the availability of raw materials' and by 'prevailing interest rates.' Unknown to himself he is headed next week for the 'surplus labor market.' A union official collects his dues; just why he doesn't know. At noontime that corporate monstrosity, Horn and Hardart, swallows him up, much as he swallows one of its automatic pies. After more activity in the afternoon, he seeks out a standardized day-dream produced in Hollywood, to rest his tense, but *not* efficient mind. At the end of his day he sinks into a tavern, and unknowingly victimized by the advertising cycle, orders in rapid succession Four Roses, Three Feathers, Golden Wedding and Seagram's which "men who plan beyond tomorrow" like to drink.

Sam has been active all day, immensely active, playing a part in dozens of impersonal cycles of behavior. He has brushed scores of 'corporate personalities,' but has entered into intimate relations with no single human being. The people he has met are idler-gears like himself meshed into systems of transmission, far too distracted to examine any one of the cycles in which they are engaged. Throughout the day Sam is on the go, implicated in this task and that,—but does he, in a psychological sense, *participate* in what he is doing? Although constantly *task-involved*, is he ever really *ego-involved?*

Now this problem is familiar to all of us, and one of the most significant developments of the past decade is its entrance into both industrial and social psychology. The way the problem has been formulated by industrial psychologists is roughly this:

The individual's desire for personal status is apparently insatiable. Whether we say that he longs for *prestige*, for *self-respect, autonomy*, or *self-regard*, a dynamic factor of this order is apparently the strongest of his drives. Perhaps it is an elementary organismic principle as Angyal (7) and Goldstein (19) would have it; perhaps it is rather a distillation of more primitive biological drives with social competitiveness somehow added to the brew. For our purposes it does not matter.

What the industrial psychologist has discovered is that when the work-situation in which the individual finds himself realistically engages the status-seeking motive, when the individual is busily engaged in using his talents, understanding his work, and having pleasant social relations with foreman and fellow-worker, then he is, as the saying goes, 'identified' with his job. He likes his work; he is absorbed in it; he is productive. In short, in McGregor's

terms he is industrially *active;* that is to say, he is participant (28).

When, on the other hand, the situation is such that the status-motive has no chance of gearing itself into the external cycles of events, when the individual goes through motions that he does not find meaningful, when he does not really participate, then come rebellion against authority, complaints, griping, gossip, rumor, scape-goating, disaffection of all sorts. The job-satisfaction is low. In McGregor's terms under such circumstances the individual is not active; he is industrially *reactive*.

In the armed forces, in federal employment, in school systems, the same principle holds. Ordinarily those at the top find that they have sufficient comprehension, sufficient responsibility, and sufficient personal status. *They* are not the ones who gripe and gossip. It is the lower-downs who indulge in tendency-wit against the brass hats, who complain, who go AWOL, become inert, or gang up against a scapegoat. When in actual combat, all the energies and training, all the personal responsibility of which a soldier is capable, are called upon, then egos are engaged for all they are worth. Men are active; they have no time to be reactive; nor have they reason to be.

Accepting this analysis as correct the problem before us is whether the immense amount of reactivity shown in business offices and factories, in federal bureaus, in schools, can be reduced, as it is when men at the front are using all their talents and are participating to the full in life-and-death combat.

We are learning some of the conditions in which reactivity does decline. Friendly, unaffected social relations are the most indispensable condition. Patronizing hand-outs and wage-incentive systems alone do not succeed. Opportunities for consultation on personal problems are, somewhat surprisingly, found to be important. And as members of this Society have shown, group decision, open discussion, and the retraining of leaders in accordance with democratic standards yield remarkable results. One of Lewin's discoveries in this connection is especially revealing. People who dislike a certain food are resistant to pressure put upon them in the form of persuasion and request; but when the individual himself as member of a group votes, after discussion, to alter his food-habits, his eagerness to reach this goal is independent of his personal like or dislike (25). In other words, a person ceases to be reactive and contrary in respect to a desirable course of conduct only when he himself has had a hand in declaring that course of conduct to be desirable.

Such findings add up to the simple proposition that people must have a hand in saving themselves; they cannot and will not be saved from the outside.

In insisting that participation depends upon ego-involvement, it would be a mistake if we were to assume that we are dealing with a wholly self-centered and parasitic ego that demands unlimited status, and power for the individual himself (33). Often, indeed, the ego is clamorous, jealous, possessive and cantankerous. But this is true chiefly when it is forced to be *reactive* against constant threats and deprivations. We all know of 'power-people' who cannot, as we say, 'submerge their egos.' The trouble comes, I suspect, not because their egos are unsubmerged, but because they are still reactive toward some outer or inner features of the situation which are causing conflicts and insecurity. Reactive egos tend to perceive their neighbors and associates as threats rather than as collaborators.

But for the most part people who are participant in coöperative activity are just as much satisfied when a teammate solves a common problem as when they themselves solve it (26). Your tensions can be relieved by my work, and my tensions by your work, provided we are co-participants. Whatever our egos were like originally, they are now for the most part socially regenerate. Selfish gratifications give way to coöperative satisfaction when the ego-boundaries are enlarged.

Nowadays we hear it said by our own colleagues that Americans will never participate in a postwar world union unless it is shown clearly to be to their self-interest to do so. Undoubtedly the statement is true, but self-interest is highly extensible. A revealing study by Lt. Leighton·conducted at a Japanese relocation center makes this point clear (23).

When the Japanese were asked to pick cotton in nearby ranches to help save the crop, very few responded. The reason was that they were expected to donate all wages above $16.00 a month to a community trust fund, to be used for the common good.

There was as yet insufficient community feeling; the over-all trust fund seemed too big, too distant, too uncertain. All that happened was endless argument for and against the trust fund, while the cotton stood in the fields.

At this point the schools asked to be allowed to go picking and to use the money for school improvements. This request was granted, and soon church groups, recreational societies and other community units showed themselves eager to go on the same basis; and the project was a success.

What we learn from this study is that self-interest may not extend to include an object so remote and impersonal as a community trust fund, but may readily embrace school improvements, church and recreational centers. For most people there is plenty of ego-relevance to be found in teamwork provided the composition of the team and its identity of interest are clearly understood.

Americans will endorse international coöperation in the future (as they do at the present moment) provided they continue to see its relevance to their own extended egos, and provided they feel that in some way they themselves are participating in the decisions and activities entailed.

Nearly everyone will bear testimony to the superiority of satisfaction that comes from successful teamwork as contrasted to solitary achievement. Membership in a group that has successfully braved dangers and surmounted obstacles together is a membership that is ego-involved, and the egos in question are not parasitic but are socialized.

An important by-product of participation, as I am using the term, is the reduction of stereotypes. Sam's mind we can be sure was a clutter of false stereotypes concerning the Dairy company, the transportation system, the abstract corporation for which he works, concerning economic laws, federal regulation, to say nothing of the tabloid conceptions begotten in Hollywood and by advertisers. Had he really participated in his employment his notions of 'the Company,' of surpluses, of labor unions would have become realistic. In recent years for some of us a job in Washington has happily shattered our previous stereotypes concerning sovereignty, bureaucracy, and other alleged attributes of 'the government.' One of the favorable results of the war will be the fact that men who have shared a common destiny, participating together in bombing crews, in life-and-death assaults, will at last be freed from their tabloid assumptions regarding the nature of Jews, Negroes, Catholics, and other American minorities.

IV. Participant Democracy

At the time of a presidential election we know that only about three in every five eligible voters go to the polls. At primary time the ratio is more likely to be one in every four. Yet voting is the irreducible minimum of participation in political democracy. People who do not vote at least once in four years are totally non-participant; those who vote only in a presidential election—these comprise at least a third of all voters— are scarcely better off. And if we wished to complicate matters we might ask whether those who go to the polls are really participating with the deeper layers of personality, or whether their voting is, so to speak, a peripheral activity instigated perhaps by fanfare or by local bosses. It would not be hard to prove that participation in political affairs, as well as in industrial, educational, and religious life, is rare. In this respect most people resemble Citizen Sam.

Two contemporary social psychologists have concerned themselves deeply with this problem. They see that increasingly since the days of the industrial revolution individuals have found themselves in the grip of immense forces whose workings they have no power of comprehending, much less influencing. One of the writers, John Dewey, states the problem in this way:

"The ramification of the issues before the public is so wide and intricate, the technical matters involved are so specialized, the details are so many and so shifting, that the public cannot for any length of time identify and hold itself. It is not that there is no public, no large body of persons having a common interest in the consequences of social transactions. There is too much public, a public too diffused and scattered and too intricate in composition" (15, p. 137).

Dewey has spent many years seeking remedies for this situation. Chiefly he has laid emphasis upon the need for face-to-face association, for evolving democratic methods within school and neighborhood so that citizens may obtain in their nerves and muscles the basic experience of relating their activities in matters of common concern. Some political writers, e.g., Mary P. Follett (16), have held that the solution lies in reconstituting political groups on a small enough scale so that each citizen may meet face-to-face with other members of a geographical or occupational group, electing representatives who will in turn deal face-to-face with other representatives. Though the town may no longer be the best unit for operation the spirit of the town-meeting is thus to a degree recaptured. "Democracy," says Dewey, "must begin at home and its home is the neighborly community" (15, p. 213).

Central to Dewey's solution also is freedom of publicity. To obstruct or restrict publicity is to limit and distort public opinion. The control of broadcasting and of the press by big advertisers is an initial source of distortion. Other groups need freer ventilation for their views, in order to reduce rigidity, hostility, and reactivity.

The second social psychologist, F. H. Allport, states the problem rather differently. He asks how an individual enmeshed within innumerable cycles of activity all imposed upon him from without can retain his integrity as a person? Like Sam, he finds himself a cog in countless corporate machines. State, county, federal governmental systems affect him, as do economic cycles, the impersonal systems known as private enterprise, conscription in wartime, social security; so too city transportation, milk production and delivery, consumption, housing, banking. But he does not affect them. How can he?

F. H. Allport points to an inherent contradiction that seems to lie in Dewey's position (1, Ch. 5). The latter hopes that the individual will participate in every public that his own interests create in common with others. That is to say, Sam should join with others who are affected by the same municipal, banking, transporting, feeding, housing cycles and work out common problems. But Sam would be a member of hundreds of segmental types of public. And in dashing from one 'common interest' meeting to another, he would not find his interests as an individual truly fulfilled by being partially included in multiple groups. He would still be a puppet of many systems. As complexities increase under modern conditions, total inclusion of the personality in specialized publics becomes increasingly difficult to achieve.

Like Dewey, F. H. Allport has given various suggestions for the solution of the problem, but chiefly his emphasis has been upon the creation of a scientific spirit in the common man encouraging him to call into question the corporate fictions, the sanctity of the economic cycles, which, unthinkingly, he takes for granted. By questioning the transcendental reality commonly ascribed to nationhood, to 'consumer competition,' to institutional fictions, and by substituting direct experience with the materials affecting his life, the individual may himself eventually work out a measure of integrity and wholeness within himself (2).

Both Dewey and F. H. Allport seem to agree that the only alternative to a keener analysis of the behavioral environment and more active participation in reshaping it, is to give way progressively to outer authority, to uniformity, to discipline, and dependence upon the leader. This battlefield exists here and now within each of us. The answer to growing complexity in the social sphere is renewed efforts at participation by each one of us, or else a progressive decline of inert and unquestioning masses, submitting to government by an élite which will have little regard for the ultimate interest of the common man.

Now, drawing together the threads of this problem, we are confronted with the following facts:

1. Since the industrial revolution there has been increasing difficulty on the part of the ordinary citizen in comprehending and affecting the forces which control his destiny.
2. Potentially the individual is a member of many, many publics, defined as groups of people having a common interest, for example, as voters, motorists, veterans, employers, consumers, co-religionists.
3. No public includes all of an individual's interests.

To these facts we add our earlier conclusions, namely, that

4. Activity alone is not participation. Most of our fellow citizens spin as cogs in many systems without engaging their own egos even in those activities of most vital concern to them.
5. When the ego is not effectively engaged the individual becomes reactive. He lives a life of ugly protest, finding outlets in complaints, strikes, above all in scapegoating; in this condition he is ripe prey for a demagogue whose whole purpose is to focus and exploit the aggressive outbursts of non-participating egos.

V. Toward a Solution

It is risky indeed to suggest in a few words the solution of such an immense social problem. Certainly it will require the combined efforts of educators,

statesmen, and scientists to rescue the common man from his predicament.

But from our preceding discussion one line of thought stands out as particularly helpful.

Is it not true that all of us find coercive demands upon our motor systems imposed by the corporate cycles in which we move, generally *without* serious frustration resulting? Speaking for myself, only the outer layers of my personality are engaged in my capacity as automobile owner, insurance holder, Blue Cross member, consumer of clothing, patron of the IRT. Perhaps, you say, I should be more interested in these cycles, but I reply one must choose, and other things are more important to me. In this age of specialization all of us are willing to delegate expert functions to experts. We simply cannot be bothered about the innumerable technical aspects of living that are not our specialty. To be sure, in matters of broad political or ethical policy-making the story is different; we cannot so easily avoid responsibility. Political reforms making possible good schools, recreation, and health are presumably the concern of all people. National policy in securing a lasting peace is a matter of great moment for each one of us. But even among these broad social and political issues I find some that excite me more than others.

What I am saying is that I cannot share Dewey's dismay at our failure to create innumerable self-conscious publics wherever there are common interests. In the first place, these publics need operate only on the broadest policy-forming level; and, in the second place, a relatively few members of a group can often serve adequately as representatives of others who are like-minded. I do not mean that a few public spirited citizens should do all the work. There should be wider distribution of responsibility. But my point is that talents differ. *What warms one ego chills another.*

Now assuming that the major fields of activity open to all normal people are the economic, the educational, recreational, political, religious and domestic, we might assert that a healthy ego should find true participation in all of them. Or allowing one blind spot to the bachelor, to the constitutional hater of sports or of politics, to the agnostic, there is still need for a balanced diet of participation in, say, five fields.

Against some such norm we might test our present situation. Do we find Citizen Sam truly participating in some *one* political undertaking; in some *one* of his economic contacts (preferably, of course, in his job where he spends most of his time); is he really involved in *some* religious, educational, recreational pursuits, and in family affairs? If we find that he is not actively involved in all of these areas of participation, we may, as I say, grant him a blind spot or two. *But unless he is in some areas ego-engaged and participant his life is crippled and his existence a blemish on democracy.*

In brief, it is neither possible nor desirable that all of our activities and contacts in our complex social order should penetrate beneath the surface of our personalities. But unless we try deliberately and persistently to affect our destinies at certain points, especially where broad political policies are concerned, and in some of the other representative areas of our life, we are not democratic personalities, we have no balance or wholeness, and society undergoes proportionate stultification.

VI. New Directions for Social Psychology

Returning to our starting point, my contention is that the earlier emphasis of American psychology on motor activity as such is now changing into an emphasis upon ego-involved participation. As time goes on it will mark increasingly the essential differences that exist between movement initiated at the surface level and at the deeper levels of personality (3). To do so will not be to abandon our dependence on the social climate in which we work. Quite the contrary: at last the genius of American psychology will be brought into line with the century of the common man (17).

What concretely are the roles that psychologists will play in this process? At least half a dozen can already be fairly well defined:

1. To those who serve in some consulting or guidance capacity Citizen Sam will come as a client. He will have this symptom or that—perhaps resentment, depression, bewilderment, or apathy. Among college students, a certain unpublished study suggests that 20 per cent are apathetic, complaining that they have no values whatever to live by. It calls for great therapeutic skill to lead such clients to commit themselves unreservedly to something. I have suggested that a balanced personality needs deep-rooted participation in all or most of the six spheres of value: the political, economic, recreational, religious, cultural-scientific, and domestic. But commitments cannot be too comprehensive. It is not politics or economics as a whole that evokes participation, but merely some one limited and well-defined issue in the total sphere. The democratic personality needs to influence *some* but not all of the factors that influence him in representative fields of his activity.

2. The consultant may go one step further. Sam should feel not only that he is a citizen participating at crucial points in common activities, but he should be oriented as well toward the inner crises that will occur, for example, in middle age when vitality recedes,

when his furious activity can no longer be sustained, when he faces old age and death itself. Sam, if I may put it in this way, needs to find that metaphors and images are more important ultimately than motor gyrations. In other words, the consulting psychologist has responsibility for encouraging subjective richness in personality. For in the broader sense participation extends beyond the days when active citizenship is possible. The ego needs to be wholesomely attached to life even after efficiency of action declines.

3. Industrial psychologists and group workers have already found a rewarding line of work in educating management, foremen, and employees in respect to the conditions that increase efficiency through participation in the job. The same type of effort is also yielding returns in other directions—especially in recreational and educational enterprises.

4. I would call attention specifically to the forum movement in this country which is one of the symptoms of the common man's awakening. Problems of group discussion lie at the very core of social psychology, and we shall do well to seize the opportunity now offered for investigation and social action in this field. I suggest that public opinion polls be geared to these neighborhood discussion meetings. Opinion recorded cold on a front porch is likely to be different and less enlightened than that recorded after a hour's participation in a people's policy forum.

5. As teachers, both in college and in adult centers, we have a job to do in encouraging the participation of the public in the progress of science itself. The layman now finds it impossible to keep pace with science. Dazed by the benefits of radio, auto, airplane and vitamins, all of which regulate his life, he stands on the sidelines and cheers as the procession of science goes by. He

has little real contact with the material from which his life is fashioned and little understanding. Exhibitions, demonstrations, and simplified experiments will help him understand (2). But the layman needs even more; he needs to know how to control the applications of science. While bestowing upon him many blessings, science has also given its bounty to tyrants and to the self-appointed élite, with the result of fabulous fortunes for the few, slums and squalor for the many, violent wars and suffering beyond endurance. The common man has not chosen these consequences. He was never consulted, was never participant in guiding the applications of science.

It would not be difficult to expand this list of services that psychology can provide in leading the common man into more effective participation during the democratic renaissance that lies ahead. The fact that so many of us have had active war experience guarantees that devices and techniques, as well as the requisite purpose, are available for this work.

Before listing my sixth and last suggestion, may I digress for a moment to call attention to the present training that psychologists are obtaining as participants?

VII. PSYCHOLOGISTS AS PARTICIPANTS

The Office of Psychological Personnel tells us that within the current year, approximately one-quarter of the 4500 psychologists listed are in the armed forces (64 per cent if we count only male psychologists between 18 and 38); another quarter works full or part time for the federal government or war agencies (27). Impressive as these figures are they do not include many others who are closely linked to the common effort through unreported community work and personal sacrifice. On the other hand, to be sure, some nominally engaged in war work may be mere idler-gears accomplishing little. Though they spin in the total chain their egos are not engaged. For the most part, however, the involvement is authentic and the experience gratifying.

One wonders what the youthful portion of the profession will do with their training. Some have lost their taste for academic life and will remain in 'practical' work. Among those who return to teach we can anticipate that the content and form of their instruction will be affected by their experiences. One of our ablest young social psychologists writes me that he intends, if it can be arranged, to teach six months in the year and spend the other six in an advertising business where social psychology is put into practice. In doing so he is not forsaking science; quite the contrary: he knows that only by observing the *installation* of psychological science can its facts be separated from its fantasies.

What the war has done for the majority of social psychologists is to provide them with a direction for future work, a direction that will not be lost in our generation. Committed to advancing democracy, we have found tools to work with, specialties that we mean to continue to use. There are polling, content analysis, group decision, leadership training, devices for alleviating minority tensions, and many other useful techniques.

There are also negative lessons we have learned. One of these has impressed me constantly since the excited summer of 1940. I dare say we have all had the experience of seeing plans manufactured too rapidly. Most of the blue-prints we drew up have become waste paper. Quick and alert minds meet in a committee; good rapport is established; solutions are rapidly designed at the verbal level. They are plausible solutions, and often seem much better than the policies and practices

that eventuate under the auspices of less expert groups. An example of what I mean is the 500 page blue-print prepared by the Committee for National Morale early in 1941 for a Federal Morale Service. It seemed like a more adequate plan than the stammering series of arrangements that followed, the OFF, COI, OSS, OWI. But obviously the blue-print was not geared to political realities. How many other plans fail because they are not suitable to the existing situation?

Granted that plans of men, like those of mice, 'gang aft agley,' should the plans of social scientists suffer as large a proportion of casualties as they do? There are plans for community work, plans for international coöperation, plans for reorganization of a faculty, for postwar rehabilitation, for this and for that. My impression is that the plans devised by social psychologists are unusually fluent, plausible, and reflect a high 'verbal factor.' But for the most part these good intentions fail in action. Our thoughts leap heavenward; our muscles remain below. Conceding that intellectual leaders should often point to goals above present probabilities of attainment, that they should be didactic, imaginative, still the mortality rate of their plans in these times of crisis is too high.

There are many occasions when an academic social psychologist evolves a bright idea, does the exploratory work, obtains rather convincing results on a limited scale, and then finds himself blocked in getting his ideas used. His participation is excellent up to a point, but it falls short of application—which means it falls very short indeed. The final chapter to the sad story is sometimes that his ego ceases to be active, and becomes reactive. He feels frustrated, becomes critical, bites at the brass hats, the Foundations, and lapses into apathy.

The roots of his difficulty are probably three in number. (1) Though he has sensed a need, no responsible organization has signified its intention to use his results. He has proceeded without adequate coöperation and guidance. (2) He has not learned to write simple, convincing, action-compelling reports of his research. (3) He is too much of a solipsist, unable to realize that because results are fascinating and significant to him, they will not appeal to men who make policies and initiate action unless these men too are worried about the problem in question, and unless the results reach them at the right *time* and in a clear *way*.

A social psychologist must not expect people to applaud his neat study because it is a neat study. Public policy will never mesh itself into the tempo of the laboratory or into the style of our technical journals. To be effective social psychology must go 100 per cent of the way in meeting the demands of policy-forming agencies in respect to the content, the style, and the timing of its work. It is sad to note that our profession, by and large, is not adept at the task of installation, whether in government bureaus, industry, or the community.

There are, of course, striking individual exceptions. In these fortunate cases the psychologist becomes effective because of his ability to combine in his own person the functions of both 'fact finder' and 'operator' (6, 31).

VIII. CONCLUSION

My final point is a plea that in future theoretical and systematic writing social psychologists give due consideration to the historical trend I have outlined. Reduced to the briefest possible statement it is this:

Half a century ago psychologists characteristically ascribed to the personality certain governing agencies: the will, the soul, the self, the moral sentiments, or some other ruling faculty. Subsequent emphasis upon the motor processes, especially in America, resulted in a kind of entropy for personality. Being deprived of its self-policing functions personality seemed to dissolve into endless cycles of motor activity controlled by stimulus or by habit. Like a taxicab its successive excursions had little relation to one another. Then gradually some principles of self-regulation returned to psychology, a bit timidly and not too clearly, under the guise of 'integration,' 'vigilance,' 'homeostasis.'

'Ego-functions' too were introduced to provide for a re-centering of personality with an increase in its stability. Ego-functions, as I have shown elsewhere, are of many kinds, and the ego is susceptible of many definitions (3).

Perhaps the most important distinction concerns reactive ego-functions which are resistant, contrary, clamorous, as opposed to active ego-functions which find full expression in participant activity. When participating the individual discovers that his occupational manipulations grow meaningful; his community contacts are understood and appreciated. He becomes interested in shaping many of the events that control his life.

Participation, as opposed to peripheral motor activity, sinks a shaft into the inner-subjective regions of the personality. It taps central values. Thus in studying participation the psychologist has an approach to the complete person.

Random movement, derived from the sensori-motor layer of the personality, has too long been our paradigm for the behavior of man. It fails to draw the essential distinction between aimless activity and participation. The concept of random movement denies dignity to human nature; the concept of participation confers dignity. As American psychology increasingly studies the conditions of participation it will elevate its conception of human nature, an event, we can be sure, that will at last gratify the man in the street.

In focusing upon problems of participation social psychology will also be advancing democracy, for, as Dewey has shown, the task of obtaining from the common man participation in matters affecting his own destiny is the central problem of democracy.

Skills learned by at least half our profession during this war are well-designed to carry out this purpose. Psychologists can employ them in diverse ways as consultants, group workers, personnel executives, teachers, writers, and community leaders. And in following this road psychologists as individuals will find their own salvation, for—common men that they are—they will discover that they too are participating in the march of democracy.

REFERENCES

1. ALLPORT, F. H. Institutional behavior Chapel Hill: University Press, 1933.
2. ——. The scientific spirit and the common man. Proc. Conf. on Sci. Spirit & Dem. Faith, New York: 2 West 64th St., 1944.
3. ALLPORT, G. W. The ego in contemporary psychology. PSYCHOL. REV., 1943, 50, 451–478.
4. ——. Dewey's individual and social psychology. Chap. 9 in The philosophy of John Dewey (Ed. by P. A. Schilpp). Evanston: Northwestern Univ. Press, 1939.
5. ——. Restoring morale in occupied countries. Publ. Opin. Quart., 1943, 7, 606–617.
6. ——, & VELTFORT, H. R. Social psychology and the civilian war effort. SPSSI Bull., J. soc. Psychol., 1943, 18, 165–233.
7. ANGYAL, A. Foundations for a science of personality. New York: Commonwealth Fund, 1941.
8. BAIR, J. H. Development of voluntary

control. PSYCHOL. REV., 1901, 8, 474–510.
9. BILLS, A. G. The psychology of efficiency. New York: Harper & Bros., 1943.
10. BOHNENGEL, C. An evaluation of psychobiologic factors in the reëducation phase of the Kenny treatment for infantile paralysis. Psychosomat. Med., 1944, 6, 82–87.
11. DEWEY, J. Psychology as philosophic method. Berkeley: University Press, 1899.
12. ——. Human nature and conduct. New York: Holt & Co., 1922.
13. ——. The need for social psychology. PSYCHOL. REV., 1917, 24, 266–277.
14. ——. Democracy and education. New York: Macmillan, 1919.
15. ——. The public and its problems. New York: Holt & Co., 1927.
16. FOLLETT, M. P. Creative experience. New York: Longmans, Green & Co., 1924.
17. FRIEDRICH, C. J. The role and the position of the common man. Amer. J. Sociol., 1944, 69, 421–429.
18. GATES, A. I. Recitation as a factor in memorizing. Arch. of Psychol., 1917, 6, No. 40.
19. GOLDSTEIN, K. Human nature in the light of psychopathology. Cambridge: Harvard Univ. Press, 1940.
20. HAGGARD, E. A., & ROSE, R. J. Some effects of mental set and active participation in the conditioning of the autokinetic phenomenon. J. exp. Psychol., 1944, 34, 45–59.
21. KÖHLER, W. Max Wertheimer: 1880–1943. PSYCHOL. REV., 1944, 51, 143–146.
22. KLEIN, D. B. Mental hygiene. New York: Henry Holt, 1944.
23. LEIGHTON, A. H. et al. The psychiatric approach in problems of community management. Amer. J. Psychiat., 1943, 100, 328–333.
24. LEWIN, K. The special case of Germany. Publ. Opin. Quart., 1943, 7, 555–566.
25. ——. The dynamics of group action. Educ. Leadership, 1944, 1, 195–200.
26. LEWIS, H. B. An experimental study of the role of the ego in work. I. The role of the ego in coöperative work. J. exp. Psychol., 1944, 34, 113–126.
27. MARQUIS, D. G. The mobilization of psychologists for war service. Psychol. Bull., 1944, 41, 469–473.
28. McGREGOR, D. Conditions of effective leadership in the industrial organization. J. consult. Psychol., 1944, 8, 55–63.
29. ROGERS, C. R. Counseling and psycho-

therapy. Boston: Houghton Mifflin, 1942.

30. ROYCE, J. *Race questions, provincialism, and other American problems.* New York: Macmillan Co., 1908.

31. SCHMEIDLER, G. R., & ALLPORT, G. W. Social psychology and the civilian war effort: May 1943–May 1944. SPSSI Bull., *J. soc. Psychol.*, 1944, 20, 145–173.

32. SPRANGER, E. *Kultur und Erziehung.* Leipzig: Quelle & Meyer, 1923.

33. SPOERL, H. D. Toward a knowledge of the soul. *The New Phil.*, 1944, 47, 71–81.

34. WYATT, F., & TEUBER, H. L. German psychology under the Nazi system—1933–1940. PSYCHOL. REV., 1944, 51, 229–247.

GENETICISM *vs* EGO-STRUCTURE IN THEORIES OF PERSONALITY

Reprinted from *British Journal of Educational Psychology*, **XVI**, June 1946, 57-68.

I.—INTRODUCTION.

UNTIL very recent years modern theories of personality have suffered from an overemphasis upon genetic determinants of conduct. Instincts, early habits, and the autochthonous Id between them have fashioned an account of motivation that is essentially archaic. The resulting theories fail to deal adequately with the *contemporary* character of human motives, neglecting especially the variety, individuality, and intentionality that are the earmarks of adult purposes.

Because I believe these statements to be true I have accepted the editor's kind invitation to participate in the present symposium, and likewise his suggestion that I might care to dip back into the preceding symposium of this JOURNAL which dealt with the portentous question, ' Is the Doctrine of Instincts Dead ? ' As I see it the same fundamental issues underlie both series of papers.

In the earlier symposium various authors dealt generously with my own views on motivation.[1] In all cases I find their expositions lucid and fair, and their criticisms trenchant and helpful. Mr. Burt, the strongest champion of instincts and the least persuaded by recent attacks upon the doctrine, is understandably a sharp, but eminently just, critic of the theory of ' functional autonomy.' Before discussing Mr. Burt's arguments may we take a brief glance backward in order to see just where, in 1946, theories of personality seem to stand ?

II.—PERSPECTIVE.

Prior to the last two decades nearly all of the important influences upon modern psychological theory stressed the importance of constitutional, instinctive, or early developmental factors. The ' New Psychology ' began in the late Nineteenth Century with lingering traces of phrenology, and sought in brain localisation to discover some unchanging determinants of behaviour in constitutional make-up. But it drew its main strength from Darwin's demonstration of the continuity of species. To Morgan, Loeb, McDougall, James, Thorndike and many others it was self-evident that the instincts of animals continued in the human species to be the prime movers. When the day of behaviourism dawned, reflexes and drives replaced instincts, without (as many critics have correctly argued) changing the essential emphasis upon innate motivation.

[1] P. E. VERNON, this *Journal*, 1942, Vol. 12, 1-9 ; T. H. PEAR, this *Journal*, 1942, Vol. 12, 139-147 ; C. BURT, this *Journal*, 1943, Vol. 13, 1-15. Mr. Pear has also presented a digest of my views in his paper ' Are there Human Instincts ? ' *Bulletin of the John Rylands Library*, 1942, Vol. 27, No. 1.

Then came the conditioned reflex. In essence this doctrine is as nativistic as is McDougall's conception of instincts. Both views allow for an extension of stimuli that will arouse an original unconditioned dynamism. A behaviourist who holds that high morale or firm ideological conviction in an adult represents a conditioning of security responses that originated, perhaps, in prolonged breast-feeding, is arguing that the hunger-drive and sucking reflexes underlie to-day's mature conduct. The argument is like McDougall's. The latter would say that high morale reflects a well-developed sentiment of self-regard, which in turn is sustained by a blend of instinctive energies, chiefly self-assertion and submission. For my part, I find it far easier to understand McDougall's conception of the channelling of instinctive energies at the successive stages of development than to imagine what dynamism is supposed to underlie contemporary motivation in terms of conditioned drives. The behaviourist traces the fear of furry objects to the infant's startle at the barking of a dog. But such conditioning, we know, lasts only a short time unless reinforced. Why do we find so much timidity and anxiety in adults without reinforcement through the unconditioned startle mechanism? Forced to choose, I should certainly elect McDougall's explanation in terms of a channelled and fixated instinct of fear.

The essential triviality of conditioning as a formula to account for persistent motives (other than prepotent reflexes or viscerogenic drives) led many early behaviourists into Freudianism. Like McDougall, Freud had a reservoir of energy to draw upon (Hormé, Libido), though Freud's instincts were less differentiated and less numerous than McDougall's. Everyone knows that Freud ascribed motivation to the Id, and said ' the structure of the Id never changes.' By insistence upon the unchanging character of the Id, Freud presented us with another archaic conception of motivation that is at once fatalistic, blind, and inescapably infantile.

By stressing, in addition, early repressions and fixations—which give the slant to the individual style of life—Freud brought on another phase of geneticism in modern psychology. Think of the vast literature accumulated in recent years to warn us that infant security, infant overdependence, sibling jealousy, and toilet training give a set to personality that can scarcely be abrogated by later experience. Psychoanalysts (both Freudian and others), behaviourists, and child psychologists of all sorts, seem agreed on the importance of early habit-formations. They view habits not only as ' second nature ' but even, according to one enthusiast, as ' the whole of human nature.'

The instinct doctrine of the McDougallian variety, as I have said, is more acceptable than the crude theories of ' concatenated reflexes ' which when appropriately conditioned are supposed to account for all behaviour. The latter theory is totally unable to provide any intelligible conception of the *present* causation of behaviour. Conditioning, as I have said, requires reinforcement (to prevent extinction), and what native sources of energy, pray tell, are called upon to reinforce the motives of patriotism, the sense of duty, or a passion for book-collecting? McDougall can at least call upon the lasting energies of the parental instinct, self-assertion, and submission to account for such complex and evolved interests. Yet the remoteness of these postulated McDougallian energies from the concrete structure of contemporary motives is a troublesome matter. It is not with McDougall's concept of purpose that one can quarrel, but only with the pre-ordained, eternal, and abstractly conceived character of the purposes proposed by him.

After the decline of phrenology, the geneticism of constitutional endowment had less influence than the geneticism of instincts, conditioning, and early fixation. Yet in recent years one marks the resurgence of constitutionalism in the work of Kretschmer, and still more recently, of Sheldon.[1] The mild merits of this approach may be appreciated even if we are forced to reject its excessive claims.

To summarise : Psychoanalysis, behaviourism, hormic psychology, constitutional psychology, and the preoccupations of child psychologists, all favour a backward emphasis. They regard motives, say at the age of fifty, as elaborated, conditioned, sublimated, or otherwise modified, editions of instincts, drives, or of an Id whose structure ' never changes.' One might as well say that the pianistic dexterity of Myra Hess is an elaboration and extension of her original grasp-reflex. Granted that there is a continuous evolution of her manual dexterity from the days when the grasp reflex was her only digital stock in trade, is the energy that sustains her skill the aboriginal energy of the grasp ? The grasp-reflex served one function in her life ; musical dexterity a wholly different function. *Historical continuity does not mean functional continuity.*

Although geneticism in one form or another has clearly dominated most modern theories of personality, it has not held exclusive sway. There is, for instance, the mathematical approach. This, surely, takes a cross-sectional view, attempting to determine the principal patterns (traits, factors, syndromes) that colour a life at the moment the anaylsis is made. Geneticism is not over-emphasised by the mathematical psychologists. But would it not be fair to say that factorists in general show very little interest in the theoretical problem of motivation ? Factorial work is infrequently applied to orectic qualities, and where it is applied the nature of the resulting units is unclear.· Though contemporaneous in its emphasis, the conception of factors, like that of instincts, seems to me remote from the specifically goal-directed behaviour of a concretely motivated individual.

Somewhere in the past twenty-five years a new orientation began to appear. The past began to lose its appeal to certain theorists, and the present and the future correspondingly to gain. Gestalt psychology illustrates the trend. To advocate ' insight ' and ' belongingness ' is to advocate current, and even momentary, dynamisms. The discovery of the motivational character of persistence in interrupted tasks, and of other closure-activities, led to an emphasis upon the immediate situation. The Field-theory of Lewin, with its topological representation, makes it almost impossible to include genetic factors in the representation of field forces. Again, a rebirth of introspective studies brought in the ' feel ' of motives as parts of the self. Koffka began to speak of the ' ego ' as a region of the personality having to do with states of tension and self-reference which are so characteristic of motivated behaviour.[2] There is virtually nothing in the writings of Köhler, Koffka, Lewin, and others of the Gestalt persuasion that would suggest that what we do to-day is a necessary product of unchanging Id, eternal instincts, or early conditioning. Belongingness, the field, the ego, closure, are the characteristic motivational concepts.

Furthermore, a shift has definitely occurred in psychoanalysis. Currently, psychoanalysts are inclined to ascribe much more *momentum* to the ego than did Freud. Elsewhere I have commented on this development.[3] I will only illustrate it here by a quotation from Heinz Hartmann, who writes :

[1] W. H. Sheldon, *The Varieties of Human Physique*, 1940, and *The Varieties of Human Temperament*, 1942. (New York and London : Harper and Bros.)

[2] K. Koffka, *Principles of Gestalt Psychology*, 1935.

[3] ' The Ego in Contemporary Psychology,' *Psychological Review*, 1943, Vol. 50. 451-478.

adaptation to reality—which includes mastery of it—proceeds to a large extent from the ego and in particular from that part of the ego which is free from conflict ; and it is directed by the organised structure of ego-functions (such as intelligence, perception, etc.) which exist in their own right and have an independent effect upon the solution of conflicts.[1]

Outside psychoanalytic circles the powerful therapeutic movement, called ' non-directive therapy, is gaining ground with a distinctly anti-genetic platform. The patient is allowed to re-structure and re-plan his life, with as little or as much reference to past motives and influences as he himself feels to be relevant. It turns out that he, unlike the geneticist, is normally interested more in the future than in the past. Indeed, if we pause to think about it, any personal problem has an *effective* relation only to one's future, since it is in the future that all problems must be solved. The ego in taking command projects itself forward into the future, and recasts its motives largely in terms of intentions and plans.

III.—Ego-structure.

Few writers on war-neuroses or morale have been able to avoid using the concept of the ego. Writings dealing with theory, like those dealing with therapy, have re-introduced the very term which long ago fell into disuse. Its period of desuetude, incidentally, coincided fairly with the supremacy of geneticism in psychology.

Over and over in the past five years we have read of the ' firm ego-structure ' and the ' weak ego-structure.' The former, it is often said, resists fear whether immediate or repressed ; the latter succumbs to the traumatic conditions of battle.[2] Prisoners best able to resist the tortures of a concentration camp are those who have firm purposes and strong political convictions.[3]

One may ask, ' Did not Freud acknowledge ego-strength in the ability of a patient to hold his impulses in check and to steer a safe course between, the tyrannies of the Id, the Superego, and the harsh environment ? ' He did, but he also claimed that the ego has no energy of its own ; it is passive. It is the mere rider on the horse.

War studies show indisputably, I think, that far from being a passive agent, the ego is a dynamic process of great positive power. What but a motivational structure of immense momentum *could* handle the fatigue, fear, anger, apathies, disgust and conflicts aroused by war-time conditions ? Morale ascribed to ego-strength is not passive, it is a matter of powerful, dominant interests, capable of promoting activity so vital that lesser, segmental, impulsive activities are inhibited effectively and without serious repression.

A few passages from one of the recent books on psychiatric combat casualties indicate that the primary purpose of treatment is to restore normal ego-strength (i.e., normal and current interests and motives) in order to offset the ravages of segmental and impulsive fears and conflicts. I quote from Grinker and Spiegel.[4]

> As the ego becomes stronger, the therapist demands increasing independence and activity from the patient (p. 94).

A soldier (or civilian) is abnormal if he cannot proceed according to the

[1] ' Ich-psychologie und Anpassungsproblem,' *Intern. J. Psychoanal.*, 1940, Vol. 21, 214-216.

[2] J. DOLLARD, *Fear in Battle*, 1943. (New Haven : Institute of Human Relations.)

[3] B. BETTELHEIM, ' Individual and Mass Behaviour in Extreme Situations,' *Journal of Abnormal and Social Psychology*, 1943, Vol. 38, 417-452.

[4] R. R. GRINKER and J. P. SPIEGEL, *War Neuroses*. 1945.

lights of his ordinary, daily motivation. Horribly shocked, he becomes fearful, uncontrollably hostile, or apathetic. In any case he finds that he cannot absorb and handle the traumatic conditions. The provocation is great :

> It is difficult to describe the intensity of these hostile feelings before which the ego recoils and withdraws (p. 96).

Yet, normally, even these incredibly severe strains are handled adequately by an ego which is so firmly attached to its present projects that it refuses to regress or to split. And even when the break comes the physician knows there is a *norm* for each person to which he must be helped to return. After treatment the physician writes with gratification :

> The ego now seemed in full control (p. 105).

It is an interesting discovery that unless the ego resumes control soon, there is special danger of malignant repression, chronicity and rigidity. In terms of theory, this finding seems to mean that the ordinary pattern of interests that comprise morale, normally balances the life, but if denied dominance for too long a time, may yield permanently to regressive mechanisms. Hence it was up to the war psychiatrist, in the words of Grinker and Spiegel, to ' put pressure on the ego ' to make it assume control as soon as possible (p. 113).

Now, is this ego-structure—emphasised so much during war-time—a mere matter of instincts or early training or constitutional make-up ? That it may be historically conditioned by these factors no one can deny. We have no data to show, for example, whether an optimum degree of security in early life correlates with ego-strength. We do know that war-time writers have emphasised rather the rôle of *group-identification* and of *ideological conviction*. Both make for resistance to combat neurosis. Both reflect the high importance of *contemporary* loyalty. The man who wants *now* to stand with his outfit, to support his commander, to win a victory for democracy, is the man who stands the strain. Even if it turns out that this man was also characteristically breast fed, secure within the family, father-identified, or (in physique) meso-morphic, the psychiatrist finds that ordinarily he cannot appeal to, or employ these factors. He invokes only the most recent, adult, motivational structure. Childhood security may or may not be a factor in resistance to breakdowns (I suspect the correlation is low), but ideological strength and loyalty are factors of proven importance. Grinker and Spiegel write :

> If the soldier could feel that the pain, the sacrifices, and death were dedicated to a larger purpose with which he was identified, his capacity to ward off anxiety would thereby increase (p. 119).

To summarise this section, I have argued that recent evidence and recent trends in theorising have drawn attention away from the ' remote control ' of instincts, early conditioning, and habit formation ; and have pointed to the decisive rôle that the present ego-structure plays in directing human conduct.

IV.—FUNCTIONAL AUTONOMY.

' Functional autonomy ' is merely a shorthand phrase designed to call attention to some of the considerations I have just reviewed. It marks a shift of emphasis in the theory of motivation from geneticism in its various forms to the present ' go ' of interests that contemporaneously initiate and sustain behaviour.

It is not necessary for me to repeat the lines of evidence I have adduced.[1] They include such diverse considerations as the high correlation between skills

---

[1] Especially in *Personality : A Psychological Interpretation*, 1937, Chapter 7. See also ' Motivation in Personality : Reply to Mr. Bertocci,' *Psychological Review*, 1940, Vol. 47, 533-554 ; ' The Psychology of Participation,' *Psychological Review*, 1945, Vol. 53, 117-132.

and interests ; ' conative perseveration,' which refers to the haunting urgency with which tasks accepted by the individual are held in mind until completed ; the obvious dynamism of sentiments which are so individual in character that they bear no ascertainable resemblance to underlying instincts. Patriotism, stamp collecting, religion, *are themselves* the needs of the person—often his *ultimate* needs.

In my earlier exposition, however, there was one defect which I have tried subsequently to remedy.[1] My picture of derived motives led some readers to accuse me of allowing for a complete anarchy among motives. A motive (I seemed to be saying) might evolve, severing itself from its root-forms, and lead a wholly independent existence, devoid not only of historical ties, but of relationship to anything else in the personality. Such a loose conception is, of course, untenable. Though motives may often be (and, I argue usually are) independent of their origins, they are obviously not independent of the contemporary ego-structure in which they are now embedded.

Let us take an example. During the war a fairly large number of illiterates turned up in the American draft. The men, negro and white, were sent to special training centres where, with the aid of ingenious methods of instruction, most of them acquired within eight weeks a degree of literacy equal to that of four years of schooling.[2] They were highly motivated to learn, the chief incentives being (1) to correspond by post with the folks at home ; (2) to avoid the shame of using an X in place of a signature when others were watching, e.g., in signing the payroll ; (3) to do what was expected of them. When these men left the special training unit, and especially after they were discharged from the army and returned home, these three incentives were completely eliminated. Yet many of the men, perhaps most, had acquired an interest in reading. The interest was a product of the three motives, but since all three became demonstrably inactive, its subsequent existence must have been autonomous of these origins. The interest in reading, we conclude, brought them *new* sources of satisfaction. It played a revised rôle in the economy of their lives. Not merely is the ego-structure somehow served by this new skill and interest, but the skill and interest are now a current *part* of the ego-structure itself. Literate interests now help to *constitute* the personality.

To say that some instinct must be sustaining the new literate interests is to invoke a remote abstraction. Even McDougall, I suspect, would grant that the interest in this case is merely an aspect of the generalized sentiment of self-regard. If so, his statement of the matter would be close to my assertion that the new interest now finds itself part of the essential economy of the ego. With the sentiment of self-regard the doctrine of functional autonomy has much in common. The chief difference is that the latter sees no necessity for invoking the energies of underlying, hypothetical instincts. An ego-structure (sentiment of self-regard) is quite sufficient to keep an individual on the move. It seems to me unnecessary to seek its dynamics, as McDougall does, in the twin and abstract propensities of self-assertion and submission.[3]

V.—MR. BURT'S CRITICISMS.

Mr. Burt no doubt is still unpersuaded. I hope, however, that he may find my relating of functional autonomy to ego-structure somewhat more to his liking than the earlier version of the theory that he has criticised.

[1] *Psychological Review*, 1940, Vol. 47, 533-554.
[2] P. WITTY, ' New Evidence on the Learning Ability of the Negro,' *Journal of Abnormal and Social Psychology*, 1945, Vol. 40, 401-404.
[3] W. McDOUGALL, *Outline of Psychology*, 1923, p. 428.

His objections are all closely reasoned and well taken. I shall list them :
(1) Mr. Burt starts with the evolutionary argument :
When the ape evolved into man, what freak of innumerable mutations abruptly obliterated all traces of the instinctive mechanisms, handed down throughout the ages through all our mammalian ancestors ? Surely the ' higher brain centres ' have been merely ' superposed ' upon the lower, not suddenly inserted into their place.[1]

Phylogenetic continuity, I grant, may not be denied. The appetites of men and animals are much alike and rest on identifiable mechanisms that are closely similar. Yet these drives and these mechanisms comprise only a fraction of the vast motivational structure of human beings. Do we not know that the ' superposed ' higher brain centres in many ways regulate and dominate the lower ? Since this is so, we have a right to expect a shift in emphasis and dominance of mechanisms as well as phylogenetic continuity.

(2) He argues that drives are, after all, instincts and, when admitted, surrender the argument to the instinctivist. A serious misunderstanding exists. Drives are primarily viscerogenic states of excess or deficit stimulation—what Woodworth calls conditions of ' tissue change.' Besides the obvious pressures that arise in body cavities, blood stream and autonomic organs, we may include among drives, the irritation of proprioceptors and sensitivity (with a customarily adient response) to external stimulation. This equipment and the attendant initial responses, let us concede, are innate, unlearned, universal. They account for the ' absolutely dependable motives ' which Klineberg finds to be the possession of every individual in every culture. What is more, their physiological foundations are clearly identifiable.[2]

If instincts are defined in this way, then, of course, instincts exist. But the doctrine of instinct generally smacks more of the ' pull ' and less of the push.' It stresses the innateness of the *purpose*, and most lists of instincts exceed by far the range of physiologically-grounded drives or ' absolutely dependable motives ' that can be universally established.

Though drives are instinctive, they don't carry us far with our theory of motivation. They account well enough for the maintenance of physiological equilibrium and for initial and vague contacts with the environment. They furnish a fairly adequate picture of *infant* motivation, but a poor picture of adult motivation. Lust and the ' activity drive,' even hunger and elimination, are so regulated by acquired habits and sentiments that they do not for long operate as Simon-pure drives but soon take their place as dynamisms in the ego-structure. The drive-force becomes fused with, and modified by, psychogenic accretions. Tastes often become inseparable from the drives.

Mr. Burt dislikes this view because he fears, to take the example of hunger, that we should :

have to abandon any notion that there might be a biological purpose in eating, because there must be as many purposes in eating as there are types of objects to eat (*op. cit.* p. 5).

I see no real difficulty here. We can take the purpose of eating at its face value, and acknowledge that hunger and other ' absolutely dependable ' drives have a uniform significance for all creatures, without denying the obvious fact that differing tastes, modes and manners, do affect the operation of the drive, and form (from the individual's point of view) a highly integral part of the total motive.

[1] This *Journal*, 1943, Vol. 13, p. 3.
[2] O. KLINEBERG, *Social Psychology*, 1940, p. 160 f.

To admit drives in the sense here defined is not to open the door to such alleged instincts as acquisitiveness, gregariousness, appeal. parental behaviour, submission, or self-assertion. These concepts are not in the least comparable with drives, but are abstractions from learned human behaviour and ascribed without evidence to the primordial Hormé.

(3) My critic wonders, naturally enough, why some acquired patterns of activity and interest become autonomous and others not. Since he doubts that a satisfactory answer is forthcoming he suggests that any adult interest is, after all, secretly fed by the springs of some instinct or other. He believes that the concept of ' instinctive reinforcement ' is more helpful to the teacher or therapist than the theory of ' functional autonomy,' for in the former case one invokes deeper dynamisms and escapes the perils of rationalisation (*op cit*. p.10).

In attempting to answer the question why some acquired motivational patterns become autonomous and others do not, I shall have to invoke the concept of ego-structure.   To take an example, one individual finds that the cause of labour, let us say, becomes his passion. Everything connected with the rights of the working man takes on an urgency. Another individual, with perhaps similar upbringing, remains cool and indifferent to the issue. My first comment on this puzzling problem is that *all* theories of motivation fail to provide a full solution.   Instinctive reinforcement applied to the riddle is certainly vague. Even assuming that in one case a bit of the parental instinct is involved and in the other case not, the question of *why* this selectivity exists between two individuals remains unanswered. The conditioned reflex theory likewise finds no solution, at least so far as the *present* absorbing rôle of the interest in the personality is concerned. Freud might invoke in the case of the labour enthusiast reaction-formation (say, a repressed hatred of the father), but he would have difficulty in either proving his point or changing the man's interest when this alleged ' reinforcement ' is uncovered.

From the point of view of functional autonomy I would approach the problem by saying that this mature interest, like all others, is now a part of the individual's style of life ; it *is* his present ego-structure. It brings satisfactions, not to this or that instinct, but to his total blended sytem of current sentiments, aspirations and intentions. It is not a channelling of the parental instinct, nor is it sublimated aggression (at least not necessarily) ; it is *he*. There are, of course, genetic reasons why he evolved this particular zeal, but now the ego-structure, in its present economy, consists of a blending of this powerful motive with many others which are not sharply separated from it. Taken together they comprise the congruent pattern of the current ego-structure in which all dynamism resides.

(4) Mr. Burt worries lest by taking motives at their face value I open the door to all the misleading rationalisations of which every skilled psychologist is properly wary. Yes, there may be such a danger. We cannot always believe an individual's account of his own motives, for people have differing degree of insight into their own ego-structures. What is more, in many cases there *are* infantile reasons for a current intense or obsessive interest. Undoubtedly *some* labour-fanatics are merely expressing a neurosis.   But without careful diagnosis we cannot tell, and there is certainly no reason to assume that *every* current interest is merely a mask for hidden instincts or early repressions.

I am inclined to believe that Mr. Burt will agree with me on this point, for he too seems impatient with the archaisms of psychoanalysis, and with the everlasting recounting of stories of early life in place of establishing a current, cross-sectional analysis of motives (*op. cit.*, p. 11).

Mr. Burt, I believe, is on solid ground when he says that in individuals who have partly regressed or never risen above infantile level, one may look for the dominance of repressed innate tendencies.   Whatever these genetic tendencies are, it is chiefly in neurotic or infantile personalities that they hold sway (*op. cit.*, p. 14).   Normal people are not prisoners of the past.

I would applaud Mr. Burt's concluding statement in the symposium, ' Is the Doctrine of Instincts Dead ? '

In studying the more normal adult the assessment of acquired interests, motives, and ideals may be far more important ; here indeed, lies a field of research which, as is generally conceded, has been sadly neglected hitherto (*op. cit.*, p. 14).

(5) Mr. Burt wonders why habits-on-the-make should show so much functional autonomy, and why habits already formed recede in motivational force.   He would think that the opposite condition ought to prevail (*op. cit.*, p.11).   My answer is that in learning a habit (driving a car, for example) the individual is distinctly *ego-involved*.   He has accepted the task, its accomplishment is important to his self-esteem.   While this condition lasts there is a peculiar urgency about acquiring the skill.   When once acquired it is relegated to the level of instrumentality and is called upon in the service of some more ego-involved motive.

(6) Mr. Burt's sharpest shafts, like those of other critics, are reserved for my contention that an unavoidable corollary of the doctrine of functional autonomy is the resulting uniqueness of mature patterns of motives.   Since this is a question of some moment I shall devote the following section to it.

VI.—The uniqueness of personality.

In the preceding contribution to this Symposium, Mr. Maberly presented persuasively the clinical point of view, and stressed the importance of evaluating any bit of behaviour in the light of the total individual's motivational pattern as it exists at any given moment.   Anyone who deals with personality in the concrete is likely to agree cordially with Mr. Maberly's emphasis.   Mr. Burt apparently agrees with it, for in the present Symposium he too writes of the need for obtaining a synoptic view of the individual with the aid of ' imaginative insight.'   Yet at the same time Mr. Burt seems to land himself in something of a contradiction, for he affirms that it is the bounden duty of the scientist to occupy himself with *universals*, even in dealing with personality.

Let us look first at Mr. Burt's definition of personality, which I find to be excellent.   For him personality is the :

entire system of relatively permanent tendencies, both physical and mental, that are distinctive of a given individual, and determine his characteristic adjustments to his material and social surroundings.[1]

Words like ' distinctive ' and ' characteristic ' should make Mr. Burt very chary of exalting universals to the extent that he does. · He would have us study also the ego-sentiment, including the ego-ideal which, he admits, is a qualitative matter, and can best be ' stated primarily in words.

All this evidence of Mr. Burt's sensitivity to the never-repeated patterns of personality does not, however, quite fit with his scientific conscience as expressed in his plans for the assessment of personality.   He wants to find a small number of independent factors, like ' key-elements in chemistry.'   He favours the

[1] This *Journal*, 1945, Vol. 15, p. 107.   In all essential features this definition is identical with my own ; *Personality : A Psychological Interpretation*, p. 48.

factorial approach. That he can easily reconcile this methodological preference with his own definition of personality I doubt.

Mr. Burt presents the dilemma, and his preference, in the following analogy: Every man's face is absolutely unique ; yet should we argue that the ' common ' features—the eyes, the nose, the mouth—are not ' true ' features at all ? We may agree that a list of facial measurements would be no substitute for a photographic reproduction of an individual face in all its concrete completeness. But equally a set of portraits, however life-like, could not by themselves suffice for scientific purposes.[1]

It is true that every man has a nose, two eyes, a mouth and chin, and that these are common and measurable features. It is also true that no method of measuring emotional expression of the face has been evolved, let alone the permanent configuration or set that *is* the person's face.

Yet, Burt insists, ' psychology, as a science, deals with universals, not with particulars.' I am tempted to reply, tartly perhaps but also justly, that as long as psychology deals only with universals and not with particulars, it won't deal with much—least of all human personality. Burt's definition of psychology as science is far more rigid and narrow that his definition of personality. The consequence can only be that psychology as science is frankly and woefully inadequate to deal with personality, its natural subject-matter. I wonder whether Mr. Burt really wants to accept this conclusion, to which he has inevitably committed himself.

Psychology, it seems to me, must be equipped to deal with the *whole* of personality, defined as Mr. Burt has defined it. What is ' distinctive,' what is characteristic ' must be included. The doctrine of functional autonomy helps to express the uniqueness of motives which confer distinctiveness to a person's characteristic adjustments.

Our difficulty here lies in the cultish conception of science which bedevils most of us simply because of the incalculable prestige of those disciplines that have dealt so successfully with *inanimate* nature. If we no longer rivet our attention to their methods (so well adapted to their subject-matter but not to ours), and if we ask what the *aims* of science are, the dilemma can be resolved. Science aims to achieve powers of understanding, prediction and control above the level of unaided common sense. From this point of view it becomes apparent that only by taking adequate account of the individual's total pattern of life can we achieve the *aims* of science. Knowledge of general laws (including, let me repeat, the law of functional autonomy), quantitative assessments, and correlational procedures, are all helpful ; but with this conceptual (nomothetic) knowledge must be blended a shrewd diagnosis of trends within an individual, an ability to transcend the isolated common variables that are obtained from current measuring devices, and an ability to estimate the ego-structure of the individual. Unless such idiographic (particular) knowledge is fused with nomothetic (universal) knowledge we shall not achieve the *aims* of science however closely we imitate the methods of the natural and mathematical sciences.[2]

In the opening article in this Symposium Mr. Burt gives a conspectus of methods and principles involved in assessing personality. The test-situations he has employed in his own original investigations are life-like and situational.

[1] This *Journal*, 1943, Vol. 13, p. 7.
[2] The point stated here so briefly I have argued more fully in the following publications: 'The Use of Personal Documents in Psychological Science,' *Bulletin of the Social Science Research Council* (230, Park Ave., New York City), 1942 ; ' The Psychologist's Frame of Reference,' *Psychological Bulletin*, 1940, Vol. 37, 1-28 ; ' Personalistic Psychology as Science : A Reply,' *Psychological Review*, 1946, Vol. 54.

He believes that the proper manner of treating the data obtained is by correlational techniques. He advocates the use of such variables as have been established by previous correlational studies. Examples are (a) a general factor of emotionality ; (b) certain bipolar dimensions including introversion, cheerfulness, social responsiveness, and their opposites ; (c) special factors or needs resembling McDougall's catalogue of instincts ; (d) a measure of integration or consistency in the individual's life. He would then add (in order to repair the ravages of analysis) a ' synoptic character sketch ' which ' calls quite as much for the imaginative insight of the artist as for the tabulated measurement of the scientist.'[1]

I deplore his sharp separation of the ' insights of the artist ' and the measurements of the scientist.' Cannot a psychology of personality in the future do a better job of understanding, prediction, and control by fusing these two modes of knowledge ? Burt comes close to doing so himself in his matching studies. He demonstrates what other studies have done—that the more information derived from many sources that goes into a sketch, the more easily is it matched with a criterion. It is not, however, the mere array of psychometric scores that makes matching successful, it is rather the *patterning* of the variables which turns the trick.[2] In short, successful scientific prediction requires knowledge of the essential relations which comprise the unique ego-structure of the individual.

The reader will ask, ' But how concretely would you overcome the opposition between "science" and "art," and bring them into a single psychological discipline ? ' Though the question cannot be answered fully for many, many years I may give one illustration. Mr. Burt seeks a few 'key-qualities.' He thinks their discovery will enhance our powers of predicting an individual's behaviour So do I. But the ' key-qualities ' we seek must, I submit, be *personal* and *not* universal. Each life seems to have a limited number of themes, a handful of ascertainable values and directions—true ' key-qualities.' In finding them there is an opportunity for analysis and even quantification (on a strictly intra-individual level) ; it is not merely by ' imaginative insight ' that we make our study of unique and individual traits. Life-history techniques, matching, personal structure analysis, i.e., the search for personal but not universal factors, and other methods are already available ; others will be invented. If the reader reflects on this point he will understand my insistence that the study of personality lies entirely within the scope of *psychological science*, and not—as Mr. Burt seems to say—half in science and half in art.

Exclusive reliance on factorial dimensions is not acceptable, for two reasons. (1) The resulting factors are completely limited by the specific kinds of tests that happened to be thrown into the matrix. One cannot draw out more than one puts in. (2) The resulting factors are a peculiar hash of the personalities of all participants, and do not necessarily represent the living ego-structure of any single participant.

In making these criticisms I am not repudiating the use of nomothetic factors, nor of test-scales, ratings and dimensions. More of my own research and writing has been devoted to this type of approach to personality than to any other. The resulting ' common traits,' I find, have utility for *comparative* purposes, for approximations to the modes of adjustment that similarly constituted individuals in similarly constituted societies can be expected to acquire, and for the training of the young psychologists in respect to a common

[1] This *Journal*, 1945, Vol. 15, pp. 110f.
[2] Cf. N. Polansky, ' How Shall a Life-History be Written ? ' *Character and Personality*, 1941, 9, 188-207.

language and in the use of analytical procedures. What I argue is that as psychologists we must include many other procedures in our store of tools, and must acknowledge the roughness and inadequacy of our universal dimensions. Thereby shall we enhance our own ability to understand, predict, and control. By learning to handle the individuality of motives and the uniqueness of personality we shall become better scientists, not worse.

VII.—SUMMARY.

Until recently various forms of geneticism have dominated theories of personality. There has been an over-emphasis upon constitutionalism, instincts, an unchanging Id, and childhood habits. Within the past few years, especially under the impact of the war, a desirable shift of emphasis to the contemporary motivational structure of the ego has occurred. One theory, in line with this modern trend of emphasis, is the doctrine of functional autonomy which holds that while the transformation of motives from infancy onward is gradual, it is none the less genuine. Just as we learn new skills, so also we learn new motives.

A consequence of this view, disturbing to those who define science rigidly as the study of universals, is that the motivational structure of adult lives is essentially unique. Egos have infinite variety. Methods are now developing that will enable psychology to catch up with and deal more adequately with this unassailable fact. The bifurcation of scientific and clinical psychology is false and undesirable, so too an over-sharp distinction between the methods of science and the methods of art.

Since Mr. Burt's views on personality are well-known, I have stated my own in comparison with his. As I see it, in many respects our views are substantially identical. My definition of personality agrees with his. Together we repudiate the theory that ' concatenated reflexes ' constitute personality. We both wish to study the total person, and regard the rubrics of abnormal psychology as inadequate to the task. We agree that goal-striving is the essence of personality, and that assessment is practicable and desirable. In yet other respects we likewise see eye to eye.

There are two chief differences. (1) In my opinion personality is a post-instinctive phenomenon, and therefore reliance upon McDougallian instincts leads us into an anachronistic conception of adult motivation. Though viscerogenic drives exist throughout life (usually in an overlaid fashion), the postulation of other instincts seems not only unnecessary but fits badly with the known facts concerning the contemporaneity and individuality of the ego-structure.

(2) Mr. Burt, I fear, sacrifices our chances of discovering in any concrete case the essential nature of the ego-structure by over-stating the case for nomothetic (chiefly correlational) methods. It seems to me improbable that a small number of uniform factors like ' key-elements in chemistry ' will account for the infinite variety of normal adult motivational patterns. I see more hope in the endeavour to find unique key factors (central traits) that animate an individual life. Common, i.e., comparable traits, whether called factors, dimensions, or what not, have a certain utility, but are at best rough approximations of what goes on in a given life, and must be used guardedly.

Instead of holding that the ' scientific ' study of personality demands the use of common variables exclusively, I argue that it is possible by broadening our theory and our procedures to avoid the sharp bifurcation of scientific and clinical psychology. Though less developed at the present time idiographic methods of study are basically more important—and are no less ' scientific '—than nomothetic methods

EFFECT: A SECONDARY PRINCIPLE OF LEARNING

Reprinted from *Psychological Review*, **53**, No. 6, November 1946, 335-347

So deftly and so incisively have Dr. Rice and Dr. Mowrer handled certain thorny problems of the law of effect that I hesitate to add my own comments lest in my efforts to clarify I may unintentionally becloud the issues that they have treated so ably.

The subject of this symposium, as all readers know, is baffling in its complexity and in its ramifications. The law of effect can scarcely be treated apart from the protean problem of learning as a whole, and this vast problem soon leads one into philosophical presuppositions which are as unavoidable as they are distasteful to most psychologists. Experiments in this area, though legion, are unfortunately not compelling so far as their theoretical interpretation is concerned.

In order to avoid as well as I can the pitfalls in the way, and to keep the discussion within the bounds set by the two preceding authors, I shall confine myself strictly to comment on the observations and interpretations offered by each of them. The reader will recognize that the discussion in this symposium is at a fairly high level of abstractness; only the broader issues are touched upon. Detailed reference to single experiments must, for the most part, be avoided lest our perspective on the problem as a whole be lost.

DR. RICE'S POSITION

Although the following summary of Dr. Rice's views is sketchy, it is, I trust, sufficiently accurate to remind us of the principal features of his trenchant argument (8).

In the past, says Dr. Rice, the law of effect has been inadequately formulated, yet in a revised form it may retain the central position accorded it in learning theory during recent years. If not actually the 'sole principle' of learning, it, along with the law of exercise, and a few other minor principles, may be considered virtually sufficient.

Its primary weakness has been the assertion, or at least the implication, that a specific response becomes set through the operation of a satisfying outcome. Such a picture is rigid and false. While something of this sort may seem to exist in animal behavior, it obviously does not apply to human reactions complicated by systems of evolved interests. For example, men who are self-assertive will seldom repeat successful acts but will seek new means to satisfy their mounting level of aspiration. Men who like novelty will deliberately shun a repetition of acts; so too will men who are set to solve new problems (since stereotyping of acts cannot contribute to new solutions).

In short, "the law cannot be upheld if it means that success or satisfaction necessarily enhances the tendency for either or both (a) the specific response sequence to be repeated, and/or (b) the particular, or even the specific, goal object to be chosen again." He agrees with my previous criticism that rigidly repetitive conduct is characteristic only of very young children, mental defectives, and compulsive neurotics (1). What adults normally do is to vary both goal and responses while holding only to the same general *kind* of response and selecting the same *kind* of goal that has brought good results in the past. The law seems to apply better to *similar* systems than to *identical* systems, at least in normal adults, and especially in those who are self-assertive, interested in novelty, or trying to solve a new problem.

Problem-solving is important. The reason men do not repeat endlessly their past success is that having succeeded, the specific problem and motive vanish. A student will not repeat a course in which he obtained an A, because he no longer has this problem to solve. When a new problem arises new determinants inevitably enter. All that success or satisfaction does is to confirm one's interest in the general range of problems (mathematical, amatory, professional).

Self-assertion, likewise, is important, for as a motive it keeps the person in a chosen channel of conduct (persistence) in spite of repeated failures. Though not succeeding (one meaning of 'effect') the person derives satisfaction (another meaning of 'effect') from his trying. For some people "to fail at a difficult task gives more satisfaction to the ego than to succeed at an easy one."

Granted that self-interest (ego-involvement) seriously alters the application of the law of effect as traditionally stated, it is none the less true that the law has a demonstrable influence upon the development of the ego itself. "Though the depth psychologists have given little explicit mention to the law of effect in dealing with such matters, their stress on the importance of satisfaction and frustrations, rewards and punishment, in character formation, suggests that the development of the ego itself may be subject to Thorndike's law." Punishment to the ego sometimes deadens it—as the ultimate brutalities of concentration camps occasionally succeeded in doing. Some form of reward is necessary to confirm an individual in his style of life and in his system of interests.

Novelty may bring satisfaction, and if it does so, it too will violate the rigid law of repetition-of-rewarded-response. Only non-recurring responses give satisfaction.

All in all, the validity of the law must depend "upon what is conceived to be satisfied or thwarted, and therefore reinforced or extinguished." Normally neither specific goals nor specific means are reinforced, but rather systems of interests become confirmed through experience of satisfaction.

New interests evolve from old (as, perhaps, an interest in poetry from an interest in sex), but this evolution of functionally autonomous motives is itself dependent upon the satisfactions that the *new* line of activity yields to the person.

Since it is often difficult to find rewards in the environment which would explain man's persistence in the face of apparent failure, or supply an evident reason why a given system of interests is so gratifying to the individual, we must invoke, with Thorndike, the concept of self-administered rewards—the O.K.—delivered by the person to his own conduct.

Whether such reinforcement is applied to an interest system and course of conduct as a whole, or whether there is some specific feature in the chain that is controlled by the law of effect is not known. Rice proposes the possibility that the 'core of the act' is symbolized for the individual in some way, and that the O.K. is directed to this core. In this manner the *purpose* behind an act can be rewarded (by the self or by others), rather than any overt sequence of responses. Rewarding the response is really less important than rewarding the purpose: "We show great flexibility in adapting our means to our ends, and we may change our goal-objects freely provided that the pursuit of them is expected to provide, somewhere in the

172

PSYCHOLOGICAL REVIEW, PAGE 337

process, those qualities or structures of the act to which satisfaction has adhered."

Through symbolic responses we may weave our approval back and forth between purpose and anticipation of response, and thus "as we are carrying out the successive phases of the act, we keep the symbolized purpose in mind, mull it over, and confirm it repeatedly; unswerving concentration on this purpose, as it begets auxiliary goals, is necessary to keep us going."

Confirming occurs continually along the way, so that it derives benefit from the 'gradient of reinforcement.' External reward is often slow to arrive or never occurs at all, but inner self-administered reward is immediate and therefore effective. Purpose and interests receive on the whole more reinforcement than do actual motor skills' and conduct patterns. Hence we should expect the law of effect to apply to interests and purposes more than to specific responses. In sub-rational learning, however, the gradient effect attaches to the reward of ultimate and penultimate responses (as experiments with animals show).

Rice admits that motivation must always be conceived as operating in the present, and that dissatisfaction rather than satisfaction is the crux of motivation. "The dynamic character of an act in progress . . . derives from an immediate dissatisfaction, ... But the interest as an enduring disposition . . . will be reinforced by repeated satisfaction. The law of effect, then, is a law of retention of interests or dispositions: it does not deal with the mechanism of the particular striving, except in so far as that is determined by past fixation or interest as one of its conditions."

Finally the operation of insight, understanding, belongingness, in learning may be explained provisionally in terms of the success that attends good solutions via the self-reward of symbols: "reinforcement may attach to the 'relevant' or 'required' features of the act."

Agreements with Dr. Rice. If my summary has been fair, I record my basic agreement with the position taken. I believe Dr. Rice is thinking in the right direction.

One feature deserves special commendation. Dr. Rice attempts, more pointedly than most authors, to account for the *refashioning* of motives. He believes the liberalized law of effect is indispensable for this purpose. Instead of assuming a rigidity of drives or instincts throughout life, he sees clearly that almost endless derivative motives must be themselves explained as products of learning. Though adult psychogenic motives are derivative they are in no sense *functionally* secondary. He holds therefore that new motives set up in their own right in proportion as satisfactions of some sort sustain them. Learning thus accounts for motives, not merely for skills and means.

Dr. Rice further spots clearly the defect in the concept of 'success.' It is certainly not objective success alone that helps to sustain a .motive. The only reward that is operative in many cases seems to be a purely subjective sense of satisfaction. A person who persists in a hopeless task by sheer grim determination, or perhaps from a sense of duty, probably derives some satisfaction from doing so, but no success. We note, however, that in such a case 'satisfaction' is a rather vague word, for along with subjective satisfaction we find plenty of painful, frustrating, punishment, whose effects somehow or other are assumed to be offset by an inner O.K.

I agree with Dr. Rice that the traditional statement of the law of effect seems to apply much better to children, imbeciles, and animals than to normal human adults. To the latter it applies badly, excepting in routine, 'blind' learning which is wholly peripheral to the central interests of a life.

I also agree that satisfaction plays *some* part in the development of central interests and purposes. An individual does mull over his purposes and plans and unless he approves of them (*i.e.*, rewards himself symbolically) he usually, in the long run, discards them.

If the law of effect can be held in this somewhat amorphous and plastic form, I favor it. But Dr. Rice, I feel, does not see fully how greatly he has attenuated the law, and how much he is forced to leave to other principles of learning. Dr. Mowrer, I believe, does see the consequences of this attenuation, and draws back into a far more conservative position, lest through conceding too much he discover that he has relegated the law to a secondary position in the economy of learning.

Problems unsolved by Dr. Rice. I should like next to call attention to certain aspects of learning (particularly the learning of motives) which elude the law of effect as Dr. Rice employs it.

He asks what can cause an individual to persist in a 'style of life.' And he answers, "Observation suggests that he does so because he has found satisfaction, actual or imaginative, from it." This statement is acceptable enough; but when we ask *why* does he derive satisfaction from it, we are again at sea. There must be formative influences (hereditary perhaps) that dispose some of us to find satisfactions from aesthetic, athletic, or humanitarian styles of life. The problem may seem to lie beyond the scope of the present discussion, yet it is really relevant. Manifestly we learn best that which fits our own style of life, but this style turns out to be determined by antecedent conditions more basic than satisfying experience. Hence effect cannot possibly be the *only* law of learning. At best it operates upon systems in part established for other reasons.

Dr. Rice admits the satisfaction that comes from varying one's performance, from non-repeated means-end solutions. He proposes that novelty itself is rewarded, but the old law of effect claims only that a "response is rewarded." How can it also claim that non-repetition of a response is rewarded? To do so would be to surrender completely the conception of a 'stamping in' process or of a 'retroflex arc.' Dr. Rice is clearly not following the classic conception of effect.

To account for learning by insight, Dr. Rice proposes that reinforcement attaches to the symbolized 'relevant' or 'required' features of an act. I am unable to follow his argument here, because insightful solutions must have occurred *before* they can yield reinforcement or satisfaction. I shall return to this problem, but mention it here to raise once more, and in a different way, the question whether satisfaction can be as basic a condition of learning as even Dr. Rice's moderate position would have us believe.

Dr. Mowrer's Position

First Dr. Mowrer wishes to re-establish the argument on familiar ground (7). He therefore takes pains to eliminate concepts which imply that new principles of learning may be needed. For him the *ego* is a matter of *interests*, interests a matter of *emotional arousal*, and emotional arousal a matter of *ordinary drives* whose tension when reduced gives rise to the operation of the law of effect. A bit hurriedly he makes this series of reductions so that 'ego-involved behavior' becomes redacted into the 'familiar drive mechanisms.' Back on familiar ground Dr. Mowrer then starts his argument proper. He believes that the law of effect provides us with "the firmest foundation on which to develop a truly adequate and comprehensive psychological theory."

His thesis is that "living organisms learn when, and only when, they solve a problem in the sense of reducing a tension, relieving a discomfort, deriving a satisfaction." This is the modern statement of the law of effect which Mowrer tenaciously defends.

Though his defense is tenacious, he realizes that many difficulties arise in the application of the law. For example, it does not tell what happens when both kinds of effects follow an act—when consequences are both rewarding and punishing, pleasurable and painful; it does not tell what happens when consequences vary in time, the effects being both immediate and remote. In such complex cases the effect must be mediated through symbolic processes of some type. The symbolic processes when well developed may be said to constitute the 'ego' and they often result in a *seeming* defiance of hedonism and the law of effect. Especially when integrative or ethical conduct is in question we find much apparent repudiation of pleasure-seeking. Yet ultimately the integrative or ethical aspects of ego-behavior are 'an outgrowth of the principles and processes of adjustment and hedonistic learning.'

There seem, then, to be no real exceptions to the proposition that "satisfaction is the cement that makes learning stick." And by a satisfaction Mowrer means pleasure and drive-reduction. This unrelenting allegiance to a hedonistic version of the law of effect reminds one of the original Thorndikean statement that "pleasure stamps in." Dr. Mowrer is orthodox; even more orthodox than Thorndike, for he has little use for the law of exercise, and even less for 'belongingness.'

One way to bring the psychology of learning and ego psychology together, Dr. Mowrer believes, is to admit "that 'interests' are secondary drives and that as such they can both motivate and reinforce behavior, in much the same fashion that primary drives do." Here Dr. Mowrer accepts Rice's demonstration that interests are a learned phenomenon (learned according to the law of effect) and they function to produce new learning.

In some connections Mowrer speaks of interests as 'cathexis,' in some as 'secondary drives,' but he much prefers to think of them as 'covert, emotional responses.' "This terminology allows us to see 'interests' as learned by past satisfaction in essentially the same way that other responses are learned." It seems to turn out, therefore, that interest-systems are nothing more than emotional responses, and thus introduce no new problems in learning.

Like Dr. Rice he endorses Thorndike's theory of self-administered rewards. In fact, it would not be possible to explain how a course of conduct, expecially of the ethical order, can be sustained, unless frequent self-administered accolades are involved.

Also like Dr. Rice he believes that the Gestalt principle of insight is to be explained by our OK'ing signs and symbols which are related to the reduction of tension or anticipated reduction of tension. The tension relieved may be secondary, and not necessarily dependent on a primary drive such as hunger. There is a constant appraising of hypotheses, censoring them and approving them along the way. Such manipulation of 'danger signals' and 'safety signals' helps us "dispel the mystery implicit in such concepts as the Gestaltists' 'goodness of figure' or Thorndike's 'belonging.'"

Satisfaction is derived in various ways; from reducing tension of a primary drive, from solving a problem, or from reducing a secondary drive. We must also admit secondary drives of a 'high level of generality' to account for the capacity of mature men and women to persist in the face of punishment. But they are not immune to the law of effect if we assume, as Rice does, that self-administered awards sustain these systems of interest.

Unsolved, to Dr. Mowrer's mind, is the riddle of response equivalence, "why living organisms do not immediately and permanently fixate upon whatever response or response-sequence has been found to lead to satisfaction, but instead continue to show a more or less behavior variability." The reason response-equivalence poses such a difficult problem seems to be that Dr. Mowrer does not really regard interests of a 'high level of generality' as true systems. If he did so equivalence would offer little difficulty (since the range of equivalence would define the degree of generality). He is clearly thinking of interests, at bottom, as a 'covert emotional response.' So long as he does not fully accept the existence of generalized autonomous interest-systems the riddle of equivalence inevitably troubles him.

Agreements with Dr. Mowrer. With Dr. Mowrer's purpose and intent I am in agreement. He wishes to find a sound, comprehensive, and adequate theory of learning. He is willing to consider open-mindedly all evidence, no matter how great a strain it may place on the law of effect. He does not insist upon holding blindly to the paradigm of animal learning even though he personally finds it rewarding and genuinely analogical with human learning. A monumental series of experiments conducted by him underlies his theories. He admits the attenuation that must come in learning theory when one considers the conflictful, symbolic, delayed, and ethical character of human conduct. Valiantly he strives to include these complex forms of learning into his

theory, and to make room for phenomena that have been hitherto neglected.

Up to a point I agree with him also on the importance of effect. In animals, young children, and in the relatively mechanical and blind learning of human adults the course of learning seems to follow fairly well the traditional statement of the law. And even in interested and ego-involved behavior I would not deny that satisfaction has *some* relation to acquisition of skills, knowledge, and new motives.

I agree also that ego-processes, whatever their nature, are not 'ultimate, unanalyzable, lawless' (Dr. Rice's terms). As Mowrer says, they develop gradually as one ascends the phylogenetic and ontogenetic scales.

Ego-Processes Are Unavoidable in Learning Theory

Dr. Mowrer's rapid reduction of ego-involved behavior to 'familiar drive mechanisms' seems to me invalid. His first step is acceptable enough, namely his insistence that the ego is not substantive, but merely a matter of process. But it is no *more* necessary to use 'ego' adjectivally than to use 'drive,' 'personality,' 'reward,' or 'intelligence' adjectivally. The ego is as valid and as necessary an intervening variable as an other. Experimental evidence shows this to be the case (1).

The second step in his reduction is much too hasty. Though ego-processes can, I agree, be considered equivalent to interests (Dr. Rice's definition in terms of a *system of interests* being acceptable), one cannot safely go further in the reduction. There is, I submit, something functionally irreducible about interest-systems, even though they are continually changing. Nor is it true, in my opinion, that interest is, as Dr. Mowrer says, a familiar term in systematic psychological literature. On the contrary, one of our greatest defects is our lack of consistent or adequate theory of interest. That interest is not the same as 'cathexis' I stoutly maintain, for interest is a motivational term (interest residing in the organism), whereas cathexis is the superficial doctrine that this or that object becomes attached to some permanent (and usually infantile) drive or instinct. The cathexis theory denies the authenticity of acquired psychogenic motives (that is to say, their functional autonomy).

Least satisfactory of all is Mowrer's reduction of ego-involvement to emotional arousal. Only *certain* emotional states are ego-involved. Literature on concentration camps proves the point over and over again. Frightful pain, terror of one's life, extreme hunger, may be perceived as 'not happening to me'; while a slap, a verbal insult, a trifling humiliation may cut to the quick, and affect the entire ego-structure of the individual. How often in recent years have wartime psychiatrists told us that strong egos handle the most intense emotional arousals, whereas weak egos are undone by trifling emotional arousals? Something here is playing a part besides mere emotional intensity.

Or consider the course of everyday life. When interest is high I find that I am learning smoothly and rapidly. At such times I certainly do not feel emotionally aroused, nor are the familiar drive mechanisms sensibly involved. Indeed when these drive mechanisms with their attendant emotions operate, then my learning is actually *interrupted,*—when, for instance, the needs for food, elimination, fresh air, or riddance from an annoying insect dominate my behavior. Drives are normally peripheral to my ego-interests, and however important they may have been for my infant learning, they seem now to impede rather than advance my adult learning.

I do not deny that some emotional arousals are ego-involved (anger, for instance, usually is). But the two states are by no means identical. Therefore, any law of learning based on 'reduction of emotional tension' does not necessarily apply without modification to learning that proceeds from ego-interests. To this subject I shall shortly return.

Neither Dr. Rice nor Dr. Mowrer denies the existence of ego-processes in some sense, though both wish to show that these processes are regulated by the law of effect. The picture they give for complex learning is like Thorndike's. *We* find *ourselves* confirming *our* purposes, symbolized in some way to *ourselves,* by administering to *ourselves* an O.K. In view of this welter of ego references it would indeed be ungracious to deny the ego some place in learning theory. We will, however, for present purposes pass over the epistemological dilemma into which even 'objective' psychologists inevitably fall, and limit ourselves to the role of the ego in Rice's sense of a 'system of interests.'

Take the case of interests that lead to grim persistence in spite of failure. No single response is rewarded, unless Dr. Mowrer is right in holding that the very core of self-esteem is itself some kind of symbolic response. But whether we regard the ego as a matter of specific symbolic cores (Mowrer) or as a system of interests (Rice), or as the sentiment of self-regard (McDougall), the fact remains that *it* (however defined) must be satisfied in order to maintain a course of conduct. No other responses need to be rewarded for learning to occur, excepting only the ego-response. This fact once more demonstrates that there is a special and selective part played in learning by ego-processes. No learning theory can do without them.

Again, as Dr. Rice points out, after

success or satisfaction we tend to adopt *similar* goals or *similar* acts in the future, but usually not both. If we retain our goal we vary the act (toward greater efficiency); if we retain the act it is usually in the service of an enhanced goal (as in the level of aspiration experiments). How can we explain this characteristic upward push in efficiency and goals unless we assume that the ego is playing some part over and beyond the repetition of a rewarded response? Dr. Rice correctly says that repetition of successful acts is ordinarily a mark of infantile, imbecilic or pathological behavior, rather than of intelligent adult activity. Blind repetition of rewarded response occurs only when the ego-structure is undeveloped or damaged.

The Question-begging Character of 'Satisfaction'

Both authors concede that in complex learning satisfaction often means nothing more than self-approval. We O.K. our own behavior. Or we find that a system of new interests is satisfying us. We are pleased with what we do and continue to do it (or something similar) because we are pleased. Does such reasoning carry us very far? We beg the question when we say that we do what we do because we are satisfied in doing it.

Dr. Mowrer hopes to avoid this circularity by holding fast to drive-reduction. Hence he defines satisfaction as 'the subjective consequence of solving a problem.' But why then, we ask, does one persist with unsolved problems? He would, I suppose, reply that we reward ourselves at each step for persisting. (If so, and if the law of effect were literally true, ought we not take the first step over and over again?) But the real difficulty here is that there is no independent evidence that we do

in fact reward ourselves. Introspectively considered the use of self-applause is so rare and so capricious that it cannot possibly sustain the heavy load that Mowrer, Rice and Thorndike are putting on it. In any case the danger of circularity is still present: we infer from our persistence that we are rewarded, simply because we persist. No independent criterion of reward or satisfaction exists.

The reef is the same one upon which all hedonism is wrecked. Man works (and learns), it is said, because of the pleasure attained. When we ask why a martyr goes to the stake, why a bomber makes suicide dives, why an anchorite forswears all earthly joys, why a member of the underground keeps silence in the face of torture, we are told that they are seeking pleasure —paradoxical though it seems. Insofar as Dr. Mowrer equates satisfaction with pleasure, he too falls into the same trap of *claiming*, without proof, that whatever a man does is *ipso facto* pleasure-seeking.

Nor does 'drive reduction' solve the problem. It is too easy to demonstrate that learning takes place when no drives have been reduced. Suppose while using a cleaning fluid I am careless with a match and an explosion follows, destroying my house and possessions. I shall certainly learn my lesson, but what drive has been reduced? Suppose I mispronounce a word in a public speech with the result that I am ridiculed, and suffer mounting shame and discomfort. Tension has been *created*, not reduced; *dissatisfaction* and not satisfaction has resulted; but in this sequence of events I shall surely learn the right pronunciation. True, I hope to avoid such suffering in the future, but there is *as yet* no drive reduction. In the year 1940 I read and learned the essential contents of *Mein Kampf* with increasing emotional tension. mounting discomfort, and acute dissatisfaction. Where was the law of effect?

These, and countless similar examples, contradict Dr. Mowrer's statement that "living organisms learn when and only when they solve a problem in the sense of reducing a tension, relieving a discomfort, deriving a satisfaction." If the examples I have just given can be manipulated to fit the hedonistic formula, then I maintain that the formula is so loose as to be worthless. In no intelligible sense in any of these cases was a tension reduced, a discomfort relieved, or a satisfaction derived.

CLASSICAL OBJECTIONS

Neither author alludes directly to the two standard objections to the law of effect: (1) that satisfaction, being both subjective and psychical, cannot legitimately intervene as a causal factor in refashioning neural states; and (2) that effect is a complete anachronism, since the attainment of satisfaction or pleasure *follows* after the crucial series of activities, and therefore cannot well work *backward* in time (especially when a long interval of time intervenes between act and effect).

It may be that the first of these venerable objections is met by an unexpressed assumption that satisfaction has some unknown physical basis which does the actual work in modifying the equally unknown physical basis of learning, so that interactionism need not be assumed. The second objection, Rice and Mowrer seem to answer through a somewhat tenuous reference to symbols. (What they would say in the case of non-symbolic learning I do not know.) Movements leading toward eventual success are accompanied by anticipations, which, being pleasant, invigorate, sustain, and reinforce the movements under way. Some such anticipatory process may well occur, but if so, it presupposes a vast amount

of foresight, intention, purpose, imagination and imagery. These presuppositions are so numerous that effect certainly cannot be said to be the sole or primary condition of learning. In order to operate it would require the ability to see relations, an intention to learn, foresight, and a sense of what signals are relevant and which irrelevant to the anticipated path to an imaged goal. There is a deal to learning besides the law of effect!

WHAT SATISFACTION DOES

Up to this point my comments have been chiefly negative. Yet I am as eager as Dr. Mowrer and Dr. Rice to discover and accord to satisfaction its rightful place in learning theory.

The evidence, as I read it, establishes two facts.

(1) It is easy to see that in animals, small children, mental defectives, and in some peripheral phases of adult human conduct, rewarded responses tend to be repeated. The bulk of experimental work on the law of effect has been done with animals, and for this reason the part played by reward in the fixation of response looms large (too large) on our theoretical horizon. Close examination of the experimental results reveals that even in these simplest instances of non-symbolic learning the repeated response varies within a narrow range. Even at its best, then, the law of effect works by approximation only.

(2) In less mechanical forms of learning, satisfaction recedes in importance. When invoked it tends to be a question-begging concept. In any case its operation is secondary to the operation of a variety of other conditions of learning. What seems to happen in normal human learning, beyond the infant stage, is that experiences of satisfaction serve as *indicators*, which, valuable as they are to the individual, are not dynamically decisive. If I am trying to be-

come a writer and am downcast by a rejection slip, I *may* thereupon cease the style of work that I was attempting. Or I *may* search the slip for encouragement between the lines, and thinking I have found it persist in my style, varying it for a better effect in the future. Knowledge of results is useful in telling me whether I am getting toward my goal. Good news tells me I am on the right road. Yet I *may* be so sure of myself (in my ego-structure) that I will persist in the face of bad news. To say that I am really 'satisfied' by bad news, or that I offset it by giving good news to myself, is dangerous reasoning. The rejection may be bitter to bear; my self-administered praise may be pallid and faint. Would it not be truer to say that in persisting I am refusing to use the indicators of pain and pleasure, and am treating 'these two impostors just the same'?

Satisfaction and dissatisfaction then are useful indicators, but according to the nature of my ego-structure I treat them in a variable manner. Having had a good meal at Restaurant X, I am likely to return when my hunger drive is uppermost. But having been highly satisfied with a score of 89 at golf, I risk failure by setting a goal of 85 for myself. Or, in carrying out some plan in which I meet a painful rebuff, I decide, conditions being what they are, that I cannot afford to take this cue but must persist in my conduct and risk repeated rebuffs. In all these cases there are other determinants at work beside the useful but not decisive indicator of effect.

I think Carr was essentially right in holding that the consequences of an act help us in the future to *perceive* the situation giving rise to the act in an altered way (5). Effect thus becomes *one* of the factors in the perceptual situation. This view, incidentally, helps us escape the paradox of the retroflex.

Satisfaction does not stamp in after the fact; it merely alters the determining situation when next it (or a similar situation) recurs.

Although Dr. Mowrer views all learning as a matter of S—R connections, he seems consistently to discount S and to magnify R. To his way of thinking an S is useful chiefly to 'trip' off a response. To my way of thinking the S (including external and internal pressures) is far more decisive.

EFFECT: A SECONDARY CONDITION OF LEARNING

In view of these many difficulties, I submit that the term 'law' is too flattering a designation to apply to the variable operation of consequences on behavior. A law should have greater and more uniform subsumptive power. The 'law of effect' is, of course, an entrenched habit of professional speech, but it would be far more accurate at the present time to speak of a *condition* rather than *law* of learning.

From the foregoing argument it appears that effect cannot be considered the primary condition of learning, certainly not its sole condition. As applied to complex forms of learning its weakness lies in its two ruinous ambiguities: *satisfaction*, as we have seen, is often a question-begging concept; and *symbols* (hopefully invoked to represent some hypothetical core-response which is somehow self-rewarded) are vague molecular constructs that taper off into a kind of aimless triviality so far as explanatory power is concerned.

To hold, as I do, that effect (as an indicator in the perceptual situation) constitutes a secondary condition of learning is, of course, to invite the natural question "What then are the primary conditions?" Since this query opens up the entire problem of learning with its crowded history of attempted solutions, it falls beyond the scope of the present discussion.

Yet we may hazard the opinion that an adequate learning theory will have to allow a prominent place to the following basic phenomena.

Typically a person learns when he is trying to relate himself to his environment, under the combined influence of his motives, the present requirements of the situation, active participation, and a knowledge of relevant facts, including a memory of his previous success and failure. In this process the role of any previous specific response (rewarded or unrewarded) is not decisive, but is only one determinant among many.

Occasionally, but not often, the process of relating oneself to the environment is so simple that only one segmental drive requires a reduction of tension (for example dust on the cornea leads ultimately to successful blinking or use of the handkerchief, and these responses under like circumstances tend to recur). In such conditions of low complexity, and in animal learning, where ego-structure is undeveloped or, for the occasion, is not engaged in the activity in question, the traditional statement of the law of effect applies fairly well.

One primary condition of learning, not reducible to effect, is the influence of motor activity and participation. Even simple motor involvement speeds up learning (6), but ego-involved participation speeds it up still more (2). There are other familiar conditions of learning which still resist various attempts to reduce them to effect, viz., recency, primacy, exercise, temporal contiguity (classical conditioning), and what Tolman calls 'sign-significance.' A certain amount of 'incidental learning' is likewise unaccounted for.

Further, before effect can be invoked as a principle of complex human learning, several *preconditions* must be assumed. In addition to the motive power of psychogenic interests, one must assume that organisms have a power of administering rewards through a self-conscious and reflective act; that they are able to imagine, foresee, and anticipate goals before they are reached; that they have 'faith' in imagined solutions; that they can test for relevance and fitness of a proposed act.

The assumption of so much rational equipment leads again into the problem of dynamics. It has never been successfully proved that complex learning may proceed without what Leibnitz called an 'active intellect.' In modern times this condition of learning has been represented under such terms as *Gestaltdrang, closure, curiosity, structuring, figure-ground, trace organization,* and *pursuit of meaning.* One thinks here too of Tolman's 'law of emphasis.' It seems impossible to write a comprehensive account of human learning without invoking intellectual dynamisms of this order. To my way of thinking, the interpretations of the law of effect offered by Rice and Mowrer *presuppose* them.

Above all, learning seems to follow the channels of acquired interests. Complex interests bear little or no resemblance to the 'familiar drive mechanisms,' even though they may originally have derived therefrom (3). It is indefensible to speak of them as 'secondary drives' unless the term secondary is used in a strictly chronological sense. Mr. X, let us say, has, in addition to his quota of primary segmental drives, a series of interests in his children's welfare, in fishing trips, in philately, in the cleaning and dyeing industry, and in Catholicism. He learns almost everything that crosses his path provided it has any perceived relevance to any of these interests.

Interest, in this sense, seems to operate almost like a sponge. Anything that has interest-relevance (= ego-relevance) is absorbed—subject, of course, to the limitations of fatigue, intellectual capacity, clear perception, and other similar conditions What is learned on the basis of this interest-relevance sometimes serves to reduce tension, but often has some other effect. Occasionally, for instance, it serves to increase tension, as when a pianist is memorizing a program for his concert début. But always the learning has some important relation to an interest. The only statement we seem able to make at present is that an interest causes learning which somewhere fits into the interest-structure.

It is true that, in the long run, continued punishment and dissatisfaction are likely to weaken or eliminate an interest system, just as the law of effect maintains. We have evidence, however, that often this result is brought about only at the price of destroying the entire ego-structure of the individual. In concentration camps it often took three to five years of uninterrupted punishment and pain to break down the desire of a person to 'remain the same' (4). In the short run, learning proceeds because it is relevant to an interest-system: it adds to knowledge, it differentiates items within the system, it broadens the range of equivalent stimuli, it does all sorts of things that tend to complete, to round out, or render the interest incisive. Pleasure attending a single response, or even concatenations of response, is not decisive.

Interests, of course, are not separate and unrelated systems. They interlock and comprise the structure of a personal life. The best designation for the resulting *pattern* of interests seems to be 'ego-structure.' Here is our reason for saying that ego-structure is a far more fundamental condition of learning than is the law of effect.

Yet, I repeat, satisfaction often enters into the process of learning as an indicator to the individual that his behavior is or is not appropriate to his own ego-structure. Dissatisfaction characteristically attends his failure to relate himself to his environment adequately; satisfaction accompanies some successful move or anticipated move. Yet it is common for the ego-structure to be so organized that these indicators are disregarded. Interests often persist in the face of continuous dissatisfaction and failure. If liberties are taken with the meaning of 'satisfaction' so that anything a person is doing is said to yield him satisfaction, then the term becomes so broad that it is question-begging, and loses its explanatory value.

In fine, effect is a useful indicator, sometimes playing a role in the total perceptual situation that guides the individual in the pursuit of his interests. But its role is contingent upon, and in this sense secondary to, the total psychological and environmental situation that prevails.

SUMMARY

The three authors in this symposium are unanimous in their desire to establish a learning theory fully adequate to the phenomena of complex human adult learning. They agree in seeing certain defects in the traditional formulations of the law of effect. They all mark, for instance, the fact that rigid repetition of successful responses practically never occurs, and that the law seems to work principally by a curious approximation, affecting 'similar' responses, 'equivalent responses' or a whole 'system' of behavior.

Dr. Rice believes that interests are the key to learning, but that they themselves are the product of past satisfaction or dissatisfaction. Dr. Mowrer believes that interests are re-

ducible to the familiar drive mechanisms and attendant symbolic core-re-
sponses. For the former author effect
is a primary law of learning, for the latter author, the sole law.

My own argument holds that the
vagueness that must result from ex-
tending the principle of satisfaction to
cover all phenomena of learning (at
the higher level of complexity) is such
as to disqualify it as a 'law.' At certain low levels of mechanical learning,
it may suffice; but at the adult human
level satisfaction is at best a *cue*, of
quite secondary importance, and often
disregarded. Its effectiveness depends
on other more important conditions of
learning. Of these the interests that
comprise the ego-structure of the individual are clearly dominant.

REFERENCES

1. ALLPORT, G. W. The ego in contemporary
   psychology. PSYCHOL. REV., 1943, 50,
   451–478.
2. ——. The psychology of participation.
   PSYCHOL. REV., 1945, 53, 117–132.
3. ——. Geneticism vs. ego-structure in
   theories of personality. *Brit. J. educ.
   Psychol.*, 1946. 16, 57–68.
4. BETTELHEIM, B. Individual and mass behavior in extreme situations. *J. abnorm.
   & soc. Psychol.*, 1943, 38, 417–452.
5. CARR, H. A. The law of effect: a round
   table discussion I. PSYCHOL. REV.,
   1938, 45, 191–199.
6. HAGGARD, E. A., & ROSE, R. J. Some effects of mental set and active participation in the conditioning of the autokinetic phenomenon. *J. Psychol.*, 1944,
   34, 45–49.
7. MOWRER, O. H. The law of effect and ego
   psychology. PSYCHOL. REV., 1946, 53,
   321–334.
8. RICE, P. B. The ego and the law of effect.
   PSYCHOL. REV., 1946, 53, 307–320.

PERSONALISTIC PSYCHOLOGY AS SCIENCE: A REPLY

Reprinted from *Psychological Review*, **53**, No. 2, March 1946, 132-135

In a recent number of this Journal Dr. E. B. Skaggs expresses his conviction that 'idiographic' knowledge does not deserve to be called 'scientific' (5). It would not be profitable to dispute this statement of semantic taste, for *science*—a 'purr word,' highly charged with positive affect—is at the present time peculiarly resistant to a dispassionate search for its most appropriate referent. And yet I cannot let Dr. Skaggs' confession of taste pass unnoticed because in stating his preferences he has unintentionally misrepresented some of my own views regarding the methods and theories suited to the study of personality.

He writes, "Now any system of personalistic psychology, such as that presented by Allport, where the effects of learning are stressed so heavily and where individual uniqueness constitutes the data of study, cannot meet the . . . criteria of scientific data or content" (5, p. 237). The criteria for scientific subject-matter, he proposes, are (*a*) durability in the phenomenon that is the object of the scientists' interest, and (*b*) the universality of this phenomenon.

My first criticism arises from his inaccurate understanding of personalistic psychology. It so happens that there is only one self-styled system of personalistic psychology, namely that set forth by William Stern. A reading of his *General Psychology from a Personalistic Standpoint* (6) shows that Stern's dimensions (or variables) almost without exception fulfill the criteria of durability and universality. In fact, Stern's writing is as nomothetic as one's heart could possibly desire. Hence, to identify personalistic psychology and

the idiographic outlook is Dr. Skaggs' first serious error.

If he wishes to label my own views 'personalistic' I cannot prevent him, but because of the many differences between Stern's 'system' and my own, I myself would hesitate to accept the label. Stern has prior rights to it. In Chapter 20 of the book that Dr. Skaggs criticizes I have explained in some detail the differences between personalistic psychology and the psychology of personality as I see it (1). Elsewhere I have summarized Stern's views at still greater length and again recorded my criticisms of them (2). Dr. Skaggs seems far more certain than I that I am a 'personalistic' psychologist.

In attacking the idiographic point of view (which, as I say, is not the same as the personalistic point of view), Dr. Skaggs writes, "Literally there would be as many separate psychologies as there are individuals, if we carried Allport's doctrine to the extreme!" (5, p. 237). Such a statement is like saying, "Penicillin is good for everything, including near-sightedness and ingrowing toenails, if we carry the penicillin-enthusiast's view to the extreme." Who wants to carry it to the extreme? Not I. In discussing the proposed distinction made by Windelband and others between the nomothetic and idiographic approaches to mental life, I state explicitly, "The dichotomy, however, is too sharp; it requires a psychology divided against itself. As in the case of the two psychologies (the analytical and the descriptive) advocated by Dilthey and Spranger, the division is too drastic. It is more helpful to regard the two methods as overlapping and as contributing to one another. . . . A complete study of the individual will embrace both approaches" (1, p. 22). The psychology of personality, I have therefore explicitly maintained, should be *both* nomothetic and idiographic.

Again, Skaggs writes, "Allport, who so severely criticizes the older scientific psychology which dealt with facts common to all mankind, ends up by *abstracting certain general laws and methodologies!*" (p. 236). Why, may I ask, is this so scandalous? Why should not a discipline that is *both* nomothetic and idiographic deal with common laws and methods? For that matter, why should not a discipline almost entirely idiographic in nature, such as history, fine arts, or medical diagnosis, employ as background laws and common methods in so far as these are helpful in comprehending uniqueness?

Dr. Skaggs goes on to state correctly my aspiration when he says that the difference between "his laws and methodologies and those of a Wundt or a Titchener lies in the fact that his are (presumably) more serviceable in giving self-understanding and understanding of other people" (p. 236). Dr. Skaggs is right. I try in my book to offer nomothetic constructs that *improve* upon those traditionally employed. While they are nomothetic in nature, many of them have an idiographic *intent*. To illustrate: such constructs as the theory of individual traits, of the ego, of functional autonomy, of congruence, of the empirical-intuitive nature of understanding, all are generalizations which if adopted would give psychologists greater predictive ability in dealing with single individuals. Similarly, among the *methods* having idiographic intent, and emphasized by me, are the case study, the personal document, interviewing methods, matching, personal structure analysis, and other procedures that contrive

to keep together what nature itself has fashioned as an integrated unit—the single personality. My whole purpose is to show how the psychology of personality can do a better job than it has traditionally done in handling the phenomenon of individuality.

But Dr. Skaggs is not pleased. To him it seems mildly treasonable to suppose that science can extend itself to the phenomenon of individuality. He writes, "If we define personalistic psychology as does Allport [the error here I have already explained] each person is a 'unique individual' " (p. 236). My reply to Dr. Skaggs is that each person *is* a unique individual regardless of who defines what how.

Although I am apparently more impressed than he by the inescapable uniqueness of personality, and by the psychologist's obligation to deal with it, I think I allow adequately for the contributions of the familiar actuarial methods of our discipline. For example, there is merit in the postulation of universal needs and capacities, and in their measurement in the customary language of individual differences. All testing (of the standardized order) must, I fully grant, proceed from the assumption of 'common traits.' Uniqueness in respect to any single variable is known only in terms of its *deviation* from the mean of the standardization group with which the individual is being compared. Where my view is 'unorthodox' is in my contention that psychological science (and I mean here the total course of psychological inquiry) cannot stop with common traits, factors, IQ's, and like nomothetic dimensions, but must admit additional methods and theories to handle the organic inter-relation of the artificialized variables with which nomothetic science deals, and must represent better than it has the personalized coloring of these variables in the individual life. I say in effect: "No doors should be closed in the study of personality. Abstract dimensions have their place. Let us use them even though they merely *approximate* the unique cleavages which close scrutiny shows are characteristic of each separate personality. Then let us add new methods and concepts where they are needed to grasp better than we have the phenomenon of individual pattern."

The most startling feature of Dr. Skaggs' position is his contention that the biological aspects of personality are legitimate data for science whereas the acquired aspects are not (p. 237). He rules out "such content as ideas, ideals, attitudes, interests, sentiments, purposes, beliefs, idealogies [sic], 'personality traits'" because these "are definitely not common to all people the world over" (p. 235). He maintains that whatever is learned cannot be the object of scientific interest, because learning results in progressive individuality. I daresay that biologists and geneticists would be glad to call Dr. Skaggs' attention to the *unique* inheritance that results from combinations of genes. An inborn temperament is certainly no less unique than acquired habit-systems, and, I suspect, not nearly so universal.

Yet he insists that "any effects wrought in man through experience or learning would be unscientific content for psychology because they would not meet the criteria of durability and commonness" (p. 237). To draw the line here would exclude from the scope of science such pursuits as market research, opinion study, vital statistics, comparative national psychology, humor, custom, much of psychopathology, and, if I understand him correctly, most of the phenomena of perception, memory, judgment, reasoning, language, and motivation, for these are all variable and socially conditioned.

To the purged hall of science he

would, however, admit such constructs as Spearman's *g* and Thurstone's 'basic factors'. (p. 235). Yet Tolman has shown clearly that nothing is more culture-bound than precisely these factors. Who, knowing the type of culturally conditioned test-matrix from which factors emerge, can deny Tolman's conclusion that "it is quite obvious that this London (or New York) *g* would not carry over, as such, to the Trobriand Islands"? (7, p. 2). And I question whether Dr. Skaggs is on safer ground with his contention that learning theory, or the Weber-Fechner law, is of eternal and universal applicability, for the operation of both, I suspect, is so basically dependent upon culture-bound and personality-bound interests, that the purely biological component is not only impossible to isolate, but worthless when isolated.

The author insists that "science as we know it to-day, thinks in terms of millions of years" (p. 238). If this be so, I doubt that any biological or psychological discipline qualifies unless its subject matter be trilobites or something else equally remote from human concern. The author's insistence upon durability and universality in the phenomena under investigation would, it seems to me, disqualify nearly every psychologist now at work. Oddly enough, Stern, the personalistic psychologist, would qualify as well as anyone, for his dimensions for the study of mental life are highly abstract and in themselves nearly content-less.

It is much more customary to define science as that form of knowledge that enhances our *understanding, prediction,* and *control* of phenomena above the level achieved by unaided common sense. Elsewhere I have argued that in order to attain a higher degree of scientific power thus defined, psychology would do well to adopt the idiographic orientation of its work (3). For **in** matters of mental life *understanding,* *prediction,* and *control* are likely to be more complete when the single organism is understood in its own special uniqueness than when exclusively nomothetic (actuarial) probabilities are applied. Although this point reaches beyond the scope of Dr. Skaggs' paper I mention it here because, if I am correct in my analysis of the situation, then according to this *more usual* definition of science, idiographic knowledge fully qualifies for a place of honor.

True, this claim that understanding, prediction and control of personality are better achieved under an idiographic than under a nomothetic mode of approach, has been disputed. But in principle, at least, the hypothesis can be submitted to experimental testing. I have already cited some evidence in its favor (3, p. 34), Sarbin some against (4). The subject is not yet closed. I shall not discuss it more fully here, because it digresses too far from Dr. Skaggs' argument.

In the last analysis his position, I regret to point out, turns on a struggle for status, the motive being revealed in several passages:

"Allport takes a bold stand for the broadening of the concept of science. This may be the proper progressive stand to take but we doubt that our fellow scientists in physics, chemistry, and astronomy will be very receptive to the idea" (p. 234).

"While the study of attitudes, beliefs, habits and skills may be of immense practical and theoretical importance, such studies are not science in the eyes of our colleagues in physics, chemistry and astronomy" (p. 237).

"Our colleagues in physics and chemistry might, and probably would resist any such change in the scientific concept" (p. 238).

"When a colleague in physiology or chemistry tells us that our data are not scientific, we become rather upset" (p. 238).

"We all want to bask in the light of the great Sun-God Science" (p. 238).

In short, psychology, the climber, must not offend those who have arrived. If it does so, it won't make the club.

This logic of appeasement has little attractiveness for me. Prestige for psychology will scarcely be won by aping those who, at this particular moment in the world's history, enjoy exalted status. Rather, when psychology has ripe wisdom to offer concerning the development of human personality, whether it offers it in a nomothetic or idiographic manner (or both), it will then merit the high position which Dr. Skaggs covets for it.

Though I have disagreed with him in his interpretations and outlook, I am grateful to Dr. Skaggs for initiating a discussion of such basic issues in the study of personality, and for the opportunity he has given me to clarify some of my own views on the subject.

REFERENCES

1. Allport, G. W. *Personality: a psychological interpretation.* New York: Henry Holt & Co., 1937.
2. ——. The personalistic psychology of William Stern. *Char. & Pers.,* 1937, 5, 231–246.
3. ——. *The use of personal documents in psychological science.* New York: Social Science Research Council, Bull. 49, 1942.
4. Sarbin, T. R. The logic of prediction in psychology. Psychol. Rev., 1944, 51, 210–228.
5. Skaggs, E. B. Personalistic psychology as science. Psychol. Rev., 1945, 52, 234–238.
6. Stern, W. *General psychology from the personalistic standpoint.* New York: Macmillan Co. (transl.), 1938.
7. Tolman, E. C. A stimulus-expectancy need-cathexis psychology. *Science,* 1945, 101, 160–166.

SCIENTIFIC MODELS AND HUMAN MORALS[1]

Reprinted from *Psychological Review*, **54**, No. 4, July 1947, 182-192

Within the span of remarkably few years, the quantity and quality of investigations in the fields of personality and social psychology have established not only their scientific dignity but likewise their popularity and promise within the psychological profession. The official formation of this large Division within the American Psychological Association is a formal recognition of these facts.

At the same time the significance of this occasion extends beyond the boundaries of the profession. In forming this Division we are, wittingly or unwittingly, stating our readiness to assume a certain responsibility. We are announcing, in effect, that as a group of scientists we believe we have a contribution to make in interpreting and in remedying some of the serious social dislocations of today. For if we did not believe in the potentialities of our science would we thus formally establish it?

The test of our fitness to exist and to prosper, I submit, will be our ability to contribute substantially in the near future to the diagnosis and treatment of the outstanding malady of our time. The malady I refer to is not war, for modern warfare is but a symptom of an underlying morbid condition; it is not the threatening fission of one world into two, ominous as this threat may be; nor is it our apparent inability to control for our safety and profit the transformation of matter into atomic energy, though this crisis too is now upon us.

I speak rather of the *underlying* ailment, of the fact that man's moral sense is not able to assimilate his technology.

While technological warfare, technological unemployment, and the atomic age—all by-products of physical science—have overtaken us, mental and moral science have made no corresponding gains in allaying the rivalries and anxieties induced by technology, in devising methods of social control, nor in enhancing human coöperation and solidarity. It is, I venture to point out, precisely our own young science, whose formal establishment we are now celebrating, that has failed to keep pace with the needs of the times.

In taking stock of the situation I observe how many of us seem so stupefied by admiration of physical science that we believe psychology in order to succeed need only imitate the models, postulates, methods and language of physical science. If someone points out the present inutility of mechanical models in predicting any but the most peripheral forms of human behavior, we are inclined to reply: Wait a thousand years if necessary and you will see that man is a robot, and that all his mental functions can be synthesized in kind as successfully as we now synthesize table salt, quinine, or a giant calculator. While we righteously scorn what one of us has called "the subjective, anthropomorphic hocus pocus of mentalism" (6), we would consider a colleague emotional and mystical should he dare speak of "the objective mechanomorphic hocus pocus of physicalism."

Let our progress be gradual, we say. By sticking to peripheral, visible operations we may some day be able to ap-

[1] Address of the Divisional President before the first annual meeting of the Division of Personality and Social Psychology of the American Psychological Association, September 4, 1946.

proach complex problems of motivation, and then come within hailing distance of the distresses of mankind. We hope that these distresses will keep a thousand years until we are ready to cope with them, and that in the meantime a free science will be permitted to linger along and take its time. But even if such improbable conditions were fulfilled, I question whether we should endorse this counsel of patience or the premises upon which it rests.

The machine model in psychology had its origin not in clinical or social experience, but rather in adulation of the technological success of the physical sciences. Since psychologists, like everyone else, are enmeshed in the prevailing ethos, they too, unless especially on guard, are likely to allow their subservience to technology to outrun their moral sense.

Besides the mechanical model, there are two other currently popular paradigms in psychology that are, in my opinion, only slightly less inept in guiding significant research or theory concerning the foundations of social morality. I refer to the phylogenetic model and to the infant mind. Although both these patterns during the past two generations have brought new insights and correctives into our work, they have not proved adequate to the needs of clinical, personnel, and social psychology.

The Current Appeal to Psychology

Public officials, confronted by postwar dilemmas, are urgently seeking the aid of psychologists. Many of us who have been approached are embarrassed by the scarcity of scientific findings, and even of serviceable concepts and well-formulated problems, that psychology has to offer *of the type that is being sought*. What is asked for is instant help in discovering the sources and conditions of man's moral sense in order that this sense may be enlarged and

brought into focus. What is asked for is aid from a science of human relationships whose assistance Franklin D. Roosevelt likewise invoked in his last speech before his death.[2] Yet we may comb the entire file of the *Psychological Abstracts* and find very little that has any bearing upon the improvement of human relationships on an international scale.

Why have we so relatively little to offer? Is it that we are young and need to follow the machine model for a thousand years? Or have we gotten off to a thoroughly bad start through our adoption of root-metaphors that lead away from, rather than toward, the problem at hand? Three generations ago psychology was commonly classified as a "moral science." Though we may not favor the aura of this term, how can we expect anything other than a science of moral conduct to discover conditions that will bring the needed counterpoise to technology run wild?

When any one of us undertakes a piece of research he inevitably adopts, according to his preference, one or another of the fundamental models available to psychologists. My thesis is that now if ever we need to test our preferred model for its capacity to yield discoveries that have some sure relevance to moral nature and to social skills.

Expectancy and Intention

If I interpret the matter correctly, American psychology naturally adopted mechanical models because our culture has always been action-oriented and technological. By and large our psychology is a motorized psychology, and is only now widening its concept of ac-

[2] "Today we are faced with the preëminent fact that, if civilization is to survive, we must cultivate the science of human relationships— the ability of all peoples, of all kinds, to live together and work together, in the same world, at peace."

tion to include the ego-involved participation of the human organism in matters affecting its own destiny (2). The earlier extreme position, represented by E. B. Holt and J. B. Watson, held personality to be essentially a battery of trigger-release mechanisms. This view paid no attention to the sustained directions of striving characteristic of moral behavior, to what in this paper I shall call "intentions."

This trigger-model, still preferred by a few, gave way gradually to a more purposive behaviorism. The concept of "sign-Gestalt expectancy" was introduced by Tolman, and mercifully shortened by Hilgard and Marquis to "expectancy" (9). It is an interesting fact that these authors seem to regard the principle of expectancy as the most purposive of all the essentially mechanical theories derived from the multitudinous experiments on the conditioned reflex (9, p. 101). In other words, some version of the principle of expectancy is as far as many psychologists have come in their conception of the nature of personal and social conduct.

The principle holds that in the presence of certain signs the organism expects a certain goal to appear if it follows the customary behavior route. If the goal is reached, the expectation is confirmed; if not, the organism may vary its behavior (9, p. 88). The principle, while allowing for the importance of attitude, is essentially stimulus-bound. We behave according to the cues we have learned, according to our expectancies.

In order not to complicate my argument I shall leave out of consideration the law of effect, which, it would be easy to show, likewise ascribes behavior wholly to past experience, to learned cues, and to mechanical reinforcements (4). Both principles, so far as I can see, accord nothing to the *un*rewarded,

*un*realized, yet persistive, intentions of man's moral nature.

The trouble with these currently fashionable concepts, drawn from the phylogenetic model, is that while they seem to apply aptly enough to animal behavior whence they were derived, they have only a limited or else a remote analogical bearing on the activities of human beings. We may know a person's expectancies and even his past rewards, and yet be singularly unable to predict or control his future behavior, unless at the same time we know also his basic intentions which are by no means a stencilled copy of his previous expectancies and rewards (3).

To take an example, the sign-Gestalten today are such that we may now reasonably expect future trouble with Russia. Does this fact tell in any degree what we can, should, or will do about it? This precise area of conflict is a novel one (as indeed all important situations are). The best predictive basis we have lies in our own national and personal *intentions* regarding Russia. It is our purposes, not our expectancies, that are now the issue.

As if aware of the scantiness of the expectancy principle, Tolman advises us to embrace also a "need-cathexis psychology" (19). But the situation here turns out to be parallel. Need-cathexis psychology—of course I oversimplify—holds essentially that a handful of physiological drives get attached to this, that, or the other object. A man who, in Tolman's pleasing vernacular, is "raised right" meshes his drive into a socially acceptable gear. A man "raised wrong" does not. But what is so striking about human motivation is that so often a desire or aspiration is meshed into no gear. It simply reaches forward hungrily into the future like the tip of a scarlet-runner bean groping for a goal that it does not know about.

The embarrassment of the need-cathexis type of psychology is reflected in the apologetic language it uses when referring to this expansive aspect of human motivation. Accustomed to work with animals or with infants, need-cathexis psychology labels adult human intentions "secondary drives," "derived drives," or "drive conversions." With such depreciating concepts both the mechanical and the phylogenetic psychologists apparently seek to dispose of those morally relevant desires and aspirations that are in fact so different from the drive-impelled excursions of the cozy robot or cozy rodent.[3]

My objection to the animal paradigm

[3] It is instructive to read the perorations of two recent presidential addresses by psychologists, one preferring the machine model, the other the rat model. Though good-humored and witty, both authors candidly acknowledge their own escapist motives. To paraphrase Carlson's quip concerning Cannon's theory of emotions: the authors seem to entertain their models because the models entertain them.

"I believe that robotic thinking helps precision of psychological thought, and will continue to help it until psychophysiology is so far advanced that an image is nothing other than a neural event, and object constancy is obviously just something that happens in the brain. That time is still a long way off, and in the interval I choose to sit cozily with my robot, squeezing his hand and feeling a thrill—a scientist's thrill—when he squeezes mine back again" (⊘, p. 192).

"And, as a final peroration, let it be noted that rats live in cages; they do not go on binges the night before one has planned an experiment; they do not kill each other off in war; they do not invent engines of destruction, and if they did, they would not be so dumb about controlling such engines; they do not go in for either class conflicts or race conflicts; they avoid politics, economics and papers on psychology. They are marvelous, pure and delightful. And, as soon as I possibly can, I am going to climb back again out on that good old philogenetic limb and sit there, this time right side up and unashamed, wiggling my whiskers at all the dumb, yet at the same time far too complicated, specimens of *homo sapiens*, whom I shall see strutting and fighting and messing things up, down there on the ground below me" (19, p. 166).

for personality and for social psychology is not so much that animals lack culture—a fact which Mr. Tolman in his sparkling paper first frankly admits and then amiably represses. My objection is rather that the motivational structure of man and of lower animals seems to be in only a slight degree similar. In this respect as with his evolutionary brain development, "Man," to quote Julian Huxley's conclusion, "stands alone" (12). Animals are demonstrably creatures of stimulus-expectancy and need-cathexis. Man, in all that is distinctive of his species, is a creature of his intentions. We may well doubt that the basic equation for intentional morality, or that for intentional learning, can be written from a study of organisms that lack propositional symbols. To this point I shall return.

While I am disapproving of current models I shall state my final grievance, this time against the rigid ontogenetic stencils that derive from Freudianism. Odd as it may appear, Freud resembles the mechanical and phylogenetic psychologists in wanting his doctrine of motivation anchored to neuro-anatomy. I assume that this is his desire because of his refusal to see anything at all in the coöperative, socialized, affiliative, undertakings of mankind excepting goal-inhibited sexuality. To the sex drive he adds principally the impulses of aggression, destruction, and death. It seems obvious that Freudianism, even though eagerly adopted by many who have found the mechanical and animal models inadequate, offers an equally meagre basis for a serviceable study of man's moral conduct.

The trouble lies chiefly in the excessive emphasis upon infantile experience. We are asked to believe that an individual's character-structure is, in all essentials, determined by the time his last diaper is changed. Even Suttie, who postulates as the foundation of morality an original and embracing instinct of tenderness, affection, and social symbiosis, believes its fate is sealed according to the manner in which the mother handles this affiliative impulse before and after weaning (17). If the chances for peace in the world depend to such a degree upon infant fixations ought we not disband this Division and register as wet nurses to the mewling citizens of tomorrow?

The concept of intention, which I am here opposing to reactivity, expectancy, and infantile fixation, is not immediately congenial to American psychology. Yet its adoption in some form or another, I argue, is necessary. With some malice aforethought I have selected the term *intention*—spiced, as it is, by an aggravating flavor of mentalism—to signify those aspects of thought and of motivation that play a leading, but now neglected, part in the complex, affiliative, moral conduct of men. I believe it is precisely the "private" worlds of desire, aspiration, and conscience that must be studied if we are to succeed in the task of social engineering.

In using the term intention, however, I am not arguing surreptitiously for phenomenology, though in order to improve our grasp on the subtleties of man's intentions we would do well to emulate the refinement of its descriptive method.[4] Nor am I arguing for a revival of Brentano, though we have neglected unduly the central proposition of

[4] An excellent example is Bertocci's analysis of man's sense of moral obligation (5). He shows that when we study the *ought-consciousness* phenomenologically we discover how entirely different it is from the *must-consciousness*. This discovery leads to a justifiable suspicion that, whatever conscience may be, it does not derive merely from fear of punishment or from social coercion. Too hastily and heedlessly have psychologists accepted Freud's identification of the Super-ego with threat of parental punishment.

Act Psychology: that at every moment man's mind is directed by some intention, be it loving, hating, comparing, understanding, desiring, rejecting, planning, or some similar mental act.

Let us define intention simply as *what the individual is trying to do*. Naïve as this definition may sound it is in reality the product of decades of sophisticated wrestling with the problems of human motivation. In this concept influences as diversified as Brentano, Darwin, Freud, Cannon, and Wertheimer are brought into focus. In essence it no longer draws the sharp distinction, advanced by both Kant and Schopenhauer, between will (or drive) on the one hand, and intellect on the other. The machine, rat, and infant models we have been following (though I am sure they'd be surprised and grieved to know it) preserve this irreconcilable Kantian dichotomy. They side somewhat more, however, with Schopenhauer in regarding the functions of the intellect as wholly instrumental and secondary. Without forgetting for a moment what we have learned about rationalizing and about the untrustworthiness of introspective reports on motives, we may safely declare that the opposing of motive and thought-process has gone much too far. Usually the individual is trying to do something in which his wants and his plans easily coöperate. Instead of being at opposite poles his emotion and his reason canalize into a single endeavor. The direction of his endeavor I designate as the intention, and offer this concept as an improvement upon the one-sided irrationalistic doctrines of drive, need, instinct, and cathexis.

In deference to the discoveries of psychoanalysis we readily admit that an individual does not always know precisely what his own intentions are. *Consciously* he may misinterpret the line of his own endeavor. A neurotic frequently does so. In such cases insight is either lacking or partially lacking. But as a rule, the "posture or lay of consciousness" reflects accurately enough that inextricable fusion of driving and planning which we find in the dynamics of mature human conduct.[5]

It is the mark of an intention that it is directed toward the future. Yet it is typical of the models we have followed that they lead to preoccupation with adjustments in the past. While people are living their lives forward, psychologists are busy tracing them backward. The model we need for our investigations of human relationships will escape from our present excessive dependence on geneticism in all its forms (3).

A geneticist, for example one who places great weight on the expectancy-principle, is inclined to define personality as a peculiar set of reaction-tendencies. An intentionist, on the other hand, sees personality as a peculiar set of subjective values. There is a difference. The one learns at best only about moral *accomplishment;* the other gains additional light on moral *potential.*

[5] McDougall specifically objected to the concept of intention on the grounds that conscious intention merely obscures the instinctive motive at work (15, pp. 121f). He had in mind the indubitable fact that men's verbal reports of their intentions may be rationalizations. But in my use of the term I do not confine intention to reportable purpose. Sometimes the essential direction of an intention is understood well enough by the subject, sometimes not. If the term, as I propose, is taken to mean *both* the understood and non-understood direction of an act I maintain that it can serve as a proper designation for "ultimate motives" and not merely for proximate or rationalized motives.

To my mind it is unnecessary to have recourse to a doctrine of underlying needs or instincts. McDougall, for example, allowed far too little for the ever-changing panorama of man's intentions which, as they evolve from an original genetic equipment, undergo complete change of form and functional significance (1).

It may be argued that the models I am presuming to criticize do deal both with "goal reactions" and with "anticipatory goal reactions." Dr. Hull, for example, offers "anticipatory goal reaction" as a "physical mechanism" which he says he regards as equivalent to the concept of "guiding ideas," or what I am calling *intention* (11). The difficulty with "anticipatory goal reaction" as with "expectancy" is that men often have values without having any specific goal in mind. They may have a consistent direction of striving, but their goals are either transient or else undefinable. All of a rat's, but only a small bit of human, behavior can be characterized in terms of concrete goals whose attainment will de-tension specific drives. For the most part the course of man's behavior runs according to certain schemata, or in prolonged channels. Only now and then are these channels marked by lights or buoys that represent specific goals.

A simple example may be borrowed from Lecky's analysis of childhood thumbsucking. The following statement distinguishes neatly between expectancy and what I am here calling intention; that is, between behavior regulated by habit and behavior ordered to non-specific schemata.

"Certainly the child who sucks his thumb gives the act plenty of exercise and gets enough satisfaction from it to fix it indelibly. Therefore if the habit theory is true, we should be able to predict absolutely that the child will continue to suck his thumb for the rest of his life. But what really happens? Every year millions of children who have industriously sucked their thumbs since birth, and who have successfully resisted every effort to force them to change their behavior, quit the practice spontaneously when they are five or six years old. The reason is that they are beginning at this age to think of themselves as big boys or girls, and they recognize that thumb-sucking is inconsistent with the effort to maintain this new idea" (13, p. 122f).

An intention often takes the form of a self-image as in the case of Lecky's reformed thumbsucker. Having adopted a conception of what we want to be we are constrained to make good in the role we have assumed. The specific goals we set for ourselves are almost always subsidiary to our long-range intentions. A good parent, a good neighbor, a good citizen, is not good because his specific goals are acceptable, but because his successive goals are ordered to a dependable and socially desirable set of values. We now know that juvenile delinquency and adult criminality were sadly misconceived so long as they were regarded as a matter of bad habit-formations. For years reformatories have trained habits, but have achieved few reformations. Only a radical shift of outlook and intention remakes a criminal, alcoholic or neurotic character.

The models we have been following lack the long-range orientation which is the essence of morality. Infant and rodent have immediate goals and indulge in anticipatory goal reactions, but have no directive schemata. By contrast, a child in puberty develops a desire to become a successful and respected man of affairs, and acquires this generalized objective long before he knows what concrete goals he has to work for. Thus customarily, image and intention seem to antedate and to define goal-reactions. The essence of moral behavior is of this sort. It presupposes long-range purposes whose directions precede their specifications.

When President Roosevelt enunciated the Four Freedoms he was speaking of certain common intentions of the human race. An important feature of his historic formulation lies in his assumption that *all* men, in *all* cultures, intend (that is, long for) freedom from

want, freedom from fear, freedom of speech and of worship. Note how this assumption contrasts with the prevailing creed of modern social science. Cultural relativity, really a doctrine of stimulus-expectancy, has laid such a heavy hand upon us that we have overlooked the possibility of universal intentions. Yet unless Roosevelt's bold assumption is found justified, we can scarcely hope to find a psychological basis for effective world organization.

In all probability Roosevelt's formulation is psychologically not the best that can be made; nor dare we underestimate the incompatibility of nationalistic intentions and rivalries. What I am saying is that the psychologists' perspective should be equally bold. It is up to us to find out whether there are in fact common purposes that might provide ground for international solidarity. To do so, social psychologists in all lands might well join in a search, through modern instruments of polling, clinical interviewing, child study, and life-histories, for existent moral bases on which international coöperation can be built.

It is conceivable—I think probable—that such research would discover the ruthless pursuit of personal and national power to be a result of the frustration of basically affiliative intentions. In clinical practice we know how often the clamorous manifestations of egotism gain the upper hand when men are denied a proper continuation of the originally friendly and symbiotic relationship with family, friends, and neighbors. It seems probable that every child in every nation, the world over, at a time when he is most plastic, wants security, affection, and an affiliative and comprehending relation to the surrounding world. It is conceivable that the same basic intentions exist in most adults, although thwarting and perversion of this relationship have engendered a vast amount of hatred, emotional instability, and warlike impulse.

Basic research would discover why the taboo on tenderness, on nurturant desires, has grown so excessive that the development of coöperative and affiliative behavior outside one's own family is, at least in our culture, generally disapproved. It would seek to discover under what conditions the impulse to love and to be loved is turned to the impulse to hate and to invite hatred. If it is the child's nature to trust everyone, why is it the nature of national or ethnic groups to distrust nearly everyone? The models we have been following tend to deflect our attention from problems of human affection and the conditions for its development. When a bit of human friendliness is discovered —and it can be discovered only accidentally with models now current—it is likely to be labeled "goal inhibited sexuality," and thus tagged, forgotten. Up to now the sexual activity of rat and man has received incomparably more attention from psychologists than has the coöperative activity of men and nations.

Besides the study of affection and hatred, the possibilities for peace require research into many other strictly human capacities—among them the use of humor, the function of creeds, the processes of communication. For moral development depends on many factors other than root-desires and intentions. But every aspect of moral conduct that one can name depends intricately upon the employment of symbols.

Signs and Symbols

Perhaps the clearest symptom of the present conceptual confusion in our field is the extent to which we confound symbols with signs, or—if one prefers Morris's terminology—symbols with signals.

We know that all animals, as well as men, respond to signals. The principle

of expectancy says so, and in this respect is right. A signal is something that exists in the physical world; it is an identifiable stimulus. But even the most behavioristically inclined theorists cannot, and do not, claim that animals can handle propositional symbols —those self-produced signs *of* signs which are man's prized and troublesome possession. An animal, says Thorndike, can "think things," but it cannot "think about things" (18, p. 119). And Yerkes asserts that symbolic processes in chimpanzees are rare and difficult to observe. One may, he says, fairly continue to question their existence, though it may be that signal responses can be regarded in some way as "antecedents of human symbolic processes" (20, p. 189). Surveying relevant investigations and opinions, Cassirer concludes:

"In all literature of the subject there does not seem to be a single conclusive proof of the fact that any animal ever made the decisive step from subjective to objective, from affective to propositional, language" (7, p. 30).

Cassirer argues, reasonably enough, that the symbolic system creates a wholly new dimension of reality for man. Instead of dealing directly with things themselves or with their visible signals, man deals with their ideational surrogates.[6]

"He has so enveloped himself in linguistic forms, in artistic images, in mythi-

---

[6] Even in human beings we occasionally encounter a sharp break between symbols and signs. Some of Goldstein's aphasic patients, for example, seem capable of responding to signs but not to symbols, as in the case of the man who could understand the word-signs "Drink it," when a glass full of water was presented to him, but was unable to go through the symbolic motions of drinking it if the glass was empty (8, p. 44).

Without symbols we could not make-believe, dissimulate, or lie; we could not form plans for our future; nor hold those schemata in mind that make possible consistency in moral conduct.

cal symbols or religious rites, that he cannot see or know anything except by the interposition of this artifical medium" (7, p. 25).

Even so behavioristic a writer as Morris admits that the theory of sign-response as developed by himself carries over with difficulty to the human sphere. These are his words:

". . . non-human beings seldom produce the signs which influence their behavior, while human individuals in their language and post-language symbols characteristically do this and to a surprising degree. Here is a basic difference between men and animals, and until behavioral theory develops a semiotic adequate to this difference it will remain what it is today: a careful study of animals and a pious hope for a science of the human person" (16, p. 198).

In this passage Morris seems to be saying with fine candor that there is a world of difference between signal and symbol; and that even his own careful system of semiotic fails adequately to bridge the gap. Though I have not actually counted the illustrations in his recent book I have the impression that a majority of them refer to animal responses to signals, and that relatively few deal with human responses to symbols. In any case it is clear that Morris, like many psychologists, is enamored of the phylogenetic model.

I venture to cite another brilliant and candid passage from his book. He writes of the fact that a sign may be *iconic*, that is to say, it may itself resemble the properties of its denotatum. Thus a motion picture is highly iconic; an onomatopoeic word less so; a wholly arbitrary sign not at all iconic. He then goes on to make this highly significant remark:

"One of the dangers of the use of models in science, for instance, arises out of the temptation to ascribe to the subject matter of a theory properties of the model illustrating the theory which are not involved in the theory itself" (16, p. 23).

From this warning would it not follow that an adequate theory of symbols can hardly be derived from the animal model in which *signals* alone predominate? How can we expect to understand human symbolism in terms of the phylogenetic type when, as Morris himself asserts, we are tempted to over-extend the properties of our type-model and force them to serve in place of the independent theory that we need to develop?

THE MODEL WE NEED

To sum up: the designs we have been using in our studies of motivation, of symbol, and hence of the foundations of moral behavior, are not—to borrow Morris's crisp term—sufficiently iconic with our subject-matter. Addiction to machines, rats, or infants leads us to overplay those features of human behavior that are peripheral, signal-oriented, or genetic. Correspondingly it causes us to underplay those features that are central, future-oriented, and symbolic.

What sort of a model then do we need? This question opens systematic vistas that lie beyond the scope of this paper. Yet, lest my numerous criticisms indicate a despair that I do not actually feel, I shall mention a few recent signs and portents that signify a newer—and, to my mind—more wholesome outlook.

Most noteworthy is the fact that the war led many psychologists to deal directly with the integrated behavior of GI Joe, of the factory worker, of the civilian. We then learned that the interests of morale, psychotherapy, personnel placement, psychological warfare, could not be pursued successfully by clinging to our threadbare models. Our inadequate root-metaphors went into the ash can for the duration. It is because of this conceptual discard, with its resultant wartime success in the promotion of social engineering, that I have presumed at this time to bring into the open a conflict that many, perhaps most of us, have secretly felt. Must we now resume the tattered stencils that we so recently abandoned with such good effect?

There are various indicators of improvement in theoretical outlook. · I have in mind the new and vital conception of the ego that has come into psychotherapy in recent years (3); the discovery and application of psychological principles involved in bringing the worker into a participant relation with his job (2); the discovery and application of procedures leading to successful administration (14). We discern an accelerated movement toward the development of such theories as can have their acid test here and now, not one thousand years hence. These theories neither strain the credulity, nor stretch an inappropriate model some distance beyond its logical breaking point.

We happily find more emphasis than before on the structuring activities of the person, on the importance of centrally initiated motive patterns, on cognitive dynamisms—including ideology, schemata of meaning, frames of reference. We find the contemporaneity of motives stressed, as well as the important functions of self-esteem and ego-involvement. Though symbols are still confused with signals, we are beginning, through content-analysis and interviewing, to study symbols both in their own right, and as the basic ingredients that they are in all complex conduct, including all morally relevant thought and behavior. We have learned, through improved polls and other methods of inquiry, to ascertain the direction of so-cial purpose as it resides in individual minds. From such knowledge it should be possible to fashion a domestic and international social policy that will be sufficiently realistic to succeed.

All these and many more signs indicate the growing dependence of modern theories upon a model that is none the less scientific for being humane. As this design for personality and social psychology gradually becomes better tempered to our subject-matter we shall cease borrowing false notes—whether squeaks, squeals, or squalls. We shall read the score of human personality more accurately, and for the benefit of the world audience that waits to listen.

REFERENCES

1. ALLPORT, G. W. Motivation in personality: Reply to Mr. Bertocci. PSYCHOL. REV., 1940, 47, 533–554.
2. ——. The psychology of participation. PSYCHOL. REV., 1945, 53, 117–132.
3. ——. Geneticism versus ego-structure in theories of personality. Brit. J. educ. Psychol., 1946, 16, II, 57–68.
4. ——. Effect: a secondary condition of learning. PSYCHOL. REV., 1946, 54, 335–347.
5. BERTOCCI, P. A reinterpretation of moral obligation. Phil. & Phenomenol. Res., 1945, 6, 270–283.
6. BORING, E. G. Mind and mechanism. Amer. J. Psychol., 1946, 54, 173–192.
7. CASSIRER, E. An essay on man. New Haven: Yale Univ. Press, 1945.
8. GOLDSTEIN, K. Human nature in the light of psychopathology. Cambridge, Mass.: Harvard Univ. Press, 1940.
9. HILGARD, E. R., & MARQUIS, D. G. Conditioning and learning. New York: D. Appleton-Century, 1940.
10. HOSLETT, S. D. (Ed.). Human factors in management. Parkville, Mo.: The Park College Press, 1946.
11. HULL, C. L. Goal attraction and directing ideas conceived as habit phenomena. PSYCHOL. REV., 1931, 38, 487–506.
12. HUXLEY, J. Man stands alone. New York and London: Harper & Bros., 1941.
13. LECKY, P. Self-consistency: a theory of personality. New York: The Island Press, 1945.

14. LEIGHTON, A. H. *The governing of men.* Princeton: The University Press, 1945.
15. McDOUGALL, W. *Outline of psychology.* New York: Scribners, 1923.
16. MORRIS, C. *Signs, language and behavior.* New York: Prentice-Hall, 1946.
17. SUTTIE, I. D. *The origins of love and hate.* London: Kegan Paul, 1935.

18. THORNDIKE, E. L. *Animal intelligence.* New York: Macmillan, 1911.
19. TOLMAN, E. C. A stimulus-expectancy need-cathexis psychology. *Science,* 1945, 101, 160–166.
20. YERKES, R. M. *Chimpanzees: a laboratory colony.* New Haven: Yale University Press, 1943.

PERSONALITY: A PROBLEM FOR SCIENCE OR A PROBLEM FOR ART?

Reprinted from *Revista de Psihologie* (Cluj, Romania, I, No. 4, 1938, 1-15)

Already in the twentieth century three great revolutions have occurred in man's thinking about his own mind. These are first, Freudian psychoanalysis, with its discovery of the depth and the emotion in mental life; second, Behaviorism, with its discovery of the accessibility of mind to objective study; and third, Gestalt psychology, with its discovery of the essential orderliness and self-regulation of mind. It is not at all unlikely that these new modes of thought will revolutionize our ways of life during the present century, much as the natural and biological sciences revolutionized ways of life during the past century. We may well expect them to affect profoundly the morals, manners, and mental health of our generation and of generations to come. Psychology, it is often said, is destined to become *the* science of the twentieth century.

Now, one of the most significant happenings in the first part of the twentieth century has been the discovery — to which Freudian, Behavioristic, and Gestalt psychologies have all contributed — that human *personality* is an accessible subject for scientific probing. It is this event, above all others, I think, that is likely to have the most practical consequences for education, for ethics, and for mental health.

But before getting into the problem of personality I should like to dwell for a moment upon the somewhat stormy state of psychological science today. It sometimes seems to me that all the four winds of the intellectual heavens had collided in one storm center, competing for mastery, with the outcome as yet unsure.

According to the division adopted by the Harvard Tercentenary celebration there are indeed exactly four winds in the intellectual heavens, springing from the four basic provinces of research and learning:

the natural sciences
the biological sciences
the social sciences
the humanities

Have you ever thought before that it is in the territory of psychology and *only there,* that all these four intellectual winds collide and run a tempestuous course? I suppose it is natural enough that they should do so, for only by the aid of all the inventions and all the resources of the mind can the creative mind itself be adequately explored.

From the *natural sciences* comes the colossal impact of scientific methodology. I suppose that in the entire history of human thought there never was a case where one science has been bullied by another science to compare with the way psychology is bullied by her elder sister science, physics. And I suppose no younger sister ever had so acute an inferiority complex as psychology has in relation to her well-groomed and socially correct elder sister. The desire to emulate the success of physics has led psychology to import at an increasing rate instruments of precision and mathematics into its treatment of mental life. Heaven help the psychologist nowadays who doesn't know his amplifiers and electrical circuits. It is, of course, particularly in the study of sensation that the physical sciences dominate psychology, though it is also true that their influence is felt throughout the entire structure of psychological science.

From the *biological sciences* also come high standards and exacting methods of research, as well as the evolutionary and organismal points of view without which psychology would still be scholastic in character. But the freshening winds of biology have not blown gently and with moderation; they have blown rather with the force of a gale; so forcefully that in many quarters they have threatened to push every vestige of humanism out, leaving psychology with a plague of rats. Today it is probably true that more rats are used in the American laboratories of psychology as subjects than men, women, and children combined. Some people feel that what psychology really needs is an efficient Pied Piper

It is, then, the impact of the natural and biological sciences upon psychology that account for its obsession to reach the eminence of scientific respectability. The methodological advances have indeed been considerable; but the sum-total of the findings from these points of approach have not as yet by any manner of means solved the problems of human personality. Their value lies chiefly in their advancement of sensory and reflex psychology, or as someone has a bit derisively called it "eye-ear-nose-and-throat" psychology.

In recent years the third wind has risen likewise to the force of a gale. *Social science* is causing a tornado all its own. It refuses to blend amicably with natural and biological science, but claims mind pretty much as its own province for study. Anthropologists and sociologists give no quarter. Mind, they insist, takes its form almost wholly in response to cultural demands. Language precedes the individual, so too do the religion, the morals, the economic system into which the individual is born. Mind then, is not a matter for instrumental or biological study, but for cultural study. A large number of psychologists have been converted, at least partially, to this view, and recently have staged a rebellion within their own ranks, four hundred of them forming a society to investigate as realistically as possible the fate of mind as it is conditioned and constrained by the gigantic movements of contemporary society.

The last wind that blows in our storm center is gentler and less voracious. Yet its presence is always felt. In spite of all counter currents it is perhaps still the prevailing wind. It is the wind of humanism. After all is said and done, it is philosophy and literature, and not the natural, biological, or social sciences, that have fostered psychology throughout the ages. It is only in comparatively recent years that psychology has detached itself from philosophy and from art to become the storm center that it is. Only five years ago in my own university it was still felt that psychology should not form a department of its own but should remain snuggly sheltered within the historic sanctuary of philosophy.

Now we come to personality. One of the outstanding events in psychology of the present century has been the discovery of personality. Personality, whatever else it may be, is the substantial concrete unit of mental life that exists in forms that are definitely single and individual. Throughout the ages, of course, this phenomenon of personal individuality has been depicted and explored by the humanities. The more aesthetic philosophers and the more philosophical artists have always made it their special province of interest.

Tardily, psychologists have arrived on the scene. One might almost say they are beginning two thousand years too late. The psychologist's work, it might seem, has been done for him, and done most brilliantly. With his scant thirty years of background, the psychologist looks like a conceited intruder. And so he is in the opinion of many literati. Stephan Zweig, for example, in speaking of Proust, Amiel, Flaubert, and other great masters of characterization, says,

"Writers like these are giants in observation and literature, whereas in psychology the field of personality is worked by lesser men, mere flies, who have the safe anchorage of a frame of science in which to place their petty platitudes and minor heresies."

It *is* true that the giants of literature make psychologists, who undertake to represent and to explain personality, seem ineffectual and sometimes a bit foolish in comparison. Only a pedant could prefer the dry collections of facts that psychology can offer regarding an individual mental life to the glorious and unforgettable portraits that the gifted novelist, dramatist, or biographer can give. The literary artist creates his account; the psychologist merely compiles his. In the one case a unity emerges, self-consistent even through its subtleties of change. In the other case a ponderous accumulation of discontinuous data piles up.

One recent critic has put the matter crisply. Psychology, whenever it deals with human personality, he remarks, is only saying what literature has always said, and is saying it much less artfully.

Whether this unflattering judgment is entirely correct we shall soon see. For the moment it serves at least to call attention to the significant fact that in a sense literature and psychology *are* competitors; they are the two methods *par excellence* for dealing with the personality. The methods of literature are those of art; the methods of psychology are those of science. Our question is: which approach is the more suitable for the study of personality?

Literature has had centuries of headstart, and it has been served by genius of the highest order. Psychology is young and has bred as yet few, if any, geniuses in the depiction and explanation of human personality. Being youthful, it would be becoming for psychology to learn a few basic truths from literature.

To show what it can profitably learn, let us take a concrete example. I have chosen one from ancient times in order to show clearly the maturity and ripeness of literary wisdom. Twenty-three hundred years ago, Theophrastus, Aristotle's pupil and successor at the Lyceum in Athens, wrote a number of brief characterizations of certain of his Athenian acquaintances. Thirty of his sketches have survived.

The sketch that I shall select is called "The Coward." Please note its timelessness. The coward of today is essentially the same kind of mortal as the coward of antiquity. Please note also the remarkable directness and economy of the portrait. No words are wasted. It is like a prose sonnet. No one could add or subtract a single sentence to its betterment.

THE COWARD

"Cowardliness is a shrinking of the soul caused by fear. The Coward is this sort of person. At sea he thinks cliffs are pirates and directly the sea gets rough inquires anxiously whether all the passengers are initiated;* as he looks up at the sky he asks the steersman if they are half-way and what he thinks of the weather; he tells the person next him that he has had a disturbing dream; he takes off his tunic and gives it to his slave;** and finally begs to be put on shore. On active service when the infantry are going into action, he calls to the men of his deme to come and stand by him and to keep a good look-out — pretending that it is hard to distinguish who is the enemy. Then hearing the noise

---

* Into the mysteries of the Cabeiri.
** So that he can swim.

of battle and seeing men fall, he tells his comrades that in the hurry he has forgotten his sword; he runs back to his tent and, after getting rid of his slave by sending him out to reconnoitre, hides the sword under his pillow and wastes time in pretending to look for it. If he sees a wounded friend carried in, he rushes up, tells him to keep cheerful, holds him under the arms to support him; then he attends him, wipes the blood off and sits down by him to keep the flies away — in short, does everything except fight. The trumpets sound the charge and, as he sits in the tent, he murmurs: "Curse you! Won't you let the poor man sleep with your everlasting trumpeting!" Covered with the other man's blood he goes out to meet the returning soldiers and tells them he has saved one of his friends at the risk of his own life; and he brings to the bedside the men of his deme and tribe and explains to each visitor that he carried the wounded man to the tent with his own hands."

There is one feature in this classic sketch that I should like to call particularly to your attention. You will note that Theophrastus selects two situations for recording his observations. In one the coward is traveling; in the other he is unwillingly engaged in a battle. In the first situation seven typical episodes are depicted: the coward's illusion of see-ing the cliffs as pirates, his superstitious fear lest some of the passengers might bring bad luck through having neglected a religious rite, his desire to be at least half-way on the dangerous journey, his consulting expert opinion on the weather, his fear of his own disturbing dreams, his prepara-tions for swimming to safety, and finally his emotional collapse in begging to be put on shore. Even more subtle are the seven telltale episodes during battle. In all there are fourteen situations described: all of them for the coward are equivalent; whatever stimulation he is exposed to arouses the same deep, dominant disposition. Although his separate acts are quite distinctive, yet each and every one is equivalent in that each is a manifestation of the same dominant cowardly disposition.

In short, Theophrastus, more than 2000 years ago, used a method, just now being glimpsed by psychologists, of defining with the aid of equivalent stimulations and equivalent responses the major dispositions of a character.

To state the point yet more broadly: Almost all the literature of character — whether sketch writing, as in the case of Theophrastus, or fiction, drama, or biography — proceeds on the psychological assumption that each character has certain traits peculiar to himself which can be defined through the narrating of typical episodes from life. In literature a personality is never regarded, as it sometimes is in psychology, as a sequence of unrelated specific actions. Personality is not like a water-skate, darting hither and yon on the surface of a pond, with its several fugitive excursions having no intrinsic relation to one another. Good literature never makes the mistake of confusing the personality of man with that of a water-skate. Psychology often does.

The first lesson, then, that psychology has to learn from literature is something about the nature of the substantial and enduring dispositions of which personality is composed. This is the problem of traits, and by and large, I maintain, it has been handled more successfully through the assumptions of literature than through the assumptions of psychology. More specifically, it seems to me, the concept of the equivalence of stimulation and the equivalence of response, seen so clearly in the ancient sketches of Theophrastus, may serve as a strikingly productive guide for the scientific study of personality — where equivalences may be determined with greater accuracy and greater verifiability than in literature itself. Using the resources of the laboratory and controlled observation outside, psychology might be able to establish for the single individual far more exactly than literature can do, the precise range wherein various life-situations are for him equivalent, and the precise range of responses which for him have equivalent significance.

A second major lesson from literature concerns the self-consistency of its products. No one ever asked their authors to prove that the characters of Hamlet, Don Quixote, Anna Karenina, Hedda Gabbler, or Babbitt were true and authentic. Great characterizations by virtue of their greatness prove themselves. They are plausible; they are even necessary. Every act seems to be in some subtle way both a reflection of, and a rounding out of a single, well-knit character. This adhesiveness of behavior meets the test known as self-confrontation; one bit of behavior supports another, so that the whole can be comprehended as a self-consistent if intricate unity. Self-confrontation is the only method of validation applied to the work of artists (excepting perhaps to the work of biographers, who indeed have certain requirements for external validation to contend with). But the method of self-confrontation, I think it may rightly be said, is barely beginning to be applied to the productions of psychology.

Once in commenting on a character of Thackeray's, Gilbert K. Chesterton remarked, "She drank, but Thackeray didn't know it." Chesterton's quip springs from the demand that all good characterizations possess "systematic relevance" within themselves. Given one set of facts about a personality, other relevant facts should follow. To be sure, a deep and intimate knowledge of a character is required before these necessary inferences can be made. One must know just what the most intimate motivational traits in each case are. For this most central, and therefore most unifying core of any personality, Professor Wertheimer has proposed the concept of the "radix" — a root from which all stems may grow. He illustrates his conception with the case of a school girl who was a zealous scholar, but at the same time addicted to vivid cosmetics. On the surface there certainly seems to be no systematic relevance here. The two lines of conduct seldom go together. But the apparent contradiction is resolved in this case by exploring beneath the surface for the basic root. In this case it turned out that the school girl had deep admiration for (a psychoanalyst might call it a fixation upon) a certain teacher who in addition to being a scholarly woman had a natural vivid complexion. The school girl simply wanted to be like her teacher. The same facts in another case might betoken a basic desire for power, or simply a double-barrelled attempt to capsize the studious boy across the aisle. Whatever the explanation in this case, the point is that with radical understanding it becomes possible to harmonize the apparent inconsistencies in a personality.

Of course, the problem is not always so simple. Not all personalities have basic unity. Conflict, changeability, even the dissociation of personality are common. Much of the *literature* we read exaggerates the consistency of personality; caricatures rather than characters emerge. Oversimplification is found in drama, fiction, and biography. The confrontation seems to come almost too easily. The characters of Dickens are a good example of oversimplification. They never have conflicts within themselves. They are always what they are. They may, and usually do, meet unfriendly forces in the environment; but they themselves are entirely perfect in consistency and devoid of inner conflict.

But if literature often errs through its selectivity in exaggerating the unity of personality, psychology through its lack of interest and restricted techniques generally fails to discover or to explore such consistency as does exist.

The greatest failing of the psychologist at the present time is his inability to prove what he knows to be true. No less than the literary artist he knows that personality is an intricate, well-proportioned, and more or less consistent mental structure — but he can't prove it. He makes no use, as the writer does, of the obvious method of self-confrontation of facts. Instead of emulating the artist in this matter he usually takes safe refuge in the thickets of statistical correlation.

One investigator, thinking to study the virility of his subjects, for a whole population of people, correlates the width of hips and shoulders with interests in sports; another, to find the bases of intelligence, carefully compares the I. Q. in childhood with the ossification of the wrist bones; a third compares phosphorous per body weight with good-naturedness or with leadership. Investigations such as these, though they are the fashion in research on personality, run their course entirely on a subpersonal level. Devotion to the microscope and to mathematics has led the investigators to shun complex patterned forms of behavior and thought, even though it is only in these complex forms that personality can be said to exist at all. Bullied by the instruments of physics, many psychologists neglect the most delicate recording instrument ever devised for the relating and proper clustering of facts — namely, their own minds.

Psychology, then, needs techniques of self-confrontation, techniques whereby the togetherness of a personality can be determined. Only a few rudimentary attempts in this direction have been made.*

One study employed the English themes of 70 college students. Nine themes were gathered from each student, three in October, three in January, and three in May. The topics for the themes were prescribed and were uniform for all students.

After being typed and divested of all identifying signs, two experimenters attempted to sort these themes carefully so that they might from style alone group all the themes written by the same student. For both experimenters the results were strikingly positive, well above chance.

The point of interest here is the method by which successful matchings were made. Occasionally, to be sure, some striking mechanical feature caught the eye and aided in identifications. Addiction to semicolons would mark the writing of one student, or some other oddity of punctuation or spelling. But most of the identifications were not made on this basis but through a diagnosis of the *personal traits* of the writers. "The investigators found themselves searching for a form-quality of the individual." They felt in each production a reflection of certain complex qualities in the writer himself. Now these qualities were different in each case and difficult for the experimenter to reduce to words.

In spite of the difficulty of expressing these hypotheses of "form-quality" in words, the fact remains that they (and not mechanical features) were ordinarily the basis of judgment, and likewise that the judgments were to a significant degree successful.

It is of interest to note some of the bases upon which this matching proceeded. The productions of one student, for example, would be felt always to reflect "a feeling for atmosphere; a well-balanced sense of humor; a quiet, amused tolerance of social relations and situations."

---

* The following experiment is described on pp. 491 ff. of my book, *Personality: a Psychological Interpretation*, New York: Henry Holt, 1937.

Another showed in all his themes "a positive self-assurance; definite, but neither prejudiced nor opinionated; sense of humor." A third was "constantly bored. Looks at life as a monotonous experience in which one follows the easiest course of action." A fourth had a "simple, optimistic attitude toward life and people; simple, direct, declarative sentences."

There is a third major lesson for psychologists to learn from literature, namely how to keep a sustained interest in one individual person for a *long* period of time. It was said of a certain famous English anthropologist that although he wrote about savages, he never actually had seen one. He admitted the charge, and added — "and I hope to Heaven I never shall." A great number of psychologists in their professional capacity have never really *seen* an individual, and many of them, I regret to say, hope they never will.

Following the lead of the older sciences they assume that the individual must be brushed aside. Science, they insist, deals only with general laws. The individual is a nuisance. What is wanted are uniformities. This tradition has resulted in the creation of a vast, shadowy abstraction in psychology called the generalized-adult-human-mind. The human mind, of course, exists in no such form; it exists only in concrete, intensely personal forms. There is no generalized mind. The abstraction that the psychologist commits in measuring and explaining a non-existent mind-in-general is an abstraction that no literary writer ever commits. The literary writer knows perfectly well that mind exists only in singular and particular forms.

Here, of course, we are facing the basic opposition between science and art. Science, it is said, always deals with the general; art always with the particular. But if this distinction is true, what are we to do about personality? Personality is never general; it is always particular. Must it then be handed over, wholly to the arts? Can psychology do nothing about it? I am sure that very few psychologists would accept this solution. But still it seems to me that the dilemma is inexorable. Either we must give up the individual or we must learn from literature to dwell longer upon him, modifying as is necessary our conception of the scope of science so as to accommodate the single case more hospitably than heretofore.

You may have remarked to yourself that the psychologists you have known, in spite of their profession, are no better than anyone else in understanding people. They are not exceptionally shrewd, nor are they always able to give advice on problems of personality. This observation, if you have made it, is certainly sound. I should go further, and say that because of their habits of excessive abstraction and generalization, many psychologists are actually inferior to other people in their comprehension of the *single* lives that confront them.

When I say that in the interests of a proper science of personality the psychologist should learn to dwell longer on the single case, it might seem that I am poaching upon the domain of biography, whose precise purpose is to dwell exhaustively upon one life.

There is indeed a remarkably close relationship between literary biography and the psychology of personality; but the two fields are by no means identical. The psychologist needs to look at the single case more ardently in his clinical, experimental, and theoretical studies as well as from the point of view of life history. Although the psychology of personality is not identical with scientific biography, the psychologist can learn much if he will read and ponder literary biography; and I predict that if he learns his lesson well he may eventually be able to write more revealing and accurate biographies than most of those that literature has produced.

In England biography began as hagiography and as a recounting of legendary deeds. Neither interest was conducive to objectivity or truthfulness. The term *biography* was first used by Dryden in 1683, and defined by him as "the history of particular men's lives." Reaching a high point in Boswell's *Life of Johnson,* and again in Lockhart's *Life of Scott,* and for a third time in Edmund Gosse's *Father and Son,* English biography has had a career of ups and downs. Some biographies are as flat and lifeless as eulogies upon a gravestone; others are sentimental and false.

Increasingly, however, biography is becoming rigorous, and objective, and even heartless. For this trend psychology has no doubt been largely responsible. Biographies more and more are coming to resemble scientific *autopsies,* performed for the sake of understanding rather than for inspiration or acclaim. There are now psychological and psychoanalytic biographies and even medical and endocrinological biographies.

The influence of psychological science is felt in autobiography as well. In recent years there have been many experiments in objective self-depiction and self-explanation, with improvement upon the disingenuous confessions of Casanova, Rousseau, or Barbellion. Two fascinating examples, illustrating the direct influence of psychology, are the *Experiment in Autobiography* by H. G. Wells (1935) and *The Locomotive God* by W. E. Leonard (1927). But for all their enhanced warmth and intimacy, autobiographers suffer one disadvantage compared with biographies. The autobiographer as a rule cannot bear to disparage himself and the reader cannot bear to read his praise of himself. Perhaps in time writers may learn how to control their powerful impulse to justify their deeds in the telling, and readers may learn correspondingly to be less suspicious of virtue when it is self-disclosed.

I have mentioned three lessons that the psychologist may learn from literature for the improvement of his own work. The first is the conception held universally in all of literature concerning the nature of traits. Each literary artist proceeds on the assumption that his characters have broadly organized inner dispositions that can be identified and defined. The method that literature uses in identifying and defining traits — namely, the study of equivalent fields of stimulation and equivalent fields of response, needs urgently to find its way into the psychologist's store of methods. The second lesson concerns the test of self-confrontation, which good literature always meets and psychology nearly always avoids meeting. Owing to their neglect of this basic principle of literary validation, psychologists generally fail to find the unity and coherence of the personalities that they study. The third lesson calls for more sustained interest in the single case, through longer periods of time. The psychologist should dwell as the biographer does upon one life more exhaustively than he does, no matter if in so doing he sacrifices his impulse to make broad, and usually premature generalizations, about the abstract, nonexistent, average human mind.

                               *   *   *

In presenting these three advantages of the literary method I have said little about the distinctive merits of psychology. In conclusion I ought to add at least a few words in praise of my profession. Otherwise you might infer that I am willing and even eager to sell psychology down the river in return for a copy of *Madame Bovary* and a free pass to the Athenaeum.

Psychology has a number of potential advantages over literature. Its disciplined character offsets the subjective dogmatism inherent in imaginative writing. Sometimes literature passes the test of self-confrontation of facts too easily. For example, in one recent comparative study of biographies of the same person it was found that each version of the life seemed plausible enough, but that in fact only a small percentage of the events and interpretations given in one biography were to be found in the others. No one could know which, if any, was the *true* portrait.

It is not necessary for good writers to agree in their observations and in their explanations to anything like the same extent that all good psychologists must agree. Biographers can give vastly different interpretations of a life without discrediting the literary method; whereas psychology is ridiculed mercilessly when its experts fail to agree with one another.

A psychologist is properly troubled by the arbitrary metaphors of literature. The implication of many metaphors is often grotesquely false, and yet they are seldom challenged. In literature one may find, for example, that the docility of a certain character is explained by the fact that "he had menial blood in his veins"; or the fieriness of another character by the fact that "his temperament he shared with all other redheads"; or the intellectuality of a third by the "height of his massive brow." A psychologist would be torn limb from limb if he made any such fantastic assumptions concerning cause and effect.

The artist, furthermore, is permitted and encouraged to be entertaining and engaging, to communicate his own images, to express his own biases. His success is measured by the responsiveness of his readers, who often demand nothing more than that they may languidly identify themelves with a character and escape from their immediate worries. The psychologist, on the other hand, is never permitted to entertain his reader. His success is measured by sterner criteria than the reader's applause.

In gathering his material, the writer draws from his casual observations of life, elides his data, and discards troublesome facts at will. The psychologist is held by requirements of fidelity to fact, and to all facts; and he is expected to use controlled and verifiable sources from which to secure his facts. He must prove his inferences step by step. His terminology is standardized and he is deprived almost entirely of the use of seductive metaphor.

These restrictions surrounding the psychologist make for reliability, verifiability, lessened bias, and relative freedom from self-projection into the products of his work.

Psychologists who study personality are, I agree, essentially striving to say what literature has always said, and they are of necessity saying it much less artfully; but so far as they have gone — and it is not very far — they are striving to speak more exactly and, from the point of view of social progress in our century, more helpfully.

The title of this essay, like the titles of many essays, is idly stated. Peronality is not a problem for science or a problem for art exclusively, but for both together. Each approach has its merits, but both are needed for even an approximately complete study of the infinite richness of personality.

If in the interests of good pedagogy I am expected to conclude with one pointed bit of advice, it would be this: If you are a student of psychology, read many, many novels and dramas of character, and read biography. If you are *not* a student of psychology, read these too, but *read psychology as well.*

BIBLIOGRAPHY
1921-1950

GORDON W. ALLPORT

Titles of books and monographs are printed in capitals

1921

Personality traits: their classification and measurement (with F. H. Allport). *J. abnorm. soc. Psychol.,* 1921 **16**, 6-40.

Personality and character. *Psychol. Bull.,* 1921, **18**, 441-455.

REVIEWS:

W. H. Pyle: *The psychology of learning. J. abnorm. soc. Psychol.,* 1921-22, **16**, 414-415.

M. S. Pittman: *The value of school supervision;* W. S. Herzog: *State maintenance for teachers in training;* A. G. Peaks: *Periodic variations in efficiency. J. abnorm. soc. Psychol.,* 1921-22, **16**, 415.

1922

REVIEWS:

L. Berman: *The glands regulating personality. J. aborm. soc. Psychol.,* 1922, **17**, 220-222.

E. S. Bogardus: *Essentials of social psychology. J. abnorm. soc. Psychol.,* 1922, **17**, 104-106.

1923

Germany's state of mind. *New Republic,* 1923, **34**, 432, 63-65.

The Leipzig Congress of Psychology. *Am. J. Psychol.,* 1923 **34**, 612-615.

1924

The study of the undivided personality. *J. abnorm. soc. Psychol,.* 1924, **19**, 132-141.

Eidetic imagery. *Brit. J. Psychol.,* 1924, **15**, 99-120.

Die theoretischen Hauptströmungen in der amerikanischen Psychologie der Gegenwart. *Zeitschrift f. Pädagog. Psychologie,* 1924, 129-137.

The standpoint of Gestalt psychology. *Psyche,* 1924, **4**, 354-361.

REVIEWS:

M. P. Follett: *Creative experience. J. abnorm. soc. Psychol.,* 1924, **18**, 426-428.

W. W. Smith: *The measurement of emotion;* and H. Eng: *Experimentelle Untersuchungen über das Gefühlsleben des Kindes im Vergleich mit dem des Erwachsenen. J. abnorm. soc. Psychol.,* 1924, **18**, 414-416.

1925

REVIEW:

W. B. Munro: *Personality in politics. J. abnorm. soc. Psychol.,* 1925, **20**, 209-211.

1926

REVIEWS:

K. Dunlap: *Social psychology. J. abnorm. soc. Psychol.,* 1926, **21**, 95-100.

O. Selz: *Uber die Persönlichkeitstypen und die Methoden ihrer Bestimmung. Am. J. Psychol.,* 1926, **37**, 618-19.

1927

Concepts of trait and personality. *Psychol. Bull.,* 1927, **24**, 284-293.

REVIEWS:

A. A. Roback: *A bibliography of character and personality. Psychol. Bull.,* 1927, **24**, 309-310.

A. A. Roback: *Psychology of character. Psychol. Bull.,* 1927, **24**, 717-723.

W. S. Taylor (Ed.) : *Readings in abnormai psychology and mental hygiene. J. abnorm. soc. Psychol.,* 1927, **21**, 445-448.

1928

The eidetic image and the after-image. *Am. J. Psychol.,* 1928, **40**, 418-425.

A test for ascendance-submission. *J. abnorm. soc. Psychol.,* 1928, **23**, 118-136.

A-S REACTION STUDY (with F. H. Allport). Boston: Houghton Mifflin, 1928.

1929

The study of personality by the intuitive method: an experiment in teaching from *The Locomotive God. J. abnorm. soc. Psychol.,* 1929, **24**, 14-27.

The composition of political attitudes. *Am. J. Sociol.,* 1929, **35**, 220-238.

REVIEWS:

E. T. Clark: *The psychology of religious awakening. Psychol. Bull.,* 1929, **26**, 710-711.

W. McDougall: *The group mind. J. abnorm. soc. Psychol.,* 1929, **24**, 123-126.

H. Meltzer and E. Bailor: *Developed lessons in psychology. Dartmouth Alumni Bull.*, 1929.

T. Munro: *Scientific method in aesthetics. Psychol. Bull.*, 1929, **26**, 711.

C. Murchison: *Social psychology. Psychol. Bull.*, 1929, **26**, 709-710.

M. Prince: *Clinical and experimental studies in personality. Psychol. Bull.*, 1929, **26**, 711-712.

L. T. Troland: *Fundamentals of human motivation. J. abnorm. soc. Psychol.*, 1929, **23**, 510-513.

1930

Some guiding principles in understanding personality. *The Family*, 1930, June, 124-128.

The neurotic personality and traits of self-expression. *J. soc. Psychol.*, 1930, **1**, 524-527.

The field of personality (with P. E. Vernon) *Psychol. Bull.*, 1930, **27**, 677-730.

Change and decay in the visual memory image. *Brit. J. Psychol.*, 1930, **21**, 133-148.

REVIEWS:

J. E. Downey: *Creative imagination. Psychol. Bull.*, 1930, **27**, 408-410.

K. Young: *Social psychology. Psychol. Bull.*, 1930, **27**, 731-733.

1931

What is a trait of personality? *J. abnorm. soc. Psychol.*, 1931, **25**, 368-372.

A test for personal values (with P. E. Vernon). *J. abnorm. soc. Psychol.*, 1931, **26**, 231-248.

A STUDY OF VALUES (with P. E. Vernon). Boston: Houghton Mifflin, 1931.

1932

REVIEWS:

W. Boven: *La science du caractère. Am. J. Psychol.*, 1932, **44**, 838-839.

J. C. Flugel: *The psychology of clothes. Psychol. Bull.*, 1932, **29**, 358-359.

D. Katz and F. H. Allport: *Students' attitudes. Psychol. Bull.*, 1932, **29**, 356-358.

F. Künkel: *Vitale Dialektik. Psychol. Bull.*, 1932, **29**, 371-373.

A. A. Roback: *Personality. Psychol. Bull.*, 1932, **29**, 359-360.

J. J. Smith: *Social psychology. Psychol. Bull.*, 1932, **29**, 360.

P. M. Symonds: *Diagnosing personality and conduct. J. soc. Psychol.*, 1932, **3**, 391-397.

1933

STUDIES IN EXPRESSIVE MOVEMENT (with P. E. Vernon). New
York: The Macmillan Co., 1933.

The study of personality by the experimental method. *Character & Pers.*,
1933, **1**, 259-264.

The determination of personal interests by psychological and graphologi-
cal methods (with H. Cantril and H. A. Rand). *Character &
Pers.*, 1933, **2**, 134-151.

Recent applications of the *Study of Values* (with H. Cantril). *J. abnorm.
soc. Psychol.*, 1933, **28**, 259-273.

REVIEWS:

C. Bühler: *Der menschliche Lebenslauf als psychologisches Problem.*
Sociologus, 1933, **9**, 336-338.

N. D. M. Hirsch: *Genius and creative intelligence. Psychol. Bull.*,
1933, **30**, 365-366.

L. Klages: *The science of character* (Transl. by W. H. Johnston).
Psychol. Bull., 1933, **30**, 370-371.

M. A. McLaughlin: *The genesis and constancy of ascendance and
submission as personality traits. Am. J. Psychol.*, 1933, **45**, 779-
780.

1934

Judging personality from voice (with H. Cantril). *J. soc. Psychol.*, 1934,
5, 37-55.

REVIEWS:

A. Goldenweiser: *History, psychology, and culture. Psychol. Bull.*,
1934, **31**, 363-364.

A. A. Roback: *Self-consciousness and its treatment. Psychol. Bull.*,
1934, **31**, 370.

1935

THE PSYCHOLOGY OF RADIO (with H. Cantril). New York:
Harper & Bros., 1935.

Attitudes. Chapter 17 in C. C. Murchison (Ed.), *A handbook of social
psychology.* Worcester: Clark Univ. Press, 1935.

The radio as a stimulus situation. *Acta Psychologica*, 1935, **1**, 1-6.

The nature of motivation. *Understanding the child*, 1935, Jan., 3-6.

1936

TRAIT-NAMES: A PSYCHO-LEXICAL STUDY (with H. S. Odbert).
   Psychol. Monogr., 1936, **47**, No. 211, 1-171.

Are attitudes biological or cultural in origin? (with R. L. Schanck).
   Character & Pers., 1936, **4**, 195-205.

REVIEW:

   G. K. Zipf: The psycho-biology of language. *Psychol. Bull.*, 1936, **33**,
   219-222.

1937

PERSONALITY: A PSYCHOLOGICAL INTERPRETATION. New
   York: Henry Holt, 1937.

The functional autonomy of motives. *Am. J. Psychol.*, 1937, **50**, 141-156.

The personalistic psychology of William Stern. *Character & Pers.*, 1937,
   5, 231-246.

1938

The Journal of Abnormal and Social Psychology: an editorial. *J. abnorm.
   soc. Psychol.*, 1938, **33**, 3-13.

William Stern: 1871-1938. *Am J. Psychol.*, 1938, **51**, 770-774.

Personality: a problem for science or a problem for art? *Revista de
   Psihologie*, 1938, **1**, **4**, 1-15.

REVIEW:

   L. B. Murphy: *Social behavior and child personality. J. abnorm.
   soc. Psychol.*, 1938, **33**, 538-543.

1939

Dewey's individual and social psychology. Chapter 9 in P. A. Schilpp
   (Ed.), *The Philosophy of John Dewey*. Evanston and Chicago:
   Northwestern Univ., 1939.

Recent applications of the A-S Reaction Study (with R. Ruggles). *J.
   abnorm. soc. Psychol.*, 1939, **34**, 518-528.

The education of a teacher. *The Harvard Progressive*, 1939, **4**, 7-9.

1940

The psychologist's frame of reference. *Psychol. Bull.*, 1940, **37**, 1-28.

Fifty years of change in American psychology (with J. S. Bruner). *Psychol.
   Bull.*, 1940, **37**, 757-776.

The psychology of newspapers: five tentative laws (with J. M. Faden).
   Publ. Opin. Quart., 1940, **4**, 687-703.

Motivation in personality: reply to Mr. Bertocci. *Psychol. Rev.*, 1940, **47**, 533-554.

Liberalism and the motives of men. *Frontiers of Democracy*, 1940, **6**, 136-137.

Foreword. H. Werner, *Comparative psychology of mental development* (transl. by E. B. Garside). New York: Harper & Bros., 1940. Revised edition, Chicago: Follett Pub. Co., 1948.

1941

Liabilities and assets in civilian morale. *The Annals* (Amer. Acad. Polit. & Soc. Sci.) , 1941, **216**, 88-94.

Psychological service for civilian morale. *J. consult. Psychol.*, 1941, **5**, 235-239.

Personality under social catastrophe: ninety life-histories of the Nazi revolution (with J. S. Bruner and E. M. Jandorf). *Character & Pers.*, 1941, **10**, 1-22. Also published as Chapter 25 in C. Kluckhohn and H. A. Murray, *Personality in nature, society, and culture*. New York: Alfred A. Knopf, 1948.

Morale: American style. *Christian Science Monitor* (Weekly Magazine Section) , 1941, Apr. 26, 1-2 and 13.

REVIEW:

J. M. MacKaye: *The logic of language*. *J. abnorm. soc. Psychol.*, 1941, **36**, 296-297.

1942

THE USE OF PERSONAL DOCUMENTS IN PSYCHOLOGICAL SCIENCE. New York: Soc. Sci. Res. Council, Bull. **49**, 1942.

The nature of democratic morale. Chapter 1 in G. Watson (Ed.) , *Civilian Morale*. Boston: Houghton Mifflin Co., 1942.

Defense seminars for morale study and morale building. *J. soc. Psychol.*, *SPSSI Bull.*, 1942, **15**, 399-401.

Report on the third front: at home. *Christian Science Monitor* (Weekly Magazine Section) , 1942, Sept. 5, 6 and 14.

Morale and its measurement. In *Public Policy*: Yearb. Littauer School of Publ. Admin., 1942, **3**, 3-17.

REVIEW:

F. C. Bartlett: *Political propaganda*. *Sat. Rev. Lit.*, 1942, **25**, 18.

1943

The productive paradoxes of William James. *Psychol. Rev.*, 1943, **50**, 95-120.

Test tube for rumors. *Coronet*, 1943, **14**, 136-140.

Psychological considerations in making the peace: editorial note. *J. abnorm. soc. Psychol.*, 1943, **38**, 131.

This clinical supplement: editorial note. *J. abnorm. soc. Psychol.*, 1943, **38**, 3-5.

Do rosy headlines sell newspapers? (with E. C. Winship). *Publ. Opin. Quart.*, 1943, **7**, 205-210.

Social psychology and the civilian war effort (with H. R. Veltfort). *J. soc. Psychol. SPSSI Bull.*, 1943, **18**, 165-233.

The ego in contemporary psychology. *Psychol. Rev.*, 1943, **50**, 451-478.

Morale research and its clearing (with G. R. Schmeidler). *Psychol. Bull.*, 1943, **40**, 65-68.

Restoring morale in occupied territory. *Publ. Opin. Quart*, 1943, **7**, 606-617.

REVIEWS:

E. P. Aldrich (Ed.) : *As William James said. J. abnorm. soc. Psychol.*, 1943, **38**, 119-120.

M. D. Allers: *The psychology of character. Am. sociol. Rev.*, 1943, **8**, 735-736.

M. A. May: *A social psychology of war and peace. The Annals* (Amer. Acad. Polit. Soc. Sci.) , 1943, **229**, 186-187.

A. A. Roback: *William James: his marginalia, personality and contribution. New England Quarterly*, 1943, **16**, 143-144.

C. Schrodes, J. van Gundy, and R. W. Husband (Eds.) : *Psychology through literature. J. abnorm. soc. Psychol.*, 1943, **38**, (No. 2, Clin. Suppl.) 203.

E. C. Tolman: *Drives toward war. J. abnorm. soc. Psychol.*, 1943, **38**, 293-296.

1944

Prefaces to: *Educational Opportunities in Greater Boston.* Prospect Union Educational Exchange, 1944 and annually thereafter.

The Quest of Nellie Wise Allport. Privately printed, 1944.

The Roots of Religion *Advent Paper*, No. 1, Boston: Church of the Advent, 1944.

ABC's of scapegoating (Ed. and author of Foreword). Chicago: Central
    YMCA College, 1944. Revised edition. *Freedom Pamphlet
    Series.* New York: Anti-Defamation League of B'Nai B'Rith,
    1948.

This clinical number: editorial. *J. abnorm. soc. Psychol.,* 1944, **39**, 147-
    149.

Social psychology and the civilian war effort (with G. R. Schmeidler).
    J. soc. Psychol., SPSSI Bull., 1944, **20**, 145-180.

The bigot in our midst. *The Commonweal,* 1944, **25**, 582-586. Also pub-
    lished in: *The Catholic Digest,* 1944, **9**, 93-96; and *Common
    Sense* (Johannesburg, South Africa), 1945, **6**, 154-156. Revised
    edition, New York: Community Relations Service, 1950.

1945

The psychology of participation. *Psychol. Rev.,* 1945, **53**, 117-132. Also
    published in: *Occupational Psychol.* (London), 1946, **20**, 54-62;
    and S. D. Hoslett (Ed.), *Human factors in management,* Park
    College Press: Parkville, Mo., 1946.

Human nature and the peace. *Psychol. Bull.,* 1945, **42**, 376-378.

Is intergroup education possible? *Harv. Educ. Rev.,* 1945, **15**, 83-86.

Catharsis and the reduction of prejudice. *J. soc. Issues,* 1945, **1**, 1-8.

The basic psychology of rumor (with L. J. Postman). *Transactions* of
    the New York Acad. of Sci., *Section of Psychology,* 1945, **8**, 61-81.

REVIEW:

    G. Gallup: *A guide to public opinion. J. abnorm. soc. Psychol.,* 1945,
    40, 113-114.

1946

Personalistic psychology as science: a reply. *Psychol. Rev.,* 1946, **53**,
    132-135.

Controlling group prejudice (Ed. & author of Foreword). *The Annals*
    (Amer. Acad. Polit. & Soc. Sci.), 1946, 244.

Psychology and Social Relations at Harvard University (with E. G. Bor-
    ing). *Amer. Psychologist,* 1946, **1**, 119-122.

Some roots of prejudice (with B. M. Kramer). Published as a separate and
    in *J. Psychol.,* 1946, **22**, 9-39. Revised edition, *Roots of Prejudice.*
    New York: Amer. Jewish Congress, Pamphlet Series *Jewish
    Affairs,* 1946, **1**, 13.

Geneticism *versus* ego-structure in theories of personality. *Brit. J. educ. Psychol.*, 1946, **16**, 57-68.

Effect: a secondary principle of learning. *Psychol. Rev.*, 1946, **53**, 335-347.

Preface. E. Simmel (Ed.), *Anti-Semitism: a social disease.* New York: International Universities Press, 1946.

The priest and the psychologist. *Bull. of General Theological Seminary,* Sept. 1946. (Commencement address at Chapel of the Good Shepherd of the General Theological Seminary, Chelsea Square, New York, May 22, 1946.)

An analysis of rumor (with L. Postman). *Publ. Opin. Quart.*, 1946-47, **10**, 501-517. Also published in *Science Digest,* 1947, **22**, 5, 58-61.

Introduction. Swami Akhilananda, *Hindu psychology.* New York: Harper & Bros., 1946.

REVIEW:
> A. H. Leighton: *The governing of men. J. abnorm. soc. Psychol.,* 1946, **41**, 89-92.

1947

THE PSYCHOLOGY OF RUMOR (with L. Postman). New York: Henry Holt & Co., 1947.

Guide lines for research in international cooperation. *J. soc. Issues,* 1947, **3**, 21-37.

El marco de referencia de los psicologos. (Transl. by A. Bernal del Riesgo from *Psychol. Bull.*, 1940) Havana: University of Havana, 1946.

Introduction. Marie I. Rasey, *Toward maturity, the psychology of child development.* New York: Hinds, Hayden and Eldredge, 1947.

The genius of Kurt Lewin. *J. Person.,* 1947, **16**, 1, 1-10. Also published in *J. soc. Issues,* 1948, **4**, 4, Suppl. series **1**, 14-21.

Scientific models and human morals. *Psychol. Rev.*, 1947, **54**, 4, 182-192.

1948

Foreword. Kurt Lewin (G. W. Lewin, Ed.), *Resolving social conflicts.* New York: Harper & Bros., 1948.

Psychology. Chapter 3 in *College Reading and Religion.* New Haven: Yale Univ. Press, 1948.

The religion of the post-war college student (with J. M. Gillespie and J. Young). Published as a separate and in *J. Psychol.,* 1948, **25**, 3-33.

Modelos cientificos y moral humana. (Transl. from *Psychol. Rev.*) *Revista de Psicologia General y Aplicada,* Madrid, 1948, **3**, 425-447.

REVIEWS:

D. Jacobson: *The affairs of dame rumor. Boston Sunday Post,* Oct. 24, 1948.

E. Mayo: *Some notes on the psychology of Pierre Janet. Survey Graphic,* 1948, **37**, 5, 267.

A. Schweitzer: *The psychiatric study of Jesus. Christian Register,* Boston: Beacon Press, Apr. 1948.

1949

PERSONLICHKEIT: STRUKTUR, ENTWICKLUNG, UND ERFASSUNG DER MENSCHLICHEN EIGENART. (Transl. by H. von Bracken of: *Personality: a psychological interpretation.*) Stuttgart: Klett Verlag, 1949.

Psychology and the fourth R. *New Republic,* Oct. 17, 1949, 23-26.

Editorial note. *J. abnorm. soc. Psychol.,* 1949, **44**, 439-442.

1950

THE INDIVIDUAL AND HIS RELIGION. New York: The Macmillan Co., 1950.

THE NATURE OF PERSONALITY: SELECTED PAPERS. Cambridge: Addison-Wesley Press, 1950.

Foreword. M. G. Ross, *Religious beliefs of youth.* New York: Association Press, 1950.

How shall we evaluate teaching? Chapter 3 in B. B. Cronkhite (Ed.), *A handbook for College Teachers.* Cambridge: Harvard Univ. Press, 1950.

The role of expectation. Chapter 2 in H. Cantril (Ed.), *Tensions that Cause Wars.* Urbana: Univ. of Illinois Press, 1950.

A psychological approach to the study of love and hate. Chapter 7 in P. A. Sorokin (Ed.), *Explorations in altruistic love and behavior.* Boston: Beacon Press, 1950.

Prejudice: a problem in psychological and social causation. (Kurt Lewin Memorial Lecture), *J. soc. Issues,* 1950, Suppl. Series.

REVIEWS:

S. A. Stouffer *et al.: The American soldier,* 2 vols. *J. abnorm. soc. Psychol.,* 1950, 45, 168-173.

A five-volume shelf about a sickness of both individuals and society: prejudice (M. Horkheimer and S. H. Flowerman, Eds.: *Studies in prejudice,* 5 vols. New York: Harper & Bros., 1950.) *Scientific American,* 1950, 182, 6, 56-58.